Jean-Baptiste Greuze / 1725-1805

D1548659

9782951448711

An exhibition organized by the Wadsworth Atheneum, Hartford
1 December 1976–23 January 1977

and also seen at The California Palace of the Legion of Honor,
San Francisco, 5 March–1 May 1977

Musée des Beaux-Arts, Dijon, 4 June–31 July 1977

Selection and Catalogue by Edgar Munhall

Jean-Baptiste Greuze

1725-1805

Wadsworth Atheneum / Hartford

Edited by Joseph Focarino

Wadsworth Atheneum Board of Trustees

Cover: *The Fowler*, see No. 12

Thomas R. Cox, Jr., *President*
James B. Lyon, *Vice-President*
Talcott Stanley, *Vice-President*
John P. Britton, *Treasurer*
Jared I. Edwards, *Secretary*
Joseph H. Allen
Homer Babbidge
Edward J. Barlow
William H. T. Bush
Mrs. Lawrence Cathles, Jr.
David L. Coffin
Robert E. Darling, Jr.
William G. DeLana
James F. English, Jr.
Daniel E. Gold
Arnold C. Greenberg
William W. Hoppin
John W. Huntington
Henry T. Kneeland
Mrs. Bernhard Kohn
Mrs. Richard Koopman
Robert H. Krieble
Horace B. Learned
William Lidgerwood
Frederick C. Maynard
Stephen B. Middlebrook
David H. Neiditz
Joseph D. Sargent
Herbert P. Schoen
Arthur L. Shipman, Jr.
James McA. Thomson
Burton G. Tremaine, Jr.
Dr. Archibald M. Woodruff

©Copyright Wadsworth Atheneum, 1976
Library of Congress Catalogue
Card Number: 76-40506

Designer:
Nathan Garland
Typesetter:
Eastern Typesetting
Printer:
Meriden Gravure

An exhibition funded in part
by the National Endowment for the Arts,
a Federal agency, the Morris Joseloff
Exhibition Fund and the Women's
Committee of the Wadsworth Atheneum

Ex-Officio:
The Governor of Connecticut
The Mayor of Hartford
The President of the Women's Committee
The Past President of the Women's Committee
The President of the Docent Council

Honorary Trustees:
Henry S. Beers
John D. Britton
Hugh S. Campbell
Charles C. Cunningham
Pomeroy Day
Mrs. James L. Goodwin
Philip Hammerslough
Susan Morse Hilles
Olcott D. Smith
Nelson White
Frazer Wilde

The following numbers will not be seen in Hartford:
26, 34, 38, 45, 53, 69, 70, 75, 87, 105, 111.
in San Francisco:
14, 15, 22, 26, 44, 45, 53, 68, 69, 75, 77, 81, 82, 84, 87, 88, 104, 105.
in Dijon:
6, 7, 8, 14, 15, 19, 20, 22, 23, 28, 34, 38, 40, 44, 54, 58, 60, 62, 70, 73, 74, 81, 82, 86, 89, 96, 101, 104, 109, 111, 112.

Lenders to the Exhibition

Amsterdam:
Amsterdam Historisch Museum
Angers:
Musée d'Angers
Baltimore, Maryland:
Baltimore Museum of Art
Private Collection
Boston, Massachusetts
Mr. David Ames, Mr. Oliver F. Ames
and Mrs. Peter S. Thompson
Museum of Fine Arts
Brunswick:
Herzog Anton Ulrich-Museum
Brussels:
Musées Royaux des Beaux-Arts de Belgique
Cambridge, Massachusetts:
Fogg Art Museum, Harvard University
Chicago, Illinois:
The Art Institute of Chicago
Dallas, Texas:
Dallas Museum of Fine Arts
Dijon:
Musée des Beaux-Arts
Musée Magnin
Durham, North Carolina:
Dr. and Mrs. James H. Semans
Edinburgh:
National Galleries of Scotland
Hartford, Connecticut:
Wadsworth Atheneum
Karlsruhe:
Staatliche Kunsthalle, Kupferstichkabinett
Lille:
Musée des Beaux-Arts
London:
Her Majesty Queen Elizabeth II
The British Museum
Collection Paul Wallraf
Private Collection
Los Angeles, California:
The Norton Simon Foundation
Lyon:
Musée Lyonnais des Arts Décoratifs
Private Collection
Mâcon:
Musée Municipal des Ursulines
Marseille:
Musée des Beaux-Arts
Musée Grobet-Labadié
Minneapolis, Minnesota:
The Minneapolis Institute of Arts
New Haven, Connecticut:
Yale University Art Gallery

New Orleans, Louisiana:
New Orleans Museum of Art
New York, New York:
Mr. and Mrs. George T. Delacorte
Mr. J. F. McCrindle
The Metropolitan Museum of Art
The Pierpont Morgan Library
Mrs. Donald S. Stralem
Mrs. Herbert N. Straus
Wildenstein & Co., Inc.
Mr. Emile E. Wolf
Private Collection
Norfolk, Virginia:
Chrysler Museum at Norfolk
Oxford:
The Ashmolean Museum
Paris:
Bibliothèque Nationale
M. Michel David-Weill
M. Fabius
Fondation Custodia (Coll. F. Lugt),
    Institut Néerlandais
Institut de France, Musée Jacquemart-André
Madame Frédéric Megret
Musée du Louvre
Musée du Petit Palais
M. Gaston Palewski
Baron Walckenaer
Five Private Collections
Phoenix, Arizona:
Phoenix Art Museum
Portland, Oregon:
Portland Art Museum
Rotterdam:
Museum Boymans-van Beuningen
San Francisco, California:
The Fine Arts Museums of San Francisco
Strasbourg:
Private Collection
Tournus:
Musée Greuze
Private Collection
Warsaw:
Muzeum Narodowe
Washington, D.C.:
National Gallery of Art
United States Department of State,
Diplomatic Reception Rooms
Williamstown, Massachusetts:
Sterling and Francine Clark Art Institute
Worcester, Massachusetts:
Worcester Art Museum

Preface

The Wadsworth Atheneum is pleased and honored to have organized the first comprehensive exhibition ever devoted to the work of Jean-Baptiste Greuze, one of the leading French painters of the eighteenth century.

It is always difficult to determine when an idea first began, but my own involvement with Greuze was launched more than sixteen years ago at Yale University when I was a student of and worked with Edgar Munhall. During that time and frequently thereafter he and I discussed the possibility of organizing such an exhibition. When my professional career brought me to the Atheneum, and when the Museum was able to undertake more ambitious exhibitions after the less active period immediately following building renovations, the thought often recurred. Approximately two years ago the decision was made to proceed with the project.

It is very much in the Atheneum tradition to organize such an exhibition around one or more major works in our permanent collection. In this case our important early painting *Indolence*, done in Rome about 1756, plus two drawings, have formed a small nucleus to which major loans from the United States and abroad have been added. With 114 works from sixty-nine lenders in seven countries, this exhibition constitutes the most ambitious temporary loan exhibition the museum has undertaken.

It is extraordinary that there never has been a Greuze exhibition. When one perceives the sheer quality of his production, his striking and subtle coloration, the bravura technical ability of his brushwork, the breadth of perception with which he approached his portrait sitters and the sophisticated compositional techniques he used, and when one considers the length of time during which he sustained a significant output (over half a century) and the sensitivity he showed to the aesthetic values of the changing times in which he lived, it is clear that the opportunity to examine an extensive selection of his work is long overdue. As Edgar Munhall so ably demonstrates in the Introduction, Biography and individual entries that comprise this catalogue, and as the works themselves evidence first-hand, Jean-Baptiste Greuze is an artist of exceptional interest and importance.

Obviously such an exhibition could not take place without the cooperation, usually at personal or institutional sacrifice, of the numerous lenders, all of whom are listed on the pages that follow. We are deeply grateful to them for allowing their works to be a part of the exhibition and catalogue. Naturally, our colleagues in French museums have been called upon most extensively, and to them and to the private lenders in France go special thanks. Because the exhibition will be seen in three widely separated locations over a long period of time, certain works will not be on view in all three installations. We feel confident that we have coordinated the selections so that each exhibiting institution will have a balanced presentation. All of the works included in the exhibition appear in the catalogue; a separate list indicates where each will not be shown.

Funding for this exhibition has been obtained from the National Endowment for the Arts, a Federal agency. We are deeply grateful to the Museum Program for their support. Certain of the European loans are being insured through the new United States Government Arts and Artifacts Indemnity Program, as administered by the Federal Council on the Arts and the Humanities, National Foundation on the Arts and Humanities; in a very real sense this constitutes a grant, and we are thankful for the Foundation's understanding and cooperation. The Morris Joseloff Exhibition Fund, a special endowment at the Wadsworth Atheneum, has also made a contribution to the exhibition, as has the Women's Committee of the Atheneum. To all of these sources of financial support go our most sincere thanks.

First and foremost among the individuals who have participated in the project is Edgar Munhall, Curator of The Frick Collection in New York and Guest Curator of the exhibition. Former teacher, colleague and friend, Mr. Munhall has spent many years studying eighteenth-century French art and culture in general and Greuze in particular. No other person could have provided the scholarly insight into the period, the connoisseurship and the knowledge of Greuze's works in collections throughout the world, as well as the professional associations and personal friendships that have led to such impressive international cooperation. The selection of the pictures and the information contained in the catalogue is his work; I am confident that the latter will long remain the standard reference in the field, while the former will bring great visual pleasure to all who see it. Both are a tribute to his abilities, perseverance and patience.

The exhibition was begun when James Elliott was Director of the Atheneum; his enthusiastic support of the project is gratefully acknowledged. The very complicated logistical problems of international and national shipments were heroically faced by the Atheneum's Registrar, David M. Parrish, and his staff. Gertrud Bourgoyne, Secretary to the Chief Curator, has been particularly helpful in coordinating the loans. The catalogue was designed by Nathan Garland and printed by Meriden Gravure under the supervision of William Glick.

The staff of the Fine Arts Museums of San Francisco, Ian McK. White, Director, and Thomas Garver, Curator of Exhibitions, has been entirely supportive of the exhibition from the outset. Emmanuel de Margerie, Director of the Musées de France, Robert Poujade, Mayor of Dijon, and

Pierre Quarré, Director of the Musée des Beaux-Arts in Dijon, have generously endorsed the project and assisted in its organization.

The staffs of the lending institutions have been most helpful in providing information and assistance. These include: *Amsterdam:* B. Haak, Michel Jonker; *Angers:* Catherine Lagrue; *Baltimore:* Tom L. Freudenheim, Brenda Richardson; *Boston:* Jan Fontein, Laura Luckey; *Brunswick:* Rüdiger Klessmann; *Brussels:* Philippe Roberts-Jones; *Cambridge, Massachusetts:* Seymour Slive; *Dallas:* Harry S. Parker, III; *Dijon:* Arnauld Brejon de Lavergnée, Monique Geiger; *Edinburgh:* John M. Sutherland, Colin Thompson; *Karlsruhe:* J. E. von Borries; *Lille:* P. H. Oursel; *London:* J. A. Gere, Sir Oliver Millar, Sir John Pope-Hennessy; *Lyon:* J. M. Tuchscherer; *Mâcon:* Jean-François Garmier; *Marseille:* Marielle Latour, Henri Wytenhove; *Minneapolis:* Samuel Sachs, II; *New Haven:* Alan Shestack; *New York:* Katharine Baetjer, Jacob Bean, M. Roy Fisher, Louis Goldenberg, Marceline McKee, Felice Stampfle, Daniel Wildenstein; *Norfolk:* Dennis R. Anderson, Walter P. Chrysler, Jr.; *Oxford:* David T. Piper; *Paris:* Jean Adhémar, Roseline Bacou, Marie-Christine Boucher, Adeline Cacan de Bissy, Carlos van Hasselt, René Huyghe, Georges Le Rider, Maurice Sérullaz, Nathalie Volle; *Phoenix:* Goldthwaite H. Dorr, III; *Portland:* Donald Jenkins; *Rotterdam:* A. W. F. M. Meij; *Tournus:* Emile Magnien; *Warsaw:* Jan Bialostocki; *Washington:* J. Carter Brown, Clement E. Conger; *Williamstown:* George Heard Hamilton; *Worcester:* Richard Stuart Teitz.

I would like to pay particular tribute to the assistance rendered by the Paintings Department of the Musée du Louvre, Michel Laclotte, Chief Curator, and Pierre Rosenberg, Curator. Without their enthusiastic support and cooperation, and without the frequent responses from M. Rosenberg when called upon for help, the exhibition would have been far less successful if not impossible.

Peter O. Marlow
Acting Director

Our colleagues whom Mr. Marlow has thanked above have, in addition to assisting us with this exhibition, generously aided me in many other ways with Greuze matters over the years. I should like to express here my gratitude to them and also to the following individuals whose friendly help has contributed to the success of this exhibition: John Abbott, Sir Robert Abdy, Valentin Abdy, Robert Allen, Edzard Baumann, Irène Bizot, Coburn Britton, Anita Brookner, Marcelle Brunet, Jean Cailleux, David Carritt, Robert A. Cecil, Richard Clair, Suzanne Damiron, Bernice Davidson, Mme. Pierre David-Weill, Peggy Davis, Danielle Demetz, James Draper, comte C. E. de Dreux-Brézé, Maître Dufour, Winthrop Edey, Bryan Essenhigh, Everett Fahy, Miss Helen C. Frick, Françoise Gardey, Elizabeth E. Gardner, Mrs. Oliver Russell Grace, Mary Ann Wurth Harris, François Heim, baron Rodolphe Hottinguer, Robert Isaacson, John Ittmann, Evelyn Joll, Philippe Jullian, Mrs. Maurice Kahn, Sylvain Laveissière, Richard di Liberto, John Maxon, Robert de Micheaux, Marcelle Minet, Geneviève Monnier, Evelyne Morant, Maurice Mourre, Ruth Maria Muthmann, Benedict Nicolson, Mark Oliver, Ann Peterson, Jacques Petit-Horry, Jean-Paul Poisson, M. and Mme. Christian Prévost-Marcilhacy, Marianne Roland-Michel, Caroline Rollins, baron Edmond de Rothschild, baronne Elie de Rothschild, Raymond Ruby, François-Gérard Séligmann, Germain Séligman, Jean Seznec, Gyde Vanier Shepherd, baronne de Soucy, Dr. Stewart Springstead, Mildred Steinbach, Mme. Maurice Stern, William Suhr, Teresa Sulerzyska, Jacques Vilain, Robert von der Lieth, Charles Walckenaer, Dean Walker, Burr Wallen, Sir Francis J. B. Watson and Eunice Williams.

I am deeply grateful to my friends at The Frick Collection for their encouragement and to the intelligent and helpful staff members of the libraries that made this catalogue possible: the Art Library and Sterling Memorial Library of Yale University, New Haven; the Frick Art Reference Library and New York Public Library, New York, and the Bibliothèque d'Art et d'Archéologie and Bibliothèque Nationale, Paris.

I owe very special thanks to Peter O. Marlow, who had the courage to make this venture possible and who was most indulgent to his Guest Curator; to Annette Ellis for sustained and patient assistance; to Carlos van Hasselt for boundless help and hospitality; to Pierre Rosenberg for unfailing cooperation and moral support, and to Joseph Focarino, ablest of editors, gifted translator and best of friends.

Edgar Munhall

Introduction

"Greuze, le grand Greuze . . . qui, encore aujourd'hui, demeure un des artistes les plus méconnus, les plus méprisés de toute l'histoire de la peinture et dont le 250è anniversaire de la naissance semble ne devoir être marqué par aucune exposition retentissante. . . ."[1]

It is entirely within the distinguished tradition of the Wadsworth Atheneum, a museum that has consistently assumed as avant-garde an attitude toward the past as toward the present, to accept the challenge offered less than a year ago by Pierre Rosenberg and to present the first comprehensive showing ever to be given the work of Jean-Baptiste Greuze.

Extolled at his death in 1805 with an understanding and enthusiasm comparable to that accorded his work when it was first presented to the Parisian public in 1755,[2] this painter's reputation has been eclipsed in our century. Surfeited with omnipresent *Heads of Girls*, most of which Greuze never painted, and prejudiced against or unfamiliar with the canons of history painting—a genre of which Greuze was an innovative and skilled practitioner—our contemporaries have failed until the last decade to give his art a fresh look and a new intellectual consideration. Thanks to our lenders' generosity, the present exhibition for the first time makes this possible.

In summing up the nature of Greuze's art, a theme developed at the end of this Introduction, the artist's contemporaries described Greuze over and over again as *"unique."*[3] Uniqueness is of course a characteristic of every great painter, yet Greuze's uniqueness seems more deliberate than accidental. He recognized at an early age the extra-ordinary skills and imagination he possessed and, driven by a fierce pride, resisted any temptation to conform his art to the ways of his time. His subjects had to be original, the execution of them would be as rapid or slow as Greuze decided, media would be mixed, the boundaries of genres would be broken and the emotional content of his work would range from the childishly timid to the demonic. Greuze gladly accepted the challenge of those masters he revered—Van Dyck, Rembrandt, Rubens, Poussin—and the artist seemed determined to join their company rather than rest comfortably among his contemporaries. Surely it is time that this highly individual attitude and the works it infused strike a sympathetic chord again.

Greuze's appearance, ideas and personality are relatively vivid to us, thanks to his many self-portraits (see for example Nos. 36, 71, 95, 114), to his writings—voluminous in comparision with those of his contemporary artists— and to the frequent references to him made by Diderot, Wille, Madame Vigée-Lebrun and their lesser-known associates. C.-L. Lecarpentier's appraisal of Greuze published shortly after the artist's death recorded his physical appearance in flattering terms: *"Greuze étoit d'une taille*

médiocre, il avoit la tête forte, le front très-grand, les yeux vifs et bien fendus, une figure spirituelle. Son abord annonçait la franchise et l'homme de génie; il étoit même assez difficile de ne pas dire, voilà Greuze, sans presque l'avoir vu. Il discourut volontiers, et avec la noble fierté d'un homme pénétré de son mérite, surtout quand on paroissoit vouloir le lui contester."[4] Charles Dufresne's description rings equally true: *"Il étoit d'une petite taille mais bien prise, la figure spirituelle, l'esprit vif, aucune infirmité à 70 ans, un petit pied qui, disoit-il à 70 ans, feroit sécher un petit maître, du reste ayant comme l'oeil de l'aigle et la main prompte comme l'éclair."*[5] Perhaps most evocatively, the author of Greuze's obituary recalled the tone of the artist's conversation: *"Sa conversation avec les hommes, étoit piquante et animée, surtout quand il parloit de son art, qu'il connoissoit à fond, et pour lequel il avoit un véritable enthousiasme. Son âme étoit naturellement élevée, même un peu fière, et cette fierté se manifestoit promptement, quand il n'obtenoit pas la justice qu'il croyoit due à ses rares talens, ou quand elle étoit provoquée par une censure amère ou peu éclairée."*[6]

These sources and others stress Greuze's small stature— often characteristic of an individual who carries a chip on his shoulder—his energy and the inordinate self-confidence that Diderot evoked so vividly and sympathetically in 1767: *"Pour l'artiste, il continue à s'enyvrer de lui-même, et tant mieux; il feroit peut-être moins bien, sans l'énorme présomption qu'il a de son talent."*[7] At the extreme, he was considered mad for his gauche utterances at court, capricious and bizarre in his dealings with subordinates, yet ultimately austere in his behavior.[8] He must never have stopped working.

Greuze was not a Parisian by birth. He was the sixth child in the large family of a roofer who lived in Tournus. The artist's early years were passed in that small town on the Saône, which was then as now dominated by the church of Saint-Philibert, once part of a Benedictine abbey (fig. 1). Built in the eleventh century, its grand scale and stern beauty characterize it as a major Romanesque monument. It was the first great work of art Greuze knew. Echoes of the artist's origins appear in the rustic settings of many of his familial subjects and in the genuine fervor of his religious sentiments, whose overtones of Protestant sobriety were typical of the Mâconnais region, as this inscription dated 1672 over a door in the rue de l'Hôpital at Tournus suggests:

"Avant le jour commence la journée
De l'éternel le Saint Nom bénissant
Le soir aussy ton labeur finissant
Loue le encor et passe ainsy l'année
Ayme Dieu et ton prochain."[9]

There were other indications of the artist's sensitive awareness of his provincial origins. Though he was baptized simply "Jean" and signed his earliest dated portrait (No. 5) "J. Greuze," he subsequently adopted the more elegant

Fig. 1 Tournus, Church of Saint-
Philibert, south side

1 "Greuze, the great Greuze . . .
who even today remains one of the
least understood, most scorned
artists in the entire history of
painting and whose 250th birthday
seems due to be marked by no
exhibition of world-wide interest
. . . ." P. Rosenberg, in *Le Siècle
de Louis XV: Peinture française de
1710 à 1774*, exhib. cat., Ottawa,
1976, p. 22
2 "*aucun artiste de cette époque . . .
n'a obtenu une réputation aussi étendue
et aussi peu contestée que la sienne. Le
prix considérable mis à ses tableaux,
et la place distinguée qu'ils occupent
dans tous les cabinets, sont un sûr
garant de l'estime de ses contemporains
et de celle de la postérité.*" ("no
artist of this era . . . achieved a
reputation so extensive and so
little contested as his. The
considerable price paid for his
pictures, and the distinguished place
they occupy in all collections,
are a sure guarantee of the esteem
of his contemporaries and of that
of posterity." "Notice sur Greuze,"
Journal des débats, March 27, 1805,
p. 2. "*Quel est ce jeune émulateur des
Téniers et des Brauer de qui le vol hardi
et subit semble tendre à la gloire si
directement? A peine il s'offre devant
le Temple de la peinture, que cette
déesse avec joye lui en ouvre les portes.*"
("Who is this young emulator of
Teniers and Brouwer whose bold
and sudden flight seems to tend so

directly toward glory? Hardly does
he present himself before the
Temple of painting than its goddess
joyfully opens its doors to him.")
[Baillet de Saint Julien],
*Caractères des peintres françois
actuellement vivans*, Paris, 1755, p. 3
3 "*Greuze . . . est unique dans
l'école française. Il n'y a été précédé ni
remplacé.*" ("Greuze . . . is unique
in the French school. He had
neither predecessor nor
replacement.") P. M. Gault de
Saint-Germain, *Les Trois Siècles de
la peinture en France*, Paris, 1808, p.
253. "*Né avec un talent original, il
n'avoit point eu de modèle, n'a point
formé d'école, et n'aura probablement
jamais que de faibles imitateurs.*"
("Born with an original talent, he
had had no model, formed no
school, and probably will never
have any but feeble imitators.")
Journal des débats, loc. cit.
4 "Greuze was of modest stature,
he had a strong head, a very high
forehead, lively, well-shaped eyes,
an intelligent face. His manner
proclaimed candor and the man of
genius; it was even rather
difficult not to say, here is *Greuze*,
almost before you had seen him.
He conversed easily, and with the
noble pride of a man imbued with
his own merit, especially when
someone appeared to want to
contest it." C.-L. F. Lecarpentier,
*Notice sur Greuze lu dans la séance de

la Société libre d'Emulation de Rouen*,
[Rouen], 1805, p. 6
5 "He was small in stature but
well proportioned, his face
intelligent, his spirit lively, no
infirmity at seventy, a little foot
that, said he at seventy, would
scare off a dandy, besides having
the eye of an eagle and a hand swift
as lightning." P. Ratouis de Limay,
"Un Chanteur à l'Opéra, graveur et
collectionneur au début du dix-
neuvième siècle," *Bulletin de la
Société de l'Histoire de l'Art français*,
1949, p. 77
6 "His conversation with men was
stimulating and animated, especially
when he was speaking of his art,
which he knew thoroughly and
for which he had a genuine
enthusiasm. His soul was by
nature exalted, even a bit proud,
and that pride showed itself
promptly when he did not obtain
the justice he believed his rare
talents deserved, or when it was
provoked by a harsh or
unenlightened criticism." *Journal
des débats, op. cit.*, p. 3
7 "As for the artist, he continues
to be intoxicated with himself,
and so much the better; he would
perhaps do less well without the
enormous presumption he has
concerning his talent." Diderot,
Correspondance, VII, p. 104
8 "*Cet homme est austère et aussi
original pour les moeurs que pour son*

talent." ("This man is austere and
as original in his manners as in his
talent.") M. G. W. Lundberg, "Le
Graveur suédois Pierre-Gustave
Floding à Paris et sa
correspondance," *Archives de l'art
français*, XVII, 1932, p. 292
9 "Before the dawn begin the
day / Blessing the Holy Name of the
eternal / At evening as well your
labor ending / Praise him again
and so pass the year / Love God
and your neighbor." Kindly
transcribed and communicated by
M. Emile Magnien in a letter dated
May 19, 1965

Fig. 2 *The Family Bible Reading*,
oil, on canvas, Paris, baron
Rodolphe Hottinguer

Fig. 3 Female Torso, study after
the antique, red chalk, Warsaw,
University Library

form of "Jean-Baptiste." The suave Mariette, appalled by
Greuze's affront to the Dauphin in 1761 (see Biography),
wrote first of that incident, *"mais cela étoit dit en sabotier,"*
and then added, *"mais étoit-il permis de manquer d'une
manière aussi ignoble au respect et aux convenances? Chacun
haussa les épaules et regarda le peintre en pitié."*[10] In addition to
the picturesque charms he regularly offered in his scenes of
country life, it would seem that Greuze as an individual
retained in Paris his earlier outspoken rustic manners and
was not at all intimidated by the more refined attitudes of
the capital.

After his initial training under Charles Grandon in Lyon,
about which very little is known, and his early days in
Paris, his meteoric rise to fame in 1755 came to the artist as
what he no doubt considered the just conclusion to an
intolerably prolonged period of neglect. Greuze's self-esteem,
which the abbé Gougenot gently called his *"trop grande
vivacité,"* obviated his following the standard training
required by the Académie as a prerequisite for membership.
Greuze sought at once to demonstrate his skills as a
draughtsman (No. 4), as a portraitist (fig. 10) and as a
genre painter (fig. 2), succeeding brilliantly at all three.
Elected an associate member of the Académie on June 28,
1755, his work was presented to the public for the first time
in the Salon later that summer. It attracted the interest of
important collectors and elicited instant critical praise:
*"Cet artiste n'a que vingt-neuf ans. Voilà des ouvrages dont un
homme peut se faire gloire; ils font honneur à son esprit, ils font
l'éloge de son coeur. On pense qu'il a une âme délicate et sensible.
On voudroit le connoître."*[11]

For various reasons none of the pictures from Greuze's
first Salon could be included in the present exhibition. The
absence of the rarely seen *The Family Bible Reading* (fig. 2)
is particularly regrettable, as this picture, in addition to
being a sophisticated pastiche of popular Dutch and Flemish
genre painters, was the first revelation of Greuze's ability
to infuse the representation of a serious moment of everyday
life with the rivetting emotional intensity that Bachaumont
would later describe thus: *"Greuze . . . un peintre qui donne
trop à penser, et remplit l'âme au point de ne pouvoir s'arréter sur
aucun autre objet."*[12]

The full impact of Greuze's Italian journey in 1755-57 is
yet to be understood, partly because of the unavailability
for study of the abbé Gougenot's manuscript "Album de
voyage en Italie." Of all the writers who have commented
on the trip, Sauerländer alone suspected any profound
consequences from Greuze's study of the monuments of
antiquity and the Renaissance, which were of crucial interest
to other travellers in Italy at the same time. Drawings such
as the previously unpublished sheet in the Warsaw
University Library (fig. 3) and echoes in Greuze's work
after the mid-1760s of antique—specifically Hellenistic—

Fig. 4 *The Well-Beloved Mother*, oil, on canvas, formerly Paris, marquis de Laborde

sculpture suggest that it took the artist many years to assimilate what he had seen on that trip. The immediate results, on the other hand, were the spectacular *Quatre Tableaux dans le costume italien* exhibited together in 1757 and reunited for the first time in the present exhibition (Nos. 9, 10, 12, 14). These complex pictures combine in their elegant design and execution precise sociological observation with witty ideas and deep moral convictions. They innaugurate as well Greuze's habit of conceiving pictures as pendants in which stylistic and dramatic differences heighten the effect of each of the pair.

The ten years following his return from Italy were among the most productive, contented and successful of the artist's career. In the four Salons between 1759 and 1765 the artist exhibited sixty-three works, ranging from polished but simple genre scenes (see No. 23) to the multi-faceted *A Marriage Contract* (No. 34), a variation of the genre picture with serious overtones presented on the scale of a history painting. The social triumph of Greuze's career as a genre painter was *The Well-Beloved Mother* (fig. 4), of which a sketch was exhibited in 1765 and the final painting completed by 1769 (see No. 46). Almost as in a pantomime, members of the family of the extremely rich marquis de Laborde act out a scene of familial bliss in a setting of rustic simplicity. For all the picture's contemporary air, it nonetheless exhibits in the group of the mother and her children reminiscences of traditional representations of Charity. In addition to this novel group portrait Greuze produced brilliant portraits of his new wife and her family (see No. 26), of influential figures at court (fig. 14), of collectors of contemporary art (Nos. 22, 35, 40) and of fellow artists such as his devoted friend Johann Georg Wille (No. 39). Perhaps as a result of Greuze's study with the latter of Rubens' Medici Series (Louvre), the artist's technique in the 1760s became less unctuous and relied increasingly on subtle glazes to set off the impasto of the highlights.[13] Diderot commented on this innovation in a letter to Falconet dated August 15, 1767: "*Il a changé toute sa manière. Vous sçavez que ses tableaux avoient tous un ciel bleuâtre. Ce n'est plus cela. Son coloris est plus franc, plus vrai, plus vigoureux.*"[14] The rapid evolution of Greuze's art during this period can be seen by comparing *Silence!* (No. 23), his masterpiece of the cabinet picture in the Dutch manner, with the roughhewn pendants of *The Ungrateful Son* and *The Punished Son* (Nos. 48, 49), which are in no manner but Greuze's alone. The unmasked emotional force of the everyday subject that simultaneously recalls the timeless theme of the Prodigal Son, the doubling of dramatic power through the pendant presentation and the implication that these were merely drawings for major paintings yet to come suggest what goals Greuze had set for himself and was announcing clearly to his public. Finally

10 "but that was said with the innocence of a country shoemaker." "but was it permissible to be disrespectful and indecorous in so ignoble a manner? Everyone shrugged his shoulders and looked at the painter with pity." P.-J. Mariette, *Abécédario*, ed. P. de Chennevières and A. de Montaiglon, *Archives de l'art français*, II, 1853 54, p. 331

11 "This artist is only twenty-nine. Here are works with which a man can attain glory; they do honor to his spirit, they speak in praise of his heart. One imagines that he has a delicate and sensitive soul. One would like to know him." Abbé J. de la Porte, *Sentimens sur plusieurs des tableaux exposés cette*

année dans le grand Sallon du Louvre, Paris, 1755, p. 17

12 "Greuze . . . a painter who gives too much to think about, and fills the soul to the point of being unable to focus on any other object." Quoted in R. Ingrams, "Bachaumont: A Parisian Connoisseur of the Eighteenth Century," *Gazette des Beaux-Arts*, January, 1970, p. 25

13 See L. Hautecoeur, "Greuze portraitiste, "*L'Art et les artistes*, IX, February, 1924, pp. 176-77

14 "He has changed his entire manner. You know how his pictures all used to have a bluish atmosphere. That is no longer the case. His coloring is purer, truer, more vigorous." Diderot, *Correspondance*, VII, p. 104

Fig. 5 Supine Male Figure,
study for *The Death of Cato of
Utica*, red chalk, Bayonne,
Musée Bonnat

Filial Piety (Hermitage), also regrettably absent from this exhibition, showed that Greuze had already established by 1763 a modern form of history painting that Diderot, along with many others, enthusiastically endorsed as a totally original invention.

Following years of such resounding public success and the satisfaction of seeing his art extend its expressive and technical limits, Greuze must indeed have been shocked by the Académie's decision not to permit him to exhibit in the Salon of 1767 for failing to present his *morceau de réception*. Still, he accepted their ultimatum and redoubled his efforts in the intervening years until the summer of 1769.

Sensing that his skills were at least equal to those of any history painter of his time, Greuze put traditional genre painting behind him and boldly entered the arena of history painting, a step he had repeatedly been advised to make from the very beginning of his career.[15] Drawing on his earlier familiarity with the antique and making fresh studies from sculpture and casts available to him, he undertook a variety of religious and historical subjects— *Lot and His Daughters* (No. 57), *Cimon and Pero* (Nos. 59, 60), *The Death of Cato of Utica* (fig. 5), *Aegina Visited by Jupiter* (No. 65), *Vespasian and Sabinus* (Chaumont, Musée d'Art et d'Histoire), *The Funeral of Patroclus* (No. 66)—and ultimately settled on the confrontation of Septimius Severus

and Caracalla as the vehicle for his reception painting (No. 70). Though it did contain echoes of the familial conflicts the artist had treated previously in contemporary dress (No. 48), it was characteristic of Greuze to select as the subject for his first official history painting not a familiar one treated by many predecessors but rather a theme never undertaken before.

Greuze's determined change of genre was accompanied by a change in painterly manner. The subtle play of transparent glazes over and around passages of impasto gave way to a flatter, mat surface reminiscent of the manner of Poussin, the master Greuze now turned to as he abandoned his earlier reliance on Rembrandt and Rubens.

The Académie's decision in 1769 to grant Greuze full membership but specifically as a genre painter, not a history painter, was the trauma of the artist's life. It seems increasingly likely that this event, which dishonored the Académie and the artist alike, was in essence a vindictive rebuke by his irritated and impatient colleagues in response to Greuze's overweaning pride and inconsiderate behavior. The humiliation resulted in Greuze's abandoning any association with the Académie until after its transformation into the Académie des Beaux-Arts in 1795, and even then he did not exhibit with that body until 1800. As a further sign of disdain Greuze regularly timed exhibitions of his

Fig. 6 *The Bed*, oil, on panel,
Paris, private collection

own work in his studio to coincide with the biennial ones of the Académie. More importantly, the event led to Greuze's largely abandoning traditional history painting to develop his own version of that exalted genre, most notably with *The Father's Curse: The Ungrateful Son* and *The Father's Curse: The Punished Son* (Nos. 84, 88). In taking this crucial step, Greuze was moving in the direction pointed out a few years earlier by the perceptive Diderot, who wrote in his *Essai sur la peinture:* "*Cependent je proteste que le* Père qui fait la lecture à sa famille [fig. 2], *le* Fils ingrat [No. 48], *et les* Fiançailles [No. 34] *de Greuze . . . sont autant pour moi des tableaux d'histoire que les* Sept Sacrements *de* Poussin, la Famille de Darius *de Lebrun ou* la Suzanne *de Vanloo.*"[16]

There remains the challenge of confronting Greuze's reception painting itself (No. 70). Seen alongside pictures spanning the artist's entire career—an experience which this exhibition for the first time permits—the austere beauty of *Septimius Severus Reproaching Caracalla* may now appear obvious, as well as its skillful evocation of an awesome event experienced by four men, each subtly differentiated by character, gesture and expression. The painting is a highly original exercise in history painting, exploiting the traditional techniques of the genre to draw the viewer imaginatively into a moral predicament which becomes momentarily his own.

Greuze stated later that the scandal of his reception into the Académie had in part been affected by his wife's involvement in 1769 with Blondel d'Azincourt, an influential member of the art world who had been made an *associé libre* of the Académie in 1767 and who could have influenced the artist's colleagues against him. This would have been neither the first nor the last time Anne-Gabrielle Babuti (fig. 11) influenced her husband's career. Following their marriage in 1759, her beauty, which Greuze found enhanced by their domestic environment, reappears in many of Greuze's portraits and genre scenes of the 1760s. It could be said that she is conspicuous by her absence in *The Bed* (fig. 6), a surprising glance the artist offered into his private world, showing perhaps one of the "*deux lits composés chacun d'une paillasse, un matelas, un lit de plume et leur baldaquin en indienne*" mentioned in an inventory of his belongings made after his divorce.[17] Madame Greuze's influence soon became negative, as she mingled in and flagrantly mismanaged Greuze's important dealings with engravers, and as her domestic quarrels and scandalous behavior, painfully observed by her husband but seemingly unchecked by him until much later, rendered him a buffoon. Of the couple's incessant squabbles, Diderot commented: "*J'aime à l'entendre causer avec sa femme. C'est une parade où Polichinelle rabat les coups avec un art qui rend le compère plus méchant. Je prens quelquefois la liberté de leur en dire mon avis, avec le leste que vous sçavez.*"[18] It is difficult to imagine how

15 "*Un peu plus bas s'offrent les essais d'un nouvel athlète . . . les talens supérieurs de M. Greuze ont fait désirer à tous ceux qui ont vu ces tableaux, que l'auteur élevât sa muse à un genre un peu plus noble, il semble qu'il seroit capable de faire quelque chose de plus grand: cependant c'est à lui de consulter ses forces: Quid valeant humer; c'est son génie qu'il doit suivre et non pas les idées du public.*" ("A little further down are offered the endeavors of a new athlete. . . . the superior talents of M. Greuze have made all those who have seen these pictures wish that the author elevate his muse to a genre a bit more noble, it seems that he would be capable of doing something more grand; however, it is up to him to take stock of his abilities: *Quid valeant humer*; it is his genius that he should follow and not the ideas of the public.") *Lettre sur le Salon de 1755 addressée à ceux qui la liront*, Amsterdam, 1755, pp. 38–39

16 "Still I protest that the *Father Reading to his Family* [fig. 2], the *Ungrateful Son* [No. 48], and the *Bethrothal* [No. 34] of Greuze . . . are for me as much history paintings as the *Seven Sacraments* of Poussin, the *Family of Darius* of Lebrun or the *Susanna* of Van Loo." D. Diderot, *Essai sur la peinture*, in *Oeuvres esthétiques*, Paris, n.d., p. 725

17 "two beds each made up of a straw mattress, an overlay mattress, a featherbed and their calico canopy." M. Barroux, ed., "Procès-verbal d'apposition de scellés chez Greuze après son divorce," *Bulletin de la Société de l'Histoire de Paris et de l'Ile-de-France*, 1896, p. 88

18 "I love to hear him chatter with his wife. It is a puppet show in which Punch returns the blows with an art that makes his partner all the nastier. Sometimes I take the liberty of giving them my opinion, with the freedom you are familiar with." Diderot, *Correspondance*, VII, p. 104

an individual possessed of such inordinate professional pride could have submitted in private to the humiliations his wife threw his way, many of which he recalled in precise detail in the legal dispositions he later made against her. But apparently it was a relationship that nourished him in a special way. Charles Dufresne recalled Greuze's recounting to him that, following one encounter in which the artist had to arm himself with a chair to fend off his wife brandishing firetongs and her lover the firedogs, Greuze rushed off: "*frappé du tableau que j'avais sous les yeux je rentre en frémissant dans mon cabinet. Je prends un crayon et je fais un croquis de cette scène d'horreur. C'est un des plus beaux dessins que j'aye faits* [see No. 96]. *Je vous invite à le venir voir.*"[19] This peculiar marriage was dissolved immediately after the legalization of divorce in 1793, leaving Anne-Gabrielle with a large settlement and her former husband to be comforted by their daughters, who remained with him the rest of his life.

Returning to Greuze's art, one of its peculiar and constant features, an element basic to its understanding, was Greuze's exploitation of expression. He used this device, which was a traditional feature of history painting derived in part from the ancients, to illuminate his dramatic subjects and to lure the viewer into a sympathetic participation in them. With his ceaseless observation of his fellow men, his unusual skill in capturing their likenesses and his intense involvement with his subjects, Greuze made expression one of his most effective tools. Comparison of his drawing of a sorrowful young man (fig. 8) with an engraving representing physical pain (fig. 7) from Charles Lebrun's *Conférence sur l'expression générale et particulière*, discussed in connection with No. 85, clearly indicates that in his studies of expression Greuze was following the traditional sources of history painting, but revivifying that tradition by adapting it to modern life. He produced a great number of such preparatory studies of expression for *A Marriage Contract* (No. 34), *Septimius Severus Reproaching Caracalla* (No. 70), *The Father's Curse: The Ungrateful Son* (No. 84), *The Father's Curse: The Punished Son* (No. 88) and *The Drunken Cobbler* (No. 94). Greuze's *têtes d'expression* were sought after by collectors, and engravings after them became standard tools of artistic instruction, leading to the existence of innumerable copies of Greuze's expressive heads.

It has been apparent to some of Greuze's admirers over the years that his art possessed an emotional force such as we associate more readily today with his contemporaries Goya and Fuseli. Around 1761 this quality was not yet fully grasped by Mariette, who loftily noted the anecdotal appeal of Greuze's everyday subjects to the masses—"*La multitude est touchée du choix du sujet qui rapproche de nos moeurs et lui sert d'entretien*"—as well as the technical finesse of their

execution: "*Les connoisseurs trouvent leur compte dans la façon dont ils sont peints. . . . Greuze a fait plusieurs portraits qui portent un caractère de vérité qui les doit faire priser.*"[20] But writing in 1776, J.-B.-P. Le Brun brilliantly summarized the ideological content of Greuze's art, as well as his manner of painting. For him the range of Greuze's realism was obvious: "*Peindre l'homme, dans la vie privée, est le grand talent de M. Greuze. L'expression des moeurs simples, de la candeur, de l'amour, du désir, de la libéralité, de la reconnaissance, de la tendresse filiale; tels sont les sujets qu'il prend dans la nature et qu'il rend avec le plus grand intérêt.*" What was unique in Le Brun's eyes was Greuze's ability to involve the viewer dramatically: "*l'intérêt et le pathétique ont étonné les connoisseurs et fait verser des larmes à des âmes indifférentes jusqu'à ce jour à la force magique de la peinture. . . . et le Peintre qui sçait nous émouvoir de la sorte est, pour nous, un nouveau Raphaël.*"[21]

Many of the eighteenth-century critics quoted throughout the entries of this catalogue, practitioners of what was then a new literary genre, insisted on Greuze's ability to draw tears from his public. Brookner has thoroughly explored the literary and artistic background of this "*sensible*" approach to painting, but it remains to be seen whether such a reaction is as operative in the late twentieth century as it was in the eighteenth.

The baron Boutard, who wrote so sympathetically of Greuze's *Saint Mary of Egypt* (No. 113), took the occasion of Greuze's last Salon in 1804 to summarize the career of this man he called "*un personnage chaque jour plus remarquable dans l'histoire de l'art*": "*Entré dans la carrière de la peinture à l'époque peut-être la moins brillante de l'école française, il sentit que pour s'élever il falloit sortir de la route commune, et il se créa une manière de faire qu'on a vainement tenté d'imiter; il fut l'inventeur du sujet de tous ses tableaux; et ses tableaux ne sont pas un assemblage fortuit de figures, mais la représentation de scènes où tout est prévu, motivé, expliqué, et qui ont presque toujours le mérite d'être ce qu'on pouvoit imaginer de mieux approprié à l'art sous le rapport pittoresque. Ses personnages, choisis d'ordinaire dans la classe commune de la société, se relèvent par la noblesse du caractère et de l'action; peu de peintres ont aussi bien fait à la figure d'expression; nul n'a eu des idées plus élevées et plus justes sur l'ordre social; aucun n'a peint de couleurs plus vives ou plus touchantes, la pudeur des premiers amours, la tendresse des épouses et des mères, les soins de la piété filiale, la dignité des pères et leur puissance terrible.*"[22]

In 1846 Théodore Thoré, who could judge Greuze at a time when eighteenth-century painting was returning to favor, stressed anew his uniqueness: "*Greuze fut un peintre très-excentrique, en dehors de l'inspiration habituelle de son temps. C'est un anneau détaché de la chaîne des peintres de Louis XV, quoique sa forme et sa ciselure soient du même style et du même travail que l'art Pompadour. . . . Boucher est le poète des petites*

Fig. 7 *Physical Pain*, engraving
after Charles Lebrun from the
Conférence sur l'expression

Fig. 8 Head of a Young Man,
red chalk, formerly Leningrad,
Hermitage

19 "struck by the picture I had
before my eyes I return trembling
to my studio. I take some chalk
and make a sketch of that scene of
horror. It is one of the most
beautiful drawings I have done
[see No. 96]. I invite you to come
see it." Michel Nitot [called
Charles Dufresne], "Cahiers,"
ms., Paris, Musée des Arts
Décoratifs, Bibliothèque, VIII, p. 49
20 "The crowd is moved by the
subject matter which relates to
our manners and customs and gives
it something to talk about." "The
connoisseurs find their reward
in the way they are painted. . . .
Greuze has done several portraits
that convey a character of truth
for which they must be prized."
Mariette, *op. cit.*, II, p. 350
21 "To paint man in his private
life is the great talent of M. Greuze.
The expression of simple manners,
of candor, of love, of desire, of
generosity, of gratitude, of filial
tenderness, such are the subjects
he takes from nature and conveys
with the greatest interest." "the
interest and the pathos have
astonished connoisseurs and brought
forth tears from souls indifferent
up until that day to the magical
force of painting. . . . and the
Painter who can move us in this
way is, for us, a new Raphael."
J.-B.-P. Le Brun, *Almanach
historique et raisonné des architectes,
peintres, sculpteurs, graveurs et
ciseleurs*, Paris, 1776, (Minkoff
reprint, 1972), p. 92–94
22 "an individual each day more
remarkable in the history of art."
"Having embarked on a career as
painter at what was perhaps the
least brilliant era of the French
school, he felt that to elevate
himself it was necessary to abandon
the common road, and he created
for himself a way of doing things
that others have tried to imitate
in vain; he was the inventor of
the subject of all his pictures; and
his pictures are not an accidental
grouping of figures, but the
representation of scenes in which
everything is planned, motivated,
explained, and which almost
always have the merit of being as
appropriate as could be imagined
to art in its picturesque aspect.
His subjects, usually chosen from
the common class of society, are
raised up by the nobility of their
character and of the action; few
painters have done as well at the
expressive head; none has had
ideas more elevated and more just
on the social order; none has
painted with colors more vivid
or touching the purity of first
loves, the tenderness of wives and
mothers, the cares of filial piety,
the dignity of fathers and their
terrible power." M. B. [baron
Boutard], "Beaux-Arts, Salon de
l'an XIII," *Journal des débats*,
January 5, 1805, p. 5

maisons et des ruelles; Greuze est le bourgeois de la ville, singeant quelquefois avec naïveté la coquetterie de la cour."[23]

Arsène Houssaye, who in 1848 extolled the beauties of *Saint Mary of Egypt* (No. 113), developed Thoré's chain imagery, stating that "*Greuze a été un petit anneau de la chaîne d'or qui unit Lesueur à Prud'hon,*" and spoke of Greuze's position in his century as crucial: "*Greuze balaya du bout de son pinceau tout ce clinquant vieilli qui déshonorait la peinture; il lui rendit une parure plus digne et plus noble: la parure des larmes.*" He concluded by citing the artist's own characteristic words describing this accomplishment: "*J'avais trempé mon pinceau dans mon coeur.*"[24]

After the mid-nineteenth century the ambiguous charms of the typical Greuze *Head of a Girl* dominated the public's impression of the artist's production. The courageous and distinguished writers who devoted themselves to Greuze were attracted primarily by the undeniable formal beauty of his work, but often at the expense of its thematic content—though Brookner has recently set the latter squarely in its place among the intellectual currents of the time. Only in the last decade have important museum acquisitions (among them fig. 9, Nos. 18, 20, 24, 65, 79, 96), the examples of Greuze's work included and sensitively analyzed in major exhibitions, and an occasional article such as Michael Fried's suggested that the totality of Greuze's vast oeuvre is ready for a new viewing and reinterpretation. One of the reasons for citing so frequently in this catalogue the opinions of the artist's contemporaries was to supply as a valid basis for such a new interpretation the enthusiastic one of Greuze's own time.

Assessing Greuze's place among the great painters of his great century will be an easier task once this exhibition has taken place. Unreasonably neglected and scorned for nearly a century, he may still be suffering in part from the negative personal impression he left behind. The exceptionally talented pupil of an artist of no distinction, he disdained the official training his natural skills could easily have obtained for him, he worked poorly with others, neglected the most flattering commissions, forgot his benefactors, treated his colleagues with scorn, led a private life of profound self-humiliation, eventually betrayed his art to earn money and was even reduced to begging. Yet this unappealing individual was driven by a powerful conviction of his own talents, which he developed ardently and with intelligence. He used his skills to express the highest moral attitudes of the past as well as the familiar emotional preoccupations of the common people of his time, doing so with an amplitude and truth that few of his contemporaries possessed. Moreover, the intensity of his expression was such that the searing familial crises, the tragedies of childhood, the anguish of lovers he evoked retain a universal significance. His pictures are not cobwebbed images of a distant time. Modern connoisseurs can derive new satisfaction from the delights of Greuze's draughtsmanship and the panache of certain of his portraits. But a deeper, often harrowing experience awaits him who follows this magician step by step into the dramatic scenes he conjured forth with such devastating effect.

Edgar Munhall

Fig. 9 Standing Female Nude,
after Jacob Van Loo, black and
red chalk, stumped, heightened
with white chalk, Lyon, Musée
des Beaux-Arts

23 "Greuze was a most eccentric
painter, beyond the customary
inspiration of his time. He is a
link detached from the chain of
the painters of Louis XV, though
his form and modelling are of the
same style and workmanship as
the art of Pompadour. . . . Boucher
is the poet of little houses and
byways; Greuze is the citizen of
the town, aping sometimes naively
the coquetry of the court." T. Thoré,
Le Salon de 1846, Paris, 1846, pp. 3-4
24 "Greuze was a small link in
the golden chain that unites
Lesueur and Prud'hon." "Greuze
swept away with the tip of his
brush all the antiquated tinsel
that dishonored painting; he
restored to it an ornament more
worthy and more noble: the
ornament of tears." "I had dipped
my brush into my heart." A.
Houssaye, *Galerie de portraits du
XVIIIè siècle*, Paris, 1848, pp.
231, 263

This summary biography lists major events in the life of Jean-Baptiste Greuze as well as a few unfamiliar incidents and some hitherto unpublished details concerning the artist's Italian journey. For further information the reader is referred to the studies by Louis Hautecoeur, Camille Mauclair and Anita Brookner listed in the Bibliography.

1697: Birth of Jean-Louis Greuze, father of the artist. In 1725 his occupation is described as *"maître couvreur,"* but in 1759 Greuze would describe him as *"entrepreneur-architecte."*[1]

August 21, 1725: Birth of Jean-Baptiste Greuze, sixth of nine children born to Jean-Louis Greuze and his wife, née Claudine Roch, in the town of Tournus near Mâcon. The baptismal certificate in the parish register of Saint-André reads: *"Jean, fils légitime de sieur Jean-Louis Greuze, maître couvreur, demeurant audit Tournus, et de Claudine Roch, sa femme, est né le vingt et unième août mil sept cent vingt-cinq, a été baptisé le même jour par moi, vicaire soussigné; le parrain a été sieur Jean Bezaud, aussi maître couvreur, et la demoiselle Antoinette Auberut [?], femme d'Hugues Brulé, boulanger en ladite paroisse; tous lesquels se sont soussignés, excepté ledit parrain qui ne le sait, de ce requis. Signé: J.-L. Greuze, Antoinette Auberut et Gornot, vicaire."*[2]

1732: Birth in Paris of Anne-Gabrielle Babuti, the artist's future wife.

July 25, 1733: Greuze reputedly shows his first signs of talent, presenting to his father on the feast of Saint James a copy of an engraving depicting that saint which the father mistakes for a print.

1745–50: At an unknown date Greuze leaves Tournus to study painting in Lyon with Charles Grandon (1691–1762).

c. 1750: Greuze arrives in Paris, where he studies drawing at the Académie under Charles Natoire (see No. 4). He wins the favor of Pigalle and, through him, of Louis de Silvestre, who is named *Directeur* of the Académie in 1752 and whose portrait (fig. 10) Greuze paints in order to prove his talents to the members of the Académie. The earliest account of these years is that given by Louis Gougenot: *"Sa trop grande vivacité ne lui permit pas de se ployer à recevoir des leçons d'aucuns maîtres. Il vint à Paris et suivit l'école sans s'assujetter à mettre à aucun prix, privé par là de la prérogative qu'ont ceux qui les ont remportés d'être placés plus avantageusement dans l'école pour dessiner d'après le modèle, il se contentit de la dernière place, que les élèves appellent par dérision le Baquet par ce qu'en étant directement dessous la lampe, celui qui l'occupe en reçoit les égoutures."* Finally Greuze *"demanda une place de distinction pour dessiner,"* which makes the other students rebel. Pigalle decides that it is time to *"recevoir Mr Greuze sur le charge de l'Académie, que c'étoit son sentiment; mais qu'il convenoit qu'il présentât auparavant de ses ouvrages à Mr Silvestre le Directeur."* Members of the Académie agree with Pigalle's opinion and go further: *"comme il avait annoncé qu'à son talent de peindre*

Bambochades, il réunissoit celui du Portrait on le chargea d'en faire un. Plusieurs envieux alors répandirent le bruit qu'il s'étoit fait aider dans quelques têtes qu'on avoit trouvé fort belles, ce qui fit qu'on se détermina pour lever tout soupçon à le charger de tirer le Directeur. Il y réussit si parfaitement et sous les yeux de toute l'Académie qu'on trouva ce portrait dans le goût de Vandec. Il joignit à ce morceau les tableaux de son élève qui s'endort en étudiant sa leçon, de l'aveugle trompé, et de son père de famille qui lit la Bible à ses enfans."[3]

June 28, 1755: Greuze is named associate member of the Académie.

Summer 1755: Greuze exhibits for the first time in the Salon. His entries include:

145 *L'Aveugle trompé* (Moscow, Pushkin Museum)

146 *Un Père de famille qui lit la Bible à ses enfans* (fig. 2)

147 *Un Enfant qui s'est endormi sur son livre* (Montpellier, Musée Fabre)

148 *Une Tête d'après nature*

149 *Le Portrait de M. de Silvestre, Directeur de l'Académie* (fig. 10)

The first three entries are purchased by Lalive de Jully, whose portrait Greuze would later paint (Nos. 6, 22), and who thus becomes the artist's first important collector.

September 1755–April 1757: Greuze travels in Italy with Louis Gougenot, abbé de Chezal-Benoît (No. 16), whom he had met probably through Pigalle.

September 22, 1755: Gougenot records that he and Greuze leave Paris *"dans une chaise ouverte italienne à laquelle j'avois fait mettre des ressorts."*[4]

October 1, 1755: Gougenot notes: *"Le 1er octobre nous fûmes à Tournus. . . . Je laissai Mr Greuze à Tournus dans le sein de sa famille où il proposait de passer quelques jours et ensuite de me rejoindre à Lyon."*[5]

October 9, 1755: The travellers spend the night in the Grande Chartreuse at Rives, *"où nous fûmes très bien traités."*[6]

October 11, 1755: On the way from Rives to Grenoble, *"Mr Greuze ne se divertit pas moins en voyant dans ce poste mal gardé une tabagie telle qu'il serait difficile d'en trouver une semblable."*[7]

October 18, 1755: The travellers cross the Mont-Cenis pass, *"chacun dans un petit fauteuil d'osier en forme de brancard. . . . Quoiqu'il ne faille que deux hommes pour porter chaque personne, on en prend ordinairement six et ils se relayent alternativement. Ces sortes de porteurs s'apellent vulgairement des Marons."*[8]

October 19, 1755: They leave Susa and fear for their lives because of floods. Gougenot recounts, *"Je donnai mes lettres de crédit à Mr Greuze et m'étant déshabillé nous prîmes le parti de nous jetter à l'eau."* They arrive safely on the other side where, *"Pendant ce temps une jeune et jolie Bergère qui étoit venuë par hasard se refugier dans la cassine, faisoit du feu à Mr Greuze et séchoit ses habits."*[9]

October 20, 1755: Passing through Rivoli the travellers reach Turin, where they see paintings by Van Dyck, Solimena, Ricci, Reni, Guercino, Bassano and others.[10]

October 28, 1755: After a week they leave Turin by coach.[11]

Fig. 10 Portrait of Louis de
Silvestre, oil, on canvas, whereabouts unknown

1 "master roofer." "contractor-architect."
2 "Jean, legitimate son of sieur Jean-Louis Greuze, master roofer, residing in the aforesaid Tournus, and of Claudine Roch, his wife, was born August 21, 1725, was baptized the same day by me, the vicar undersigned; the godfather was sieur Jean Bezaud, also master roofer, and demoiselle Antoinette Auberut [?], wife of Hugues Brulé, baker in the said parish; all of whom have signed below, except the said godfather who does not know how, as required. Signed: J.-L. Greuze, Antoinette Auberut and Gornot, vicar."
3 "His excessive vivacity would not permit him to stoop to taking lessons from any masters. He came to Paris and attended school without competing for any prizes, deprived thereby of the prerogative held by those who have won them

of being placed more advantageously in the life drawing classes; he contented himself with the most distant spot, which the students derisively call the Bucket because, being directly under the lamp, whoever occupies it catches the drippings." "requested a prime spot to draw from." "receive Mr Greuze on the Académie's roll, that such was his feeling; but that it was proper that he should first present some of his works to Mr Silvestre the Director." "as he had announced that to his talent for painting Genre scenes he added that of the Portrait, he was asked to do one. Several envious persons then spread the rumor that he had had someone help him with some heads that had been judged very beautiful, as a result of which it was determined, in order to remove all suspicion, to assign him to

portray the Director. He succeeded in this so perfectly, and before the eyes of all the Académie, that this portrait was considered to be in the manner of Van Dyck. He added to this piece his pictures of the student who falls asleep while studying his lesson, the blind man deceived, and the head of the family reading the Bible to his children." L. Gougenot, abbé de Chezal-Benoît, "Album de voyage en Italie," ms., Paris, collection of the baronne de Soucy, I, pp. 138–41
4 "in an open Italian carriage in which I had had some springs installed." Ibid., p. 144
5 "October 1st we were at Tournus. . . . I left Mr Greuze at Tournus in the bosom of his family, where he proposed to spend a few days and then rejoin me in Lyon." Ibid., p. 156
6 "where we were very well treated." Ibid., p. 178

7 "Mr Greuze was no less amused to see in this ill-kept post a saloon the likes of which it would be difficult to find." Ibid., pp. 180–81
8 "each in a little wicker chair in the form of a handbarrow. . . . Although only two men are required to carry each person, one normally takes six and they work in relays. Porters of this type are called in the vernacular Growlers." Ibid., p. 194
9 "I gave my letters of credit to Mr Greuze, and having undressed we resolved to throw ourselves into the water." "During this time a pretty young Shepherdess who had come by chance to take shelter in the hut made a fire for Mr Greuze and dried his clothes." Ibid., pp. 207–09
10 Ibid., pp. 226–27
11 Ibid., p. 249

19

October 30–November 4, 1755: They journey from Novi to Genoa and back.[12] During the visit to Genoa Greuze executes a drawing of a woman in local dress which is included in this exhibition (No. 7).

November 6, 1755: They arrive in Parma, where Greuze executes another costume drawing (No. 8) and sees the work of Parmigianino and Correggio.[13]

November 11, 1755: In Modena they see works by Guercino, Correggio and Sacchi. Gougenot makes his usual careful notes on local fashions, which correspond to Greuze's *Divers Habillements suivant le costume d'Italie* (see No. 7).[14]

November 14, 1755: To Bologna, where they admire the paintings of the Carracci, Guercino, Domenichino, Cavedone and Tiarini.[15]

November 21, 1755: Gougenot and Greuze leave Bologna for Florence.[16]

January 10, 1756: In Paris Gougenot is named an honorary associate of the Académie for having taken Greuze to Italy.

January 28, 1756: Natoire, previously Greuze's teacher in Paris and now *Directeur* of the Académie de France in Rome, announces to Marigny the arrival there of Gougenot and Greuze. The abbé Barthélémy mentions that the two had visited Naples prior to being in Rome.

May 12, 1756: The abbé Barthélémy describes *The Broken Eggs* (No. 9) and mentions that Greuze has painted portraits of the French ambassador and his wife, the future duc and duchesse de Choiseul. He writes to the comte de Caylus telling him of the imminent departure of Gougenot from Rome. He reports that *"Greuze reste à Rome; l'abbé Gougenot voulait le ramener. Il a répondu que, l'académie lui ayant fait l'honneur de l'agréer, il devoit reconnoître ses bontés par de nouveaux efforts; qu'en se renfermant dans son genre, il trouveroit, dans les sites et les ruines de Rome, des richesses piquantes pour ses compositions et qui sait si la vue et l'étude des tableaux de Raphaël ne l'élèveront pas au-dessus de lui-même. . . . Il est donc décidé qu'il reste à Rome, pour briller davantage à Paris; et qu'après un séjour de plusieurs mois, il ira s'établir à Venise pour plusieurs mois encore."*[17] Barthélémy's words are confirmed by an autograph letter of Greuze also dated May 12, 1756, expressing many of the same ideas: *"J'ai parcouru toute l'Italie avec beaucoup de soins jusqu'à Rome que j'ai été sur le point de quitter pour retourner satisfait de toutes les belles choses que j'ai vu, mais au désespoir du peu de tems qui ne me paroissait pas suffisant pour en tirer tout l'avantage qu'un artiste se doit proposer dans un voiage d'un si long cour. J'ai communiqué à M. Gougenot le désir que j'avois de rester, il a bien voulu se rendre à mes instence."*[18] An additional reason for Greuze's desire to remain in Rome may have been the romance he is said to have commenced with an aristocratic woman, possibly a member of the Pignatelli family. Fragonard, who knew Greuze in Rome, called him a *"chérubin amoureux"* (amorous cherub).

May 25, 1756: Natoire informs Marigny that Gougenot is returning to Paris.

November 28, 1756: Marigny instructs Natoire to give Greuze lodgings in the Palazzo Mancini, home of the Académie, and commissions two paintings from Greuze for Madame de Pompadour (see No. 24).

February 22, 1757: The abbé Barthélémy describes the significance and style of *The Neapolitan Gesture* (No. 14).

April 20, 1757: Natoire informs Marigny that Greuze has left for Paris. His earlier intention to visit Venice seems not to have been fulfilled.

Summer 1757: Greuze shows at the Salon the products of his Italian journey and other works:
Quatre tableaux dans le costume italien—

112 *Une Mère grondant un jeune homme pour avoir renversé un panier d'oeufs que la servante apportoit du marché. Un enfant tente de raccommoder un oeuf cassé.* (No. 9)

113 *Une Jeune italienne congédiant (avec le geste napolitain) un cavalier portugais travesti, et reconnu par sa suivante: deux enfans ornent ce sujet, l'un retient un chien qui abboye.* (No. 14)

114 *La Paresseuse italienne* (No. 10)

115 *Un Oiseleur qui, au retour de la chasse, accorde sa guitarre* (No. 12)

116 *Le Portrait de M. Pigalle, sculpteur du Roi*

117 *Le Portrait de M.*** en ovale* (No. 16?)

118 *Le Matelot napolitain* (London, Wallace Collection)

119 *Un Ecolier qui étudie sa leçon* (No. 15)

120 *Deux Têtes; l'une un petit garçon, l'autre une petite fille*

121 *Esquisse à l'encre de la Chine, représentant des Italiens qui jouent à la More* (Moscow, Pushkin Museum)

122 *Autres ouvrages du même auteur*

January 31, 1759: Greuze signs a marriage contract with Anne-Gabrielle Babuti (fig. 11), whom he marries on February 3 in Saint-Médard, Paris. He had met her in her father's bookstore shortly after his return from Rome (see No. 26).

June 11, 1759: Johann Georg Wille (No. 39) mentions Greuze for the first of many times in his *Journal*.

Summer 1759: Greuze shows twenty works in the Salon:

103 *Un tableau représentant le Repos, caractérisé par une Femme qui impose silence à son fils, en lui montrant ses autres enfans qui dorment* (No. 23)

104 *La Simplicité représentée par une jeune fille* (see No. 24)

105 *La Tricoteuse endormie*

106 *La Dévideuse* (New York, The Frick Collection)

107 *Une Jeune Fille qui pleure la mort de son oiseau* (see No. 44)

108 *Le Portrait de M. de ***, jouant de la harpe* (No. 22)

109 *Portrait de Madame la Marquise de ***, accordant sa guitarre* (No. 21)

110 *Portrait de M. ***, Docteur de Sorbonne*

111 *Portrait de Mademoiselle de ***, sentant une rose* (No. 20)

Fig. 11 Anne-Gabrielle Babuti
Asleep, red chalk, Karlsruhe,
Staatliche Kunsthalle

12 *Ibid.*, pp. 255, 299
13 *Ibid.*, p. 313
14 *Ibid.*, pp. 351–52
15 *Ibid.*, p. 365
16 *Ibid.*, p. 425
17 "Greuze remains in Rome; the abbé Gougenot wanted to take him back. He replied that, the Académie having paid him the honor of making him an associate, he was obliged to return their kindness by some new efforts; that in confining himself to his genre, he would find, in the sites and ruins of Rome, a wealth of stimulation for his compositions, and who knows whether the sight and study of Raphael's pictures will not raise him above himself. . . . It is therefore decided that he remain in Rome, in order to shine all the more in Paris; and that after a stay of several months, he will go to reside in Venice for several months more." Abbé J.-J. Barthélémy, *Voyage en Italie*, Paris, 1801, p. 133
18 "I travelled through all of Italy with great care as far as Rome, which I was about to leave to return

satisfied with all the beautiful things I had seen, but despairing over the short time, which did not seem to me sufficient to draw the full advantage an artist should propose to take during such a protracted journey. I expressed to M. Gougenot my desire to remain, he was kind enough to grant my request." Letter with the dealer Lambert, Paris, in 1964
19 Greuze would state in 1791 or 1792, "*nous avions eu trois enfants, il nous en restaient deux.*" ("we had had three children, two of them survived.") J. Boilly, ed., "Mémoire de Greuze contre sa femme," *Archives de l'art français*, II, 1852–53, p. 160
20 Wille, I, p. 164
21 "I don't like faces that are painted already." "You had given me to understand that this painter was a peculiar man, but you had not told me he was mad." M. G. W. Lundberg, "Le Graveur suédois Pierre-Gustave Floding à Paris et sa correspondance," *Archives de l'art français*, XVII, 1932, p. 292

112 *Portrait de Mademoiselle de Amici, en habit de caractère* (Leighton Buzzard, Mentmore, Lady Rosebery)
113 *Portrait de M. Babuti, Libraire* (see No. 26)
114 *Trois Têtes*
115 *Deux Têtes*
116 *Une Tête*
117 *Autre Tête*
118 *Deux Esquisses à l'encre de Chine*

November 1759: Birth of Greuze's first child, Marie-Anne Claudine, whose presumably early death is not recorded.[19]

September 30, 1760: Diderot (No. 50) refers to Greuze in a letter to Sophie Volland. He seems to have known him for some time.

April 1761: Greuze takes on as a pupil Pierre-Alexandre Wille, son of his good friend.[20] Greuze's portrait of the boy is in the Musée des Beaux-Arts, Strasbourg.

1761: Greuze paints a portrait of the Dauphin Louis but not of the Dauphine, Marie-Josèphe de Saxe, to whom the artist had been presented by Lalive de Jully. Asked by her whether he likes to paint women, Greuze replies, "*Je n'aime pas les visages plâtrés.*" The Dauphin remarks to Lalive, "*Vous m'aviez donné ce peintre comme un homme particulier, mais vous ne m'aviez pas dit qu'il était fou.*"[21]

Summer 1761: Greuze enjoys great success with his Salon entries, especially *The Marriage Contract*, which does not appear in the exhibition until September 20:
96 *Le Portrait de Monseigneur le Dauphin*
97 *Le Portrait de M. Babuti* (No. 26)
98 *Le Portrait de M. Greuze, peint par lui-même*
99 *Le Portrait de Madame Greuze en vestale*
100 *Un Mariage, et l'instant où le père de l'Accordée délivre la dot à son gendre* (No. 34)
101 *Un jeune Berger qui tente le sort pour sçavoir s'il est aimé de sa Bergère* (No. 24)
102 *Une jeune Blanchisseuse* (Wanäs, Axel Wachtmeister)
103 *Une Tête d'une Nymphe de Diane*
104 *Plusieurs Têtes peintes, sous le même numéro*
105 *Un Dessein représentant des enfans qui dérobent des Marrons*
106 *Autre Dessein d'un Paralytique soigné par sa famille, ou le fruit de la bonne éducation* (Le Havre, Musée des Beaux-Arts)
107 *Autre, un Fermier brûlé, demandant l'Aumône avec sa famille* (Chantilly, Musée Condé)

April 1762: Birth of Anne-Geneviève (Caroline) Greuze.

Summer 1763: Greuze shows fourteen works in the Salon:
128 *Les Portraits de Monseigneur le Duc de Chartres et de Mademoiselle*
129 *Le Portrait de M. le Comte d'Angévillé* (fig. 14)
130 *Le Portrait de M. le Comte de Lupé*
131 *Le Portrait de M. Watelet* (see No. 35)
132 *Le Portrait de Mlle de Pange*
133 *Le Portrait de Mme Greuze*
134 *Une petite Fille, lisant la Croix de Jésus*

135 *Une Tête de petit Garçon*
136 *Une Tête de petite Fille*
137 *Autre Tête de petite Fille*
138 *Le Tendre Ressouvenir* (London, Wallace Collection)
139 *Une jeune Fille qui a cassé son miroir* (London, Wallace Collection)
140 *La Piété filiale* (Hermitage)

November 11, 1763: A Russian businessman pays Greuze for his portrait. According to Wille, this is Greuze's second Russian commission (see No. 39).

April 9, 1764: Greuze and his wife form a corporation with Jean-Jacques Flipart to engrave *The Marriage Contract* (No. 34).[22]

May 15, 1764: Greuze's third child, Louise-Gabrielle, is baptized in Saint-Benoît, with Wille and his wife as godparents.

Summer 1765: Sixteen works appear in the Salon:
110 *Une Jeune fille, qui pleure son oiseau mort* (No. 44)
111 *L'enfant gâté* (Hermitage)
112 *Une Tête de fille*
113 *Une autre petite Fille, tenant un petit Capucin* (Dublin, National Gallery of Ireland)
114 *Autre tête de petite Fille*
115 *Une Tête en pastel*
116 *Le Portrait de M. Watelet, Receveur Général des Finances* (see No. 35)
117 *Le Portrait de M. Wille, Graveur du Roi* (No. 39)
118 *Le Portrait de M. Caffiery, Sculpteur du Roi* (New York, Metropolitan Museum of Art)
119 *Le Portrait de M. Guibert*
120 *Le Portrait de Mme Tassart*
121 *Le Portrait de Mme Greuze*
122 *Le Portrait en Pastel de M. de la Live de July, Introducteur des Ambassadeurs* (see No. 22)
123 *La Mère bien-aimée*
124 *Le Fils ingrat* (No. 48)
125 *Le Fils puni* (No. 49)

1765: Stung by Madame Geoffrin's description of his sketch of *The Well-Beloved Mother* (see fig. 4) as a "*fricassé d'enfants*," Greuze depicts her as a severe schoolmistress surrounded by members of her salon shown as timorous children (fig. 12).[23] In 1768 this would be his first drawing to enter the Russian Imperial collection.

1766: Ingouf's *Têtes de différents caractères*, a set of engravings after expressive heads in paintings by Greuze, appears with a dedication to Wille. Catherine II purchases *Filial Piety;* Mariette had predicted that its sad subject would make it difficult to sell. Greuze rejects an offer to paint an allegory on the death of the Dauphin, whose portrait he had painted in 1761.

1767: Cochin informs Greuze that because of his failure to present his reception picture he is barred from exhibiting in the Salon. According to Diderot, Greuze's reply was "*un modèle de vanité et d'impertinence.*"[24]

August 15, 1767: Through a letter to Falconet, Diderot advises Catherine II not to invite Greuze to Russia: "*Tenez, mon ami, tout bien considéré, je crois que nous n'enverrons point Greuze en Russie. C'est un excellent artiste, mais une bien mauvaise tête. Il faut avoir ses dessins et ses tableaux, et laisser là l'homme. Et puis, sa femme est, d'un consentement unanime, (et quand je dis unanime, je n'en excepte ni le sien, ni celui de son mari), une des plus dangereuses créatures qu'il y ait au monde. Je ne désespérerois pas qu'un beau jour, sa Maj. Imp. ne l'envoyât faire un tour en Sibérie. Je vous dis clairement ici ce que je vous ai fait entendre haut.*"[25]

October 12, 1767: Catherine II tells Falconet she is resigned to Greuze's absence.

December 2, 1767: Greuze, his wife and Flipart renew their corporation, planning an engraving of *Filial Piety.*

1768: Greuze's first book illustration is published, the frontispiece of Billardon de Sauvigny's *La Rose, ou la fête de Salency.*

March 6, 1769: Greuze writes to Jean Tupinier in Tournus from an address in the Louvre, which he apparently used only as a studio since on engravings of 1769 his address is still given as rue Pavée.

July 23, 1769: Greuze presents to the Académie his reception painting, *Septimius Severus Reproaching Caracalla,* and suffers the humiliation of being received as a genre painter rather than a history painter. He would subsequently refer to this event as his "*désagrément à l'Académie.*" See No. 70 for details.

September 11, 1769: Horace Walpole sees Greuze at Madame Geoffrin's.[26]

Summer 1769: The controversial *Septimius Severus* and other works appear in the Salon, Greuze's last exhibition there until 1800:
151 *L'Empereur Sévère reproche à Caracalla son fils, d'avoir voulu l'assassiner dans les défilés d'Ecosse, et lui dit: Si tu désires ma mort, ordonne à Papinien de me la donner avec cette épée* (No. 70)
152 *La Mère bien-aimée, caressée par ses Enfans* (fig. 4) (see No. 46)
153 *Une jeune Fille qui fait sa prière au pied de l'autel de l'Amour* (London, Wallace Collection)
154 *Une jeune Fille qui envoie un baiser par la fenêtre, appuyée sur des fleurs, qu'elle brise* (Pregny, baron Edmond de Rothschild)
155 *Un Jeune Enfant qui joue avec un chien* (No. 55)
156 *Le Portrait du Prince héréditaire de Saxe*
157 *Le Portrait de M. Jeaurat* (Louvre)
158 *Le Portrait de M. de ****
159 *Trois Têtes d'Enfans, sous le même numéro*
Dessins

Fig. 12 *The Schoolmistress*, brush,
gray ink wash, over pencil,
Leningrad, Hermitage

160   *La Mort d'un père regretté par ses enfans* (No. 51)

161   *La Mort d'un père dénaturé abandonné de ses
enfans* (No. 52)

162   *L'Avare et ses Enfans*

163   *La Bénédiction paternelle* (Art Institute of Chicago)

164   *Le départ de Barcelonnette* (see No. 53)

165   *La Consolation de la Vieillesse*

1769: Greuze's frontispiece for Madame Benoist's novel
Sophronie is published in London. His drawing for it was
executed the previous year (see No. 62).

1769: Greuze's father dies.[27] The artist may have returned
to Tournus this year (see No. 71).

March 9, 1771: Greuze and his wife sign a contract with
Charles Porporaty to engrave *The Well-Beloved Mother* (fig. 4),
after a drawing by the artist; Porporaty breaks the contract
on April 24 and returns his advance.[28]

1771: Exhibiting concurrently with the Académie but
independently of it in his studio at the Louvre, Greuze
receives the visit of Gustav III of Sweden.

c. 1775: Publication of the Baskerville edition of Ariosto's
Orlando furioso with Greuze's illustration for Canto XXIX
(fig. 13).[29]

June 20, 1776: Madame du Deffend tells Horace Walpole
how much Greuze had admired an amateur English
painter.[30]

22 H. Macqueron, *Procès d'artistes,*
Abbeville, 1911, p. 5

23 "fricassee of children." See T.
Kamenskaya, "Greuze et Madame
Geoffrin," *Gazette des Beaux-Arts,*
November, 1934, pp. 221–23,
citing Diderot's quotation of
Greuze: "*Je la peindrai en maîtresse
d'école, le fouet à la main, et elle fera
peur à tous les enfants présents et à
naître.*" ("I shall paint her as a
schoolmistress, whip in hand, and
she will strike fear in all the
children present and yet to be born.")

24 "a model of vanity and
impertinence." Diderot, *Salons,*
IV, p. 105

25 "Listen, my friend, everything
considered, I think we shall
definitely not send Greuze to Russia.
He is an excellent artist, but a
thoroughly unruly person. One
must take his drawings and his
pictures, and leave the man at that.
Furthermore, his wife is, by
unanimous consent, (and when I
say unanimous, I leave out neither
hers nor that of her husband), one
of the most dangerous creatures on
earth. I should not give up hope

that one fine day, her Imperial
Majesty might not send her on tour
to Siberia. I tell you clearly here
what I have given you to understand
orally." Diderot, *Correspondence,*
VII, p. 98

26 H. Walpole, *Correspondence with
Madame du Deffend and Wiart,* ed.
W. S. Lewis and W. H. Smith,
New Haven, 1939, p. 329

27 J. Renouvier, *Histoire de l'art
pendant la Révolution,* Paris, 1863,
II, p. 511; J. Tupinier, "Histoire
d'un portrait," *Annales de
l'Académie de Mâcon,* XXIX, 1934,
p. 361

28 G. Wildenstein, "Quelques
documents sur Greuze," *Gazette des
Beaux-Arts,* October, 1960, pp.
232–34

29 E. Mongan, P. Hofer and J.
Seznec, *Fragonard Drawings for
Ariosto,* New York, 1954, p. 37.
The title page of the Ariosto gives
the publication date as 1773.

30 M.-A. de Vichy Chamrond,
marquise du Deffend de La Lande,
Lettres à Horace Walpole, ed. P.
Toynbee, London, 1912, II, p. 232

1776: The chevalier de Corberon, French *chargé d'affaires* in Russia, sees *Filial Piety* and states that it is in poor condition.[31]

June 1777: Greuze visits Benjamin Franklin at Passy and executes his portrait (No. 82). The artist receives the visit of Joseph II of Austria, brother of Marie-Antoinette, travelling as the comte de Falkenstein; the Emperor sends Greuze in August a patent of nobility, which he would never use.

November 28, 1778: During the controversial celebration of an *"Apothéose de Voltaire,"* Greuze is initiated into the Masonic lodge Les Neuf Soeurs.

August 1779: Greuze exhibits with Houdon at Les Neuf Soeurs, as well as in the Salon de la Correspondance and at the Société des Beaux-Arts, Montpellier.

January 27, 1780: Pierre, *Directeur* of the Académie, informs d'Angiviller, *Surintendant des Bâtiments du Roi* (fig. 14), that Greuze is offering to give up his apartment in the Louvre, *"trop serré pour son genre de travail, qui, vu ses nombreuses études, demande un plus grand local."* He proposes in exchange that Greuze be given an annual pension of 1,000 livres.[32]

January 31, 1780: D'Angiviller reports that Louis XVI agrees to grant Greuze a pension in exchange for his apartment in the Louvre.[33]

February 2, 1780: Pierre reports to d'Angiviller that Greuze has handed over all the documents concerning his apartment in the Louvre and that the artist has received d'Angiviller's letter with great satisfaction: *"La lettre qu'il a reçue est une nouvelle couronne dont il est enchanté et pénétré de la plus vive sensibilité parce qu'il la tient de vous."*[34]

1782: Catherine II's son, the Grand Duke Paul Petrovitch, travelling as the comte du Nord, visits Greuze and probably acquires at this time the important collection of the artist's drawings most of which is now in the Hermitage.

June 12, 1782: In a letter to Pierre, d'Angiviller speaks of commissioning tapestries from the Manufacture des Gobelins after paintings by either Leprince or Greuze for an intended Royal gift to the comte and comtesse du Nord, but notes: *"Je sens qu'on n'a pas de modèles, mais il seroit peut-être facile et aussi prompt de faire faire des copies en grand."*[35]

September 14, 1782: D'Angiviller tells Pierre that he feels the subjects of Greuze's paintings, except for *The Marriage Contract* (No. 34), are too serious to be appropriate for the Royal gift of tapestries and too difficult to copy.[36]

April 24, 1783: In the Vassal de Saint-Hubert sale in Paris, lot 106 is described as *"dans le goût de J.-B. Greuze,"* indicating that imitations of the artist's work were already recognized and sold as such at this date.

1785: In 1791 Madame Greuze would make a legal request to recover from her husband 36 livres she claims to have lost *"lors d'un déménagement qu'elle fit, il y a environ six ans."*[37] This suggests that by 1785 the couple were already separated.

December 11, 1785: Following a particularly humiliating encounter with one of his wife's visitors, Greuze lodges a complaint over her behavior with Gilles Pierre Chenu, *commissaire de police.* The text suggests that the artist and his wife are living apart and also that Greuze intends to make a fuller report on his problems: *"Mais que n'a-t-il point éprouvé jusqu'à présent et combien sa fortune n'a-t-elle pas souffert, c'est ce qu'il se réserve de détailler plus amplement par la suite."*[38]

1785–89: Greuze has business dealings with Prince Nikolai Borisovitch Yussupov, to whom he sells his own pictures as well as those of other French artists including Vincent, Fragonard and Vigée-Lebrun.

1786: Greuze exhibits three drawings in the Salon des Arts at Lyon.

December 5, 1786: Greuze describes in a letter published in the *Journal de Paris* the engraving of his *Widow and Her Priest.*

December 5, 1789: Anne-Gabrielle Babuti, *"épouse séparée de fait de J.-B. Greuze,"* obtains from the police, following her husband's refusal, *"le droit d'ester en justice pour répondre à une action intentée contre elle à l'occasion d'un partage."*[39]

1790: Greuze exhibits in the Salon de l'Encouragement des Arts. Romney visits Paris and dines with Greuze and David.

1791–92: Possibly with divorce in mind, Greuze dictates a lengthy account of his marital woes.[40]

July 16, 1792: Louis XVI grants Greuze a pension of 1,537 livres 10 sols, retroactive to January 1, 1790.[41]

August 4, 1793: Greuze's divorce is granted, with Madame Greuze receiving a large settlement. The artist's two daughters remain with him.

August 27, 1793: Following the divorce Anne-Gabrielle Babuti requests an inventory and appraisal of Greuze's possessions, which he and she are to divide. The inventory is begun September 2, the pictures are evaluated on September 13 and Greuze takes possession of his lodgings again on September 18.[42]

October 1793: Greuze joins the powerful Commune Générale des Arts, led by Restout and David.

1796: Desain de Saint-Gobert records nineteen sittings for his portrait by Greuze between April 29 and November 21.[43]

1797: A lengthy lawsuit over Greuze's brother's will is settled. Greuze rewards his lawyer, Jean Tupinier, by painting his portrait, which is completed on March 19.[44]

Summer 1800: For the first time since 1769 Greuze exhibits in the Salon. His works include:

173 *Le Départ pour la chasse, portrait du C. *** et de sa femme, dans un paysage* (No. 112)

174 *Deux tableaux faisant pendans*
Même numéro
Un enfant hésitant de toucher un oiseau dans la crainte qu'il ne soit mort (see No. 44)
Une jeune femme se disposant à écrire une lettre d'amour

Fig. 13 Illustration for Canto XXIX of Ariosto's *Orlando furioso*, brush, gray ink wash, Frankfurt, Städelsches Kunstinstitut

31 L. Réau, "Greuze et la Russie," *L'Art et les artistes*, 1920, I, p. 275

32 "too cramped for his type of work, which, considering his numerous studies, requires larger premises." M. Furcy-Raynaud, ed., "Correspondance de M. d'Angiviller avec Pierre," *Nouvelles Archives de l'art français*, XXI, 1905, p. 275

33 *Ibid.*, p. 277

34 "The letter he received is a new crown with which he is enchanted and full of the keenest feeling because it came from you." *Ibid.*, p. 279

35 "I am aware that we have no models, but it would perhaps be easy and just as quick to have some full-scale copies made." *Ibid.*, p. 347

36 *Ibid.*, pp. 354-55

37 "during a change of residence she made about six years ago." M. Barroux, ed., "Procès-verbal d'apposition de scellés chez Greuze après son divorce," *Bulletin de la Société de l'Histoire de Paris et de l'Ile-de-France*, 1896, pp. 84-85, n. 4

38 "But what has he not been through to date and how much has his fortune not suffered, that is what he awaits to detail more amply in the future." J. J. Guiffrey, "Plainte de Greuze au sujet de l'inconduite de sa femme, suivie de diverses pièces sur le même artiste," *Bulletin de la Société de l'Histoire de l'Art français*, 1875-78, p. 165. Guiffrey notes suspiciously that Greuze's own behavior might not have been "*à l'abri de toute reproche*" ("entirely beyond reproach"). The only evidence on that side is to be found in the *Carnets* of David d'Angers: "*J'ai su par un des intimes du célèbre peintre Greuze qu'il allait souvent visiter des filles publiques. Il aimait à leur prodiguer les plus belles et les plus suaves appellations: l'une c'était Diane, l'autre c'était Vénus. Et il trouvait toujours un nom de divinité païenne, selon son inspiration du moment, ce qui étonnait beaucoup ces pauvres filles de la Champagne, de la Normandie et du Faubourg Saint-Marceau, et enfin ces pauvres créatures arrachées par le vice de tous les coins de la France. Ce souvenir de la Grèce était bien curieux d'un homme qui a voué sa vie à la représentation de la nature réelle et positive des drames de la vie active de son époque. Ceci pourrait indiquer qu'il sentait le besoin de poétiser le plaisir des sens, en les portant vers l'idéalisation. Cet ami qui m'a rapporté cette particularité est M. Walckenaer [No. 102].*" ("I learned through one of the intimates of the celebrated painter Greuze that he often went to visit prostitutes. He loved to lavish on them the most beautiful and urbane titles: for one it was Diana, for another Venus. And he always found a name from pagan divinity, according to his inspiration of the moment, something that greatly astonished those poor girls from Champagne, Normandy and the Faubourg Saint-Marceau, and finally those poor creatures torn up by vice from all the corners of France. This reminiscence of Greece was most curious coming from a man who devoted his life to the representation of the real and factual nature of the dramas of the daily life of his time. All this could indicate that he felt the need to poeticize the pleasure of the senses, by carrying them toward idealization. That friend who reported this peculiarity to me is M. Walckenaer [No. 102]." A. Bruel, ed., *Les Carnets de David d'Angers*, Paris, 1958, I, p. 254, entry dated February 14, 1847

39 "formally separated wife of J.-B. Greuze." "the right to go to court to reply to a suit brought against her in reference to a partition of property." Guiffrey, *op. cit.*, pp. 166-67

40 Boilly, *op. cit.*, pp. 154-72

41 Paris, Fondation Custodia, Institut Néerlandais

42 Barroux, *op. cit.*, p. 84

43 Wildenstein, *op. cit.*, pp. 230, 233. The portrait is with Wildenstein and Co., New York

44 Tupinier, *op. cit.*, p. 382, repr. facing p. 344

175 *Portrait. Une jeune fille préludant sur un forte-piano*

176 *Deux portraits d'hommes. Même num.*

177 *Trois têtes de différens caractères*

Même numéro

La peur de l'orage

La crainte et le désir[45]

Le sommeil

178 *Deux pendans. Même numéro*

L'Innoncence tenant deux pigeons[46]

Une jeune fille bouchant ses oreilles pour ne pas entendre ce qu'on lui dit (formerly Paris, baronne Edouard de Rothschild)

Summer 1801: Greuze shows five works in the Salon:

158 *Le Repentir de sainte Marie l'Egyptienne dans le désert* (No. 113)

159 *Un cultivateur remettant la charrue à son fils, en présence de sa famille* (Moscow, Pushkin Museum)

160 *Un enfant*

161 *Portrait d'homme*

162 *Portrait d'un vieillard*

Summer 1804: At the age of seventy-nine, Greuze exhibits for the last time in the Salon:

219 *Le repentir de Sainte Marie l'Egyptienne* (No. 113?)

220 *Ariane dans l'île de Naxos* (London, Wallace Collection?)

221 *Le portrait de l'auteur* (No. 114)

222 *Un portrait de femme*

223 *Deux têtes de jeunes filles: la Timidité, la Gaïeté*

March 21, 1805: Greuze dies in his studio in the Louvre. At his sparcely attended funeral Constance Mayer-Lamartinière places on his coffin a bouquet of immortelles. The artist is buried in the cemetery of Montmartre.

March 1805: A few days after Greuze's death a letter addressed to him by Bidau, *commissaire* of the town of Tournus, announces that a street in which the artist's family had lived has been renamed "rue Greuze."

1811: Death of Anne-Gabrielle Babuti. According to the inscription on No. 71, her remains were placed in the same tomb as those of her former husband in the 1850s.

1812: Death of Louise-Gabrielle Greuze, buried with her father.

November 5, 1842: Death of Anne-Geneviève (Caroline) Greuze, buried with her father.

January 25–26, 1843: Caroline Greuze sale, Paris. The important catalogue prepared for the sale by Théophile Thoré lists the contents of Greuze's studio that his daughter had preserved.

45 Possibly the picture signed and dated 1799 formerly in the David-Weill collection, Neuilly. See G. Henriot, *Collection David Weill*, Paris, 1926, I, pp. 167–69

46 A version is in the Wallace Collection, London. See Wallace Collection Catalogues, *Pictures and Drawings*, London, 1968, No. P 428, p. 135

Fig. 14   Portrait of Charles-Claude
de la Billarderie, comte d'Angiviller,
oil, on canvas, New York,
Metropolitan Museum of Art

1   Portrait of an Old Woman

Oil, on canvas, 26¾ x 22⅜ in. (68.0 x 56.8 cm)
Paris, private collection

Collections: Johann Georg Wille, Paris (?); his sale, Paris,
December 6, 1784, lot 61, sold for 180 livres (?)

This little-known portrait must be one of the earliest
surviving works by Greuze, executed probably in his native
Tournus. Its somewhat stiff air relates it to what appear to
be the still earlier portraits of Pierre Piot and Madame Piot
(Tournus, Musée Greuze),[1] but its forthright, indeed
overwhelming presentation of the distinctive features and
powerful hands of the old woman points toward Greuze's
later naturalistic work.

   This may have been lot 61 in the 1784 sale of Greuze's
friend Johann Georg Wille (see No. 39), described as:
*"Portrait d'une vieille femme, les mains croisées, tenant un Livre;
la tête caractérisée et couverte d'une grande coëffe noire."*[2] An old
copy of the portrait is in the Musée des Beaux-Arts, Beaune.[3]

1 Brookner, Pls. 3, 2
2 "Portrait of an old woman, her
hands crossed, holding a Book; her
features distinctive and her head
covered with a large black
head-dress."
3 J. Vergnet-Ruiz and M. Laclotte,
Les Petits et Grands Musées de France,
Paris, 1962, p. 238

2 Seated Man Holding a Book
(Study for *The Family Bible Reading*)
Brush, brown ink wash, over pencil, on white paper,
15⅝ x 9⁹⁄₁₆ in. (39.7 x 24.3 cm)
Inscribed: *Greuze fecit*
Lyon, Musée Lyonnais des Arts Décoratifs

Collections: Musée d'Art et d'Industrie, Lyon (Lugt S 1699 a)
  Bibliography: J. Chalon, "Greuze n'est pas le peintre que
vous croyez," *Le Figaro littéraire*, August 6–12, 1964, p. 1

This drawing is a study related to *The Family Bible Reading*
(fig. 2), which Greuze exhibited in 1755. Like the other
study for that painting included in this exhibition (No. 3),
the present one may have been executed in Lyon. The
differences between the figure shown on this sheet and the
comparable one seen in the compositional drawing for the
picture (Paris, baron Rodolphe Hottinguer) and in the

finished painting are numerous: here the man faces right
instead of left, he appears somewhat younger, he wears
buttoned gaiters rather than stockings, the book he holds
is less massive and the basket at his feet is of a different
shape. With the additional book shown on the table, he
could be a schoolteacher calmly addressing a class rather
than an old man overwhelmed by the content of his reading.
These differences of detail and dramatic concept may be
explained by different locales of execution for the study and
the painting.

A red chalk study for the same figure was sold in Paris,
November 25, 1927, lot 105.

3 Seated Old Woman with Hands Clasped

(Study for *The Family Bible Reading*)
Brush, brown ink wash, over pencil, on white paper,
15 x 9¹¹⁄₁₆ in. (38.0 x 24.5 cm)
Inscribed: *Greuze fecit*
Lyon, Musée Lyonnais des Arts Décoratifs

Collections: Musée d'Art et d'Industrie, Lyon (Lugt S 1699 a)
  Bibliography: J. Chalon, "Greuze n'est pas le peintre que vous croyez," *Le Figaro littéraire*, August 6–12, 1964, p. 13

This drawing, like No. 2, is a study for *The Family Bible Reading* (Paris, baron Rodolphe Hottinguer), the painting with which Greuze was received into the Académie and which he exhibited in the Salon of 1755. In the painting (fig. 2), the old woman, who here seems to be listening with peaceful interest, is shown at right with less caricatured features, clutching a spindle and trying to restrain a playful child who reaches for a dog. She wears the same voluminous apron but a different headdress. The same old woman, again holding a spindle and keeping the child from the dog, appears in Greuze's compositional study for the picture (Paris, baron Hottinguer).[1]

Nothing is known of the early history of this drawing. Because of its presence in Lyon, it is tempting to think that Greuze executed it in that city where he received his early training, especially since Madame de Valori stated that "*Ce fut après avoir fait son intéressant tableau de la* Lecture de la Bible, *l'un de ses premiers ouvrages, que Greuze vint à Paris.*"[2] While few have accepted Madame de Valori's statement, it must be admitted that the style of the present drawing is unlike that of Greuze's Parisian work, combining as it does a bold, free treatment of draperies with an almost macabre registering of the decrepit details of the face and hands. Perhaps Greuze executed the drawing in Lyon and completed the painting in Paris.

1 Sale, Paris, June 15, 1938, lot 12, sold for 23,100 francs
2 "It was after having done his interesting picture of the *Bible Reading*, one of his first works, that Greuze came to Paris." Valori, p. 249

4 Seated Male Nude with Left Leg Outstretched

Black and red chalk, stumped, on cream paper, 14¹⁵⁄₁₆ x
19⁵⁄₁₆ in. (38.0 x 49.0 cm)
Signed and dated: *Greuze 1758;* inscribed on mount (see below)
Paris, Bibliothèque Nationale, Cabinet des Estampes

Collections: Nicolas de Livry, Bishop of Callinique, Sens,
eighteenth century; Paris, Bibliothèque de l'Arsenal, 1858;
transferred to the Bibliothèque Nationale between 1861 and
1864 (Lugt 248)
   Bibliography: Martin-Masson, No. 1303; A. de Montaiglon,
ed., "Pièces communiquées par M. Leperlier, et annotées
par M. A. de Montaiglon," *Archives de l'art français*, VI,
1858–60, p. 236; Munhall, 1966, pp. 88–89, fig. 10

The eighteenth-century mount on this drawing bears the
following inscription: "*Cette figure est de Mʳ Greuze; quand
il la fit, Mʳ Natoire etoit professeur; Celuici après lavoir louée,
lui fit remarquer cependant quelle etoit estropiée. Le Sieur Greuze
mécontent lui répondit; Monsieur, vous seriez heureux si vous
pouviez en faire une pareille.*"[1] If this anecdote is accurate, it
would seem that the date on the drawing (1758) was added
later, perhaps when de Livry acquired it, for Greuze could
have been working under Natoire as "*professeur*" only until
1751, when the latter was appointed *Directeur* of the
Académie in Rome. This would thus be one of the earliest
known drawings by Greuze executed in Paris, and a revealing
document of his budding personality.
   Although the drawing, particularly in the treatment of
the left foot, demonstrates remarkable anatomical
knowledge and skill in rendering, Greuze was later to
express a limited appreciation of the value of anatomical
study for an artist. He told the engraver Charles Dufresne:
"*cette science étoit poussée trop loin,* [it] *convenoit mieux à un
chirurgien qu'à un peintre.*"[2]
   Nicolas de Livry, Bishop of Callinique, the first recorded
owner of this drawing and of Greuze's study for *The Fowler*
(No. 11), was a close friend of the artist's associate Johann
Georg Wille (No. 39). From 1749 until at least 1785 Wille
purchased for the Bishop a variety of art works, sending
them to his abbey of Sainte-Colombe in Sens. However,
Wille makes no mention of ever selling any of Greuze's
work to de Livry.

1 "This figure is by Mʳ Greuze;
when he did it, Mʳ Natoire was
professor; the Latter, after having
praised it, nevertheless called to his
attention that it was out of
proportion. Sieur Greuze, displeased,
answered him; Monsieur, you would
be happy if you could do one equal
to it."

2 "this science was pushed too
far, [it] was more suitable to a
surgeon than to a painter." Quoted
in P. Ratouis de Limay, "Un
Chanteur de l'Opéra, graveur et
collectionneur au début du dix-
neuvième siècle," *Bulletin de la
Société de l'Histoire de l'Art français,*
1949, p. 70

5   Portrait of Joseph (*Joseph, Modèle de l'Académie Royale, tenant une poële à feu*)

Oil, on canvas, 27$\frac{3}{16}$ x 22$\frac{13}{16}$ in. (68.8 x 58.0 cm)
Signed and dated: *J. Greuze f. 1755*
Paris, Musée du Louvre

Collections: comte de Vence, Paris, 1759; his sale, Paris, February 9, 1761, lot 148, sold for 177 livres to Rémy; C.-H. Watelet, Paris; his sale, Paris, June 12, 1786, lot 26; Detaille, Paris; his sale, Paris, January 16–17, 1818 (?); de Vèze, Paris; his sale, Paris, 1851 (?); M. C. Trembley; acquired from him by the museum in 1898

Bibliography: Brookner, pp. 60–61, Pl. 11; Goncourt, I, p. 345; L. Hautecoeur, "Greuze, portraitiste," *L'Art et les artistes,* February, 1924, p. 171; Munhall, 1966, pp. 88–89, fig. 11; Rosenberg, Reynaud and Compin, I, No. 314

The subject of this portrait was identified in the de Vence sale catalogue of 1761 as "*Joseph, Modèle de l'Académie Royale, tenant une poële à feu.*"[1] Considering that he is depicted holding a brazier filled with coals, it is probable that the portrait was executed in the first months of the year it is dated, 1755, at a time when Greuze was still struggling to establish his reputation. Within a few years, however, it would be described as a worthy pendant to Rembrandt's *Self-Portrait* of 1634 (Louvre),[2] which hung beside it in the distinguished collection of the comte de Vence. A catalogue of that collection published in 1759 stated: "*Dans la façade du côté de la cheminée, et sur le rang le plus élevé, sont cinq portraits; celui du milieu est d'un peintre François nommé* Greuze, *qui ne se trouve point déplacé, quoi qu'il aye des voisins d'une grande réputation. A droite est un portrait de* Rembrandt. *Et à gauche un* de Porbus, *qui vient du Cabinet de M. le Prince de Carignan.*"[3]

As the Greuze and Rembrandt portraits show a general similarity of pose and dramatic lighting and are nearly identical in size, it is conceivable that Greuze executed his as a challenge to Rembrandt's. The *Portrait of Joseph* subsequently belonged to the engraver Watelet, whose own portrait by Greuze in imitation of Rembrandt is included in this exhibition (No. 35).

1 "Joseph, Model at the Académie Royale, holding a coal-pan"
2 See F. Erpel, *Die Selbstbildnisse Rembrandts,* Berlin, 1967, No. 52, Pl. 35
3 "On the wall by the fireplace, and on the highest level, are five portraits; the one in the middle is by a French painter named *Greuze,* who finds himself not at all out of place, though he has neighbors of great reputation. To the right is a portrait by *Rembrandt.* And to the left is one *by Pourbus,* which comes from the collection of M. the Prince de Carignan." *Catalogue des tableaux du cabinet de Monsieur le comte de Vence,* Paris, 1759, pp. 20–21

6 Study for the *Portrait of Ange-Laurent de Lalive de Jully*
Oil, on canvas, 9$\frac{13}{16}$ x 6$\frac{7}{8}$ in. (25.0 x 17.5 cm)
London, Mr. Paul Wallraf

Collections: Couvreur, Paris; his sale, Paris, May 26–28, 1875, lot 217, as Boucher, sold for 180 francs; acquired, as Boucher, in 1946

Though Louis Réau[1] and others have attributed this small *grisaille* to Boucher, David Carritt has suggested that it might be a preparatory study by Greuze for the portrait of Lalive de Jully included in this exhibition (No. 22). Indeed the pose of the man at the harp has obvious similarities with that of the figure in the Lalive portrait, and the small size and intimate flavor of the study resemble as well Greuze's portrait of Watelet (No. 35).

The most striking differences between the two compositions are the absence here of Lalive's celebrated neoclassical furniture *à la grecque*, the presence of such details as the Rococo candle-branch alongside the mirror, the conventional Louis XV footstool and the draped dressing table and the introduction of the woman reading a letter. The crucial difference in the style of the furnishings represented in the two works would suggest that Greuze painted this small one a considerable while before the other, which appeared in the Salon of 1759. Lalive had known Greuze since at least 1755, when he acquired *The Family Bible Reading* (fig. 2).

The identity of the woman represented in the study is uncertain. Lalive's first wife died in 1752, before he knew Greuze, and he remarried only in 1762, after Greuze had executed the portrait of 1759. It is possible that the lady is Lalive's sister-in-law, Louise-Florence Pétronille de Lalive d'Epinay (1726–1783), protectress of Rousseau, friend of Grimm and author of a book of *Mémoires*.

At some time the upper corners of the canvas were painted in, beyond the artist's original rounded top. The overpaint has been removed.

1 Inscription on a photograph, dated July 12, 1931

7 Genoese Woman Selling Flowers (*Génoise, avec le mezzo rabattu, vendant des fleurs*)
Pen and brush, India ink, on white paper, 7⁵⁄₁₆ x 5⅝ in. (20.2 x 13.5 cm)
Signed, dated and inscribed on mount: *Greuze f. 1755, Donna Genovese cól mezzo calato che vende fiori*
Rotterdam, Museum Boymans-van Beuningen

Collections: Louis Gougenot, abbé de Chezal-Benoît, 1767; Randon de Boisset, Paris; his sale, Paris, February 27 — March 25, 1777, lot 376, one of twenty drawings for the *Divers Habillements* sold for 1,099 livres 19 sols to Desmarest; Vassal de Saint-Hubert, Paris; his sales, Paris, March 29—April 13, 1779, lot 164, one of twenty drawings (bought in?), and Paris, April 24—May 5, 1783, lot 159, one of twenty drawings; anonymous sale, Paris, January 12, 1784, one of lots 294-298 (?); anonymous sale, Paris, March 13-14, 1908, lot 48; Georges Lasquin, Paris (Lugt 1139 a); his sale, Paris, June 7-8, 1928, lot 85; F. Koenigs, Rotterdam (Lugt 1023 a)

   Bibliography: Brookner, p. 96; Martin-Masson, No. 410; Portalis-Béraldi, III, pp. 112-14; Smith, p. 443

   Engraving: Moitte, 1768

Greuze executed this drawing between October 30, 1755, when the abbé Louis Gougenot noted in his "Album de voyage en Italie" (see No. 16) that he and the artist had left Novi, and November 4, when the two returned to Novi from Genoa. Gougenot's precise description of Genoese women's clothing corresponds to the artist's image: "*Les bourgeoises* [of Genoa] *n'en diffèrent point par leurs coiffures. Mais elles portent un Mezzo qui est une pièce de soye ou d'indienne dont elles se servent comme de voile et de mantille, en se couvrant la tête et les épaules. Les femmes du commun portent leurs cheveux nattés et entourés en rond au haut de leur chignon, où ils sont arrêtés avec une éguille d'argent qui les traverse; elles y mêlent quelquefois des fleurs naturelles.*"[1] To illustrate this passage Greuze executed a pencil and gouache drawing of a figure similar to the present one. Contained in Gougenot's "Album," it is inscribed: "*Bourgeoise de Gènes avec le Mezzo rabattu sur les épaules.*"[2] The *mezzo* is pink with a gold edge; the woman's skirts are blue and lavender.

   In 1768 members of the Moitte family engraved a title page and twenty-four drawings, including this one and No. 8, for the *Divers Habillements suivant le costume d'Italie*, with landscape backgrounds added after Jean-Baptiste Lallemand.[3] As images of picturesque local fashions, they belong to a tradition practiced by Watteau, Wleughels and Barbault; in fact the engraving of the *Bourgeoise de Bologne* in the series is inscribed "*Barbault pinx.*" As a record of the art centers Greuze and Gougenot visited, the *Divers Habillements* refers to Chambéry, Genoa, Parma, Bologna, Florence, Pisa, Lucca, Naples and Frascati.

1 "The townswomen [of Genoa] differ not at all in the way they fix their hair. But they wear a Mezzo, which is a piece of silk or calico they use as a veil or mantilla, covering their head and shoulders. The common women wear their hair braided and wound up in a circle at the top of their chignons, where it is held in place with a silver needle which crosses it; they sometimes mix in fresh flowers." L. Gougenot, "Album de voyage en Italie," ms., Paris, collection of the baronne de Soucy, I, p. 266
2 "Townswoman of Genoa with the Mezzo lowered onto the shoulders."
3 See P. Quarré, "J.-B. Greuze et J.-B. Lallemand," *XXVè Congrès de l'Association Bourguignonne des Sociétés savantes*, Tournus, 1954, pp. 21-22

8 Peasant Woman of Parma (*Paysanne parmesane*)
Pen and brush, India ink, on white paper, 7⅚₁₆ x 5⅝ in.
(20.2 x 13.5 cm)
Signed, dated and inscribed on mount: *Greuze f. 1755,*
Parmeggiana
Rotterdam, Museum Boymans-van Beuningen

Collections: same as No. 7
  Bibliography: same as No. 7
  Engraving: same as No. 7

Greuze executed this drawing between the 6th and 9th of
November, 1755, during the brief visit he and the abbé
Gougenot made to Parma on their way from Piacenza to
Colorno (see No. 7).[1] As usual it was the art treasures of
the city—the decorations and paintings of Parmigianino and
Correggio—that attracted the travellers, but Gougenot's
notes record as well the peculiarities of local dress. In the
gouache drawing Greuze made for Gougenot's "Album," a
figure similar to the one in the present drawing wears
yellow sleeves, a white apron and a blue skirt.

1 L. Gougenot, "Album de
voyage en Italie," ms., Paris,
collection of the baronne de Soucy,
I, pp. 313–32

9 The Broken Eggs (*Une Mère grondant un jeune homme pour avoir renversé un panier d'oeufs que la servante apportait du marché. Un enfant tente de raccomoder un oeuf*)
Oil, on canvas, 28¾ x 37 in. (73.0 x 94.0 cm)
Signed and dated: *Greuze f. Roma 1756*
New York, The Metropolitan Museum of Art, William K. Vanderbilt Bequest

Collections: Louis Gougenot, abbé de Chezal-Benoît, Paris, with pendant; Prince Nicolas Nikitich Demidoff (d. 1828), with pendant; his son Prince Anatole Demidoff, San Donato Palace near Florence, with pendant; his sale, Paris, February 21–22, 1870, lot 107, sold for 12,600 francs to the fourth Marquess of Hertford; Marquess of Hertford, London and Paris; his son, Sir Richard Wallace, London and Paris; sold by him in April, 1875, for £5,292 to Lord Dudley;[1] William K. Vanderbilt, New York, after 1914; bequeathed by him to the museum in 1920
   Exhibitions: Salon of 1757, No. 112, with pendant; London, Victoria and Albert Museum, Bethnal Green Branch, Collection of Sir Richard Wallace, 1872–75; New York, Metropolitan Museum of Art, French Painting and Sculpture of the Eighteenth Century, 1935–36, No. 32; Toledo Museum of Art and Art Gallery of Toronto, The Spirit of Modern France, 1946–47, No. 8; Boston Museum of Fine Arts, Masterpieces of Painting in The Metropolitan Museum of Art, 1970, p. 70; New York, Metropolitan Museum of Art, Masterpieces of Fifty Centuries, 1970, No. 305
   Bibliography: Brookner, pp. 58, 59, 97, 98, Pl. 16; Fried, p. 163, fig. 15; Hautecoeur, p. 22; Mauclair, p. 40; Martin-Masson, No. 181; Sauerländer, pp. 148–49; Smith, No. 113; C. Sterling, *Metropolitan Museum of Art: A Catalogue of French Paintings XV-XVIII Centuries*, Cambridge, Massachusetts, 1955, pp. 174–75
   Engravings: P.-E. Moitte, 1763, with pendant; J.-E. Haïd; J.-J. Veyrassat, 1870, with pendant

The same four principal figures who are seen again in this picture's pendant, *The Neapolitan Gesture* (No. 14), are here engaged in a dramatic scene the sexual overtones of which will be apparent to twentieth-century viewers, the broken eggs symbolizing a loss of virginity. Though the costumes and setting are Italian, the iconographic *double-entendre* is as Dutch in origin as is the formal source for the figure of the

servant girl—an engraving by Moitte after Frans van Mieris the Elder's *The Broken Egg*, which in the eighteenth century belonged to Count Brühl and is now in the Hermitage.[2] The boy trying to repair one of the eggs, a detail spelled out in the Salon title, is intended to suggest the uncomprehending innocence of childhood. The roughhewn bow and arrow by his side allude to the dangers of Cupid's darts.
   Dated 1756, *The Broken Eggs* must have been painted sometime between January 28, when Natoire informed Marigny of Greuze's arrival in Rome,[3] and May 12, when the abbé Jean-Jacques Barthélémy described the picture to the comte de Caylus in glowing terms: "*Il a fait un autre tableau que vous verrez bientôt à Paris, et qui nous a paru charmant. Une jeune fille avait un panier d'oeufs; un jeune homme a joué avec elle, le panier est tombé et les oeufs se sont cassés. La mère de la fille arrive, saisit le jeune homme par le bras et demande réparation des oeufs; la fille interdite est assise par terre; le jeune homme embarrassé donne les plus mauvaises excuses du monde, et la vieille est en fureur; un petit enfant jeté sur le coin du tableau, prend un de ces oeufs cassés et tâche de le rajuster. Tout cela me paroît joli; et la figure de la fille a une position si noble, qu'elle pourrait orner un tableau d'histoire.*"[4]
   The Broken Eggs may be one of the works Marigny referred to when he wrote to Natoire on June 17, 1756, that he had seen pictures sent from Rome that pleased him.[5] Perhaps it had been brought back from that city by the abbé Gougenot, its first owner (see No. 16), who left there in May.
   When *The Broken Eggs* appeared in the Salon of 1757, Fréron described its qualities in the *Année littéraire*: "*Avec quel plaisir on considère une jeune fille aimable affligée d'avoir renversé un panier d'oeufs! Sa tête est charmante; elle est peinte avec une belle douceur et pleine d'expression. On trouve dans le reste du tableau, avec la plus grande vérité, une force singulière de couleur, et un effet très-piquant.*"[6] It is indicative of Greuze's efforts at this time to attract distinguished collectors that Moitte's engraving of *The Broken Eggs* was dedicated by Gougenot de Croissy, the abbé's brother, to the Prince de Condé, whom Croissy was then serving as *secrétaire des commandements*.[7]
   Martin lists two preparatory drawings which appeared in nineteenth-century sales: a study in an anonymous sale, Paris, March 18, 1890, and a chalk drawing in an anonymous sale, Paris, March, 16–17, 1898, lot 143, signed and dated 1756.

1 Correspondence between Sir
Richard Wallace and the first Earl
of Dudley (London, Wallace
Collection). Kindly communicated
by Mr. Robert A. Cecil
2 See Brookner, p. 158, Pls. 34, 35
3 Paris, Archives Nationales o¹
1940, cited in Brookner, p. 57
4 "He has done another picture
which you will soon see in Paris,
and which struck us as charming.
A girl had a basket of eggs; a
young man toyed with her, the
basket fell and the eggs were broken.
The girl's mother arrives, seizes the
young man by the arm and demands
compensation for the eggs; the
bewildered girl is seated on the floor;
the embarrassed young man makes
the worst excuses in the world,
and the old woman is in a fury;
a child thrown into the corner
of the picture takes one of the
broken eggs and tries to repair it.

All this seems pretty to me;
and the figure of the girl has a
pose so noble that she could
embellish a history painting."
Abbé J.-J. Barthélémy, *Voyage en
Italie*, Paris, 1801, pp. 133–34
5 Paris, Archives Nationales o¹
1940, cited in Brookner, p. 59
6 "With what pleasure one studies
an amiable young girl distressed at
having overturned a basket of eggs!
Her head is charming; she is
painted with a beautiful sweetness
and full of expression. One finds
in the rest of the picture, with the
greatest truth, a singular strength
of color and a very lively effect."
E.-C. Fréron, "Lettre XV:
Exposition des ouvrages de peinture,
de sculpture et de gravure,"
L'Année littéraire, 1757, pp. 347–48
7 M. Salé, "Nécrologe de l'abbé
Gougenot, amateur," *Revue
universelle des arts*, XII, 1860, p. 175

10 Indolence (*La Paresseuse italienne*)

Oil, on canvas, 25½ x 19¼ in. (64.8 x 48.8 cm)
Hartford, Wadsworth Atheneum, Ella Gallup and Mary
Catlin Sumner Collection

Collections: Jean-Baptiste-Laurent Boyer de Fonscolombe,
Aix-en-Provence, 1757, with pendant; his sale, Paris,
January 18, 1790, lot 101, with pendant; Prince Radziwill
Branicki, Rome, Paris and Warsaw, with pendant, before
1874; acquired by the museum from Wildenstein and Co.,
New York, in 1934

Exhibitions: Salon of 1757, No. 114, with pendant;
Springfield, Massachusetts, Museum of Fine Arts, Opening
Exhibition, 1933, No. 52; New York, Metropolitan
Museum of Art, French Painting and Sculpture of the
Eighteenth Century, 1935–36, No. 31; Pittsburgh, Carnegie
Institute, A Survey of French Painting, 1936, No. 21;
New York World's Fair, Masterpieces of Art, 1939, No.
164; New York World's Fair, Masterpieces of Art, 1940,
No. 204; New York, Parke-Bernet, French and English
Art Treasures of the Eighteenth Century, 1942, No. 27;
Middletown, Connecticut, Wesleyan University, Exhibition
of Eighteenth-Century Art, 1948; Pittsburgh, Carnegie
Institute, French Painting 1100–1900, 1951, No. 96;
New York, Wildenstein and Co., and Minneapolis
Institute of Arts, French Eighteenth-Century Painters,
1954, No. 13; Hartford, Wadsworth Atheneum, Hommage
to Mozart, 1956, No. 23; New York, M. Knoedler and
Co., and Hartford, Wadsworth Atheneum, A. Everett
Austin, Jr: A Director's Taste and Achievement, 1958,
No. 37; Northampton, Smith College Art Museum, 1761:
Diderot and the Salons des Beaux-Arts, 1961, No. 12;
Indianapolis, Herron Museum of Art, The Romantic
Era—Birth and Flowering, 1750–1850, 1965, No. 2; R. A.,
1968, No. 302; Toledo Museum of Art, Art Institute of
Chicago and Ottawa, National Gallery of Canada, The
Age of Louis XV: French Painting from 1710 to 1774,
1975–76, No. 41

Bibliography: Brookner, pp. 59, 97, Pl. 13; Lady Dilke,
French Painters of The Eighteenth Century, London, 1889, p.
197; Fried, p. 163, fig. 16; Goncourt, I, pp. 81, 89; Martin-
Masson, No. 187; Munhall, 1966, p. 87; Portalis-Béraldi,
III, p. 114; Smith, No. 96

Engraving: P.-E. Moitte, 1765, with pendant

Painted in Rome in 1756 or early 1757 and exhibited in
the Salon of 1757 as one of "*Quatre tableaux dans le costume
italien*," *Indolence*, with its pendant *The Fowler* (No. 12),
belonged to Greuze's early patron J.-B.-L. Boyer de
Fonscolombe, whose handsome château still stands not
far from Aix-en-Provence. Boyer's brother, to whom P.-E.
Moitte dedicated his engravings of both paintings, was a
diplomat in the duc de Choiseul's entourage during
Greuze's sojourn in Rome.

Greuze provides here a memorable illustration of
indolence, or sloth, as it was defined in Diderot's contemporary *Encyclopédie:* "*une nonchalance qui empêche l'homme
de travailler . . . et de remplir ses devoirs.*"[1] The artist's
fascination with human frailties and his ability to evoke
aberrant states of mind through facial expression, pose
and details of setting demonstrate his debt to Dutch
prototypes, such as Nicolaes Maes' *The Idle Servant*
(London, National Gallery), rather than to the more
immediate examples of Chardin, who stressed the positive,
thoughtful qualities of women of the same class (compare
The Kitchen Maid, Washington, National Gallery, Kress
Collection). It is more in his exquisite still-life details
that Greuze follows Chardin's path, accentuating with
virtuosity the *trompe l'oeil* effects of glistening terracotta,
worn linens and soft raffia. That this relationship of
Greuze to Chardin was deliberately stressed in the
installation of the two artists' entries at the Salon is
suggested by Renou, secretary of the Académie: "*On a
placé* [Chardin] *sur la même ligne . . . comme pour faciliter
la comparaison de ce peintre avec M. Greuze; ils gagnent et
perdent tour à tour; il* [Greuze] *prend séparément ce qu'il veut
peindre; on trouve à la vérité dans chaque objet des détails les
plus satisfaisans, mais qui considérés avec le tout, ne font point
d'accord et ne peignent point l'air et la lumière . . . . il nous
prouve que le style le moins noble a pourtant de la noblesse mais
il n'a pas toujours l'ignénuité de M. Chardin.*"[2]

From Italy Greuze seems to have taken only the
picturesque details of his subject, though Glenway
Wescott has pointed out the possible influence on this
work of Giuseppe Maria Crespi's famous *The Flea* (Uffizi),
which Greuze might have seen in Florence on his way
to Rome.[3] The pose also recalls Caravaggio's *Magdalen*
(Rome, Palazzo Doria.)

A black chalk drawing related to the figure in *Indolence*,
who seems to be the same model Greuze employed for
Nos. 9 and 14 in this exhibition, is in the Hermitage;[4]
it appeared as lot 103 in the Boerner sale, Leipzig, April
29, 1931, apparently bought in. A red chalk drawing of a
"*Buste d'une italienne*" which appeared in the Vassal de
Saint-Hubert sale, Paris, March 27—April 13, 1779, lot
167, may be another study for this painting.

1 "a lack of concern that prevents
man from working . . . and from
fulfilling his duties." Diderot,
Encyclopédie, XI, p. 939
2 "They have placed [Chardin] in
the same row . . . as though to
facilitate the comparison of that
painter with M. Greuze; they gain
and lose in turn; he [Greuze]
choses separately what he wants to
paint; in truth one finds in each
object details that are most
satisfying but which, considered
in terms of the whole, do not at all
achieve harmony and do not at all
paint air and light . . . . he proves
to us that the least noble style has
nobility all the same, but he does
not always have the ingenuity of
M. Chardin." M. Renou,
*Observations sur la physique et les
arts*, Paris, 1757, pp. 15–16
3 G. Wescott, "Poor Greuze,"
Wadsworth Atheneum Bulletin, XIII,
No. 1, 1935, p. 7
4 Monod-Hautecocur, No. 70,
Pl. XXVII

11 **Seated Man Tuning a Guitar** (Study for *The Fowler*)
Black chalk, heightened with white gouache, on gray
paper, 21¾ x 18¾ in. (55.2 x 47.7 cm), including
additions
Signed: *Greuze*
Paris, Bibliothèque Nationale, Cabinet des Estampes

Collections: Nicolas de Livry, Bishop of Callinique, Sens,
eighteenth century; Paris, Bibliothèque de l'Arsenal,
1858; transferred to the Bibliothèque Nationale between
1861 and 1864 (Lugt 248)
   Exhibitions: Paris, Musée de l'Orangerie, L'Art français
et l'Europe aux XVIIè et XVIIIè siècles, 1958, No. 77
   Bibliography: J. Vallery-Radot, "Le Dessin préparatoire
de Greuze pour 'L'Oiseleur accordant sa guitare,' "
Gazette des Beaux-Arts, October, 1959, pp. 215–18

This highly interesting drawing from Greuze's Roman
period reappeared only in 1958, although its existence
was known a century earlier when Anatole de Montaiglon
described the subject as *"une molle figure de faux espagnol
assis et jouant de la guitare."*[1] The drawing corresponds
clearly in pose and detail to the figure in *The Fowler* (No.
12), though the face is not quite so agitated as in the
painting and no accessories of the fowler's trade are
included. The additions the artist made at the sides of the
sheet in order to complete the figure suggest that this was
a working study and was not conceived as a polished
product for collectors.
   Sauerländer relates the contorted pose to one of
Michelangelo's *ignudi* in the Sistine Chapel.[2]
   The subject of a drawing in the Hermitage, probably
also executed in Rome, is dressed similarly.[3]

1 "a soft figure of a false
Spaniard seated and playing a
guitar." A. de Montaiglon, ed.,
"Pièces communiquées par M.
Leperlier, et annotées par M. A. de
Montaiglon," *Archives de l'art
français*, VI, 1858–60, p. 236
2 Sauerländer, p. 148
3 Monod-Hautecoeur, No. 55,
Pl. XXI

45

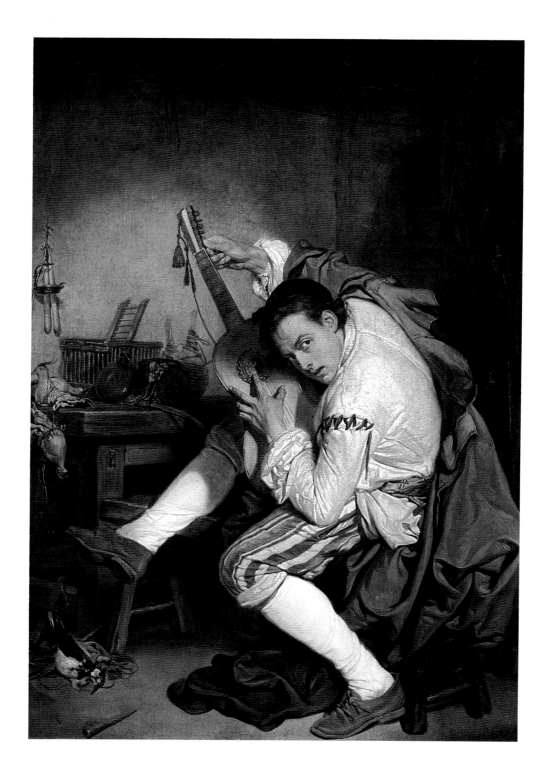

1 Listed as No. 22 in the ms.
inventory of this collection drawn
up by M. Zmigrodzki in 1882
2 Portalis-Béraldi, III, p. 114
3 "Fowling . . . means to cast
nets, set snares, or use a mirror and
traps to catch birds." "It is also
the fowler who makes cages,
aviaries, and cots, be they of wire,
brass or iron." Diderot, Encyclopédie,
XI, p. 444
4 "A merry bird-catcher am I, /
Aye merrily tra-la I cry; / As
bird-catcher it is my pride / That
I'm renowned on every side. / And
yet I'd love to catch a maid, / A
score would in my snare be laid; /
I'd mew her up and make her fast, /
And then they'd all be mine at last."
Original text by Emmanuel
Schikaneder, anon. trans., The
Magic Flute, Deutsche Grammaphon,
No. 2709 017, n.d.

12   The Fowler (*Un Oiseleur qui, au retour de la chasse, accorde sa guitarre*)
Oil, on canvas, 24⅞₁₆ x 18⅞ in. (62.0 x 48.0 cm)
Warsaw, Muzeum Narodowe

Collections: Jean-Baptiste-Laurent Boyer de Fonscolombe, Aix-en-Provence, 1757, with pendant; his sale, Paris, January 18, 1790, lot 101, with pendant; Prince Radziwill Branicki, Rome, Paris and Warsaw, with pendant, before 1874; Ksawery Branicki, Paris, 1882;[1] Branicki, Warsaw, about 1900; Branicki, Palace of Wilanów; inherited after 1918 by Countess Jadwiga Branicka, who married Stanislaw Rey; Rey, Przeclaw, until 1944; conveyed to the museum by the Ministry of Culture in 1954

Exhibitions: Salon of 1757, No. 115, with pendant; Paris, 1874; Warsaw, Muzeum Narodowe, Exposition de l'art français, 1923; Bordeaux, Paris et les ateliers provinciaux, 1958, No. 78; Paris, Musée de l'Orangerie, L'Art français et l'Europe aux XVIIè et XVIIIè siècles, 1958, No. 18; Rome, Palazzo delle Esposizioni, Il Settecento a Roma, 1959, No. 277; R. A., 1968, No. 304; Bregenz, Landes-museum and Vienna, Osterreichisches Museum für angewandte Kunst, Angelika Kauffmann und ihre Zeitgenossen, 1968–69, not in catalogue; Poznań, Muzeum Narodowe, Sztuka francuska w zbiorach polskich, 1973, No. 27

Bibliography: J. Bialostocki and M. Walicki, *Malarstwo europejskie w zbiorach polskich*, Warsaw, 1955, p. 559, Pl. XII; Brookner, pp. 59, 97, Pl. 15; Martin-Masson, No. 115; R. Michéa, "Quelques détails inédits sur le voyage en Italie de Greuze et de Gougenot, *"Etudes italiennes,* January–March, 1934; Muzeum Narodowe, *Malarstwo europejskie*, Warsaw, 1966, I, p. 160, No. 456; M. Nalecz-Dobrowolski, *Tygodnik Ilustrowany*, 1923, I, pp. 381–82; J.-F. Revel, "Les Instruments de musique, thème en trois mouvements," *Connaissance des arts*, December, 1958, p. 108; A. Ryszkiewicz, *Polonica na zamku w Montrésor*, Poznań, 1975, p. 44; Sauerländer, pp. 147–48; Smith, No. 95; J. Vallery-Radot, "Le Dessin préparatoire de Greuze pour 'L'Oiseleur accordant sa guitare,'" *Gazette des Beaux-Arts*, October, 1959, pp. 215–18

Engraving: P.-E. Moitte, 1765, with pendant[2]

Greuze must have had considerable experience with fowlers and their wares, considering the frequency with which he treated the subjects of birds and their cages (see for example fig. 2, Nos. 44, 100). The paraphernalia of the fowler are described in Diderot's contemporary *Encyclopédie:* "*Oiseler . . . veut dire tendre des filets, préparer des gluaux, ou se servir du miroir et des trébuchets pour prendre des oiseaux."* "*C'est aussi l'oiseleur qui fait les cages, les volières, et les cabanes, soit de fil, de léton ou de fer."*[3]

It is not, however, the picturesque gear of the fowler's trade but the birdcatcher's apparently pathological state of mind that makes this picture a logical pendant to *Indolence* (No. 10), which it mirrors closely in dimensions and loosely in setting and pose. In extreme contrast to the seated woman's lethergy Greuze opposes the seated man's acute nervous energy, so intensely convoluted that it seems incapable of normal expression. The twisting disorder of the pose and the confusion of the setting suggest the futility of the fowler's attempt at harmony and hint ultimately at the brutality of the senses.

The trap on the wall, the nets hanging from a cord and the cage and decoy bird on the table may have been intended to underscore the untrustworthy character of the subject by recalling the popular expressions "*prendre quelqu'un dans ses rets"* (to catch someone in one's net) and "*se faire prendre à l'appeau"* (to be lured by a decoy). Greuze's message appears to be that innocent creatures risk ensnarement by the ploys of the perverse. It is possible that music is but one more snare of the sinister fowler and that, after returning from his hunt for birds, he is preparing to seduce a human victim with a serenade—a theme advanced by the title of Moitte's engraving of the picture, *Le Donneur de sérénade.* A further insight into the eighteenth-century attitude toward the birdcatcher is offered by Papageno in *The Magic Flute*, the most familiar of all fowlers, who sings:

" *Der Vogelfänger bin ich ja,*
Stets lustig, heissa, hopsassa!
Ich Vogelfänger bin bekannt
Bei alt und jung in ganzen Land.
Ein Nets für Mädchen möchte ich
Ich fing sie dutzendweis für mich!
Dann sperrte ich sie bei mir ein,
Und alle Mädchen wären mein."[4]

A drawing for the figure of the fowler is in this exhibition (No. 11). The same model reappears in *The Broken Eggs* (No. 9) and *The Neapolitan Gesture* (No. 14).

Other versions of this painting are in the Musée des Beaux-Arts, Nantes (canvas, 71.0 x 57.0 cm), and with Wildenstein and Co., New York (panel, 59.0 x 48.0 cm). The dimensions of the Warsaw version correspond to those given in the Boyer de Fonscolombe sale and, of the three versions, its facture mostly closely resembles that of its pendant.

Greuze. f. Romae an. 1756.

13 Old Woman with Arms Outstretched
(Study for *The Neapolitan Gesture*)
Black chalk, stumped, heightened with white chalk, on
faded blue paper, 18¼ x 12½ in. (46.4 x 31.6 cm)
Signed and dated: *Greuze. f. Romae an. 1756*
New York, Mr. J. F. McCrindle

Collections: Sale, London, April 13, 1965, lot 51; acquired
from Colnaghi, London
   Exhibitions: London, Colnaghi, Old Master Drawings,
1965, No. 34

This is one of several studies related to *The Neapolitan
Gesture* (No. 14), which Greuze painted in Rome probably
early in the year after the date on this drawing. The same
model posed for the scolding old woman in *The Broken
Eggs* (No. 9), another of the four Italian scenes the artist
exhibited in the Salon of 1757. She is among the earliest
representatives of the picturesque aged types who fascinated
Greuze throughout his career and whose expressive faces
and dramatic gestures he employed to convey drama to
his subjects.

14 The Neapolitan Gesture (*Une Jeune italienne congédiant avec le geste napolitain un cavalier portugais travesti, et reconnu par sa suivante: deux enfans ornent ce sujet, l'un retient un chien qui abboye*)
Oil, on canvas, 28¾ x 37⅛ in. (73.0 x 94.3 cm)
Signed and dated: *Greuze, Roma 1757*
Worcester Art Museum, Charlotte E. W. Buffington Fund

Collections: Louis Gougenot, abbé de Chezal-Benoît, Paris, with pendant;[1] Prince Nicolas Nikitich Demidoff (d. 1828), with pendant; his son Prince Anatole Demidoff, San Donato Palace near Florence, with pendant; his sale, Paris, February 21–22, 1870, lot 108, sold for 5,300 francs to Philips, probably for William, first Earl of Dudley (d. 1885); acquired by Agnew, London, in the 1890s for Lord Masham (d. 1924); Viscountess Swinton; David Koetser Gallery, New York, 1956; Acquavella Galleries, New York; Alberto Reyna, Caracas; acquired by the museum from French and Co., New York, in 1964

Exhibitions: Salon of 1757, No. 113, with pendant; R. A.,
1871, No. 393; New York, Finch College, French Masters of the Eighteenth Century, 1963, No. 28; R. A., 1968, No. 303; Toledo Museum of Art, Art Institute of Chicago and Ottawa, National Gallery of Canada, The Age of Louis XV: French Painting from 1710 to 1774, 1975–76, No. 42

Bibliography: C. Blanc, *Histoire des peintres de toutes les écoles: Ecole française*, Paris, 1862, II, p. 16; Brookner, pp. 59, 97, Pl. 14; L. Dresser and D. C. Rich, "The Worcester Art Museum," *Antiques*, November, 1966, p. 650; Goncourt, I, p. 339; A. Graves, *A Century of Loan Exhibitions, 1813–1912*, London, 1918, I, p. 448; Hautecoeur, pp. 22–23; Martin-Masson, No. 152; H. Mireur, *Dictionnaire des ventes d'art*, Paris, 1911, III, p. 361; J. Renouvier, *Histoire de l'art pendant la Révolution*, Paris, 1863, II, p. 505; D. C. Rich, "Delights of the Dix-huitième," *Apollo*, December, 1971, p. 58; Sauerländer, p. 149; Smith, No. 150; B. A. Waldram, *Jean-Baptiste Greuze, 1725–1805*, New York, 1923, pp. 31, 94; Worcester Art Museum, *Annual Report*, 1965, pp. x, xiv, *Handbook to the Worcester Art Museum*, 1973, p. 113, and *European Paintings from the*

Collection of the Worcester Art Museum, 1974, I, pp. 254–56, II, p. 590; "Accessions of American and Canadian Museums," Art Quarterly, Spring-Summer, 1965, p. 107; "La Chronique des arts," Gazette des Beaux-Arts, October, 1965, Supplement, p. 4
Engravings: P.-E. Moitte, 1763, with pendant; J.-J. Veyrassat, 1870, with pendant

The same models who posed for the slightly earlier pendant of this picture, *The Broken Eggs* (No. 9), here enact a complicated drama with sociological overtones.[2] A Portuguese gentleman, disguised as a pedlar, is exposed by a servant and gracefully mocked by the girl he was attempting to seduce. Her gesture of passing the back of her hand under the chin was of Neapolitan derivation but was popular in Rome at the time of Greuze's visit, and is still current today. It signifies rejection, of various degrees of intensity according to the force with which the gesture is delivered.

In a letter to the comte de Caylus dated February 22, 1757, the abbé Barthélémy described this picture, which probably had only recently been completed:

"C'est un Portugais, déguisé en marchand d'allumettes, qui veut s'introduire dans une maison pour voir une jeune demoiselle. La servante soupçonne quelque fourberie, tire son manteau et découvre l'ordre de Christ (que Greuze appelle sa dignité*). Le Portugais est confus, et la fille, qui est présente, se moque de lui à la napolitaine, c'est-à-dire en mettant ses doigts sous son menton. C'était pour mettre en valeur ce geste qui est très joli, que Greuze a fait son tableau."*[3] De Lalande is even more explicit about the gesture, which, along with the costumes, sculptural fragments and architecture, constitute the most specific evidence of Greuze's Italian experience to this date:

"On remarque chez les Napolitains un geste particulier qui est fort agréable; il se fait en passant le revers des doigts avec vitesse sous le menton; il exprime la négation, comme notre geste de tourner la tête à droite et à gauche, mais il est plus gracieux; il donne occasion à une femme de faire paroître une belle main ou de faire briller un beau diamant; il est aussi en usage à Rome, où on l'a emprunté des Napolitains qui la tiennent, dit-on, des Orientaux; mais il est peu usité dans les autres parties de l'Italie. M. Greuze a trouvé ce geste si agréable, si

piquant, qu'il l'a exprimé dans deux tableaux qu'il a faits à Rome pour M. Gougenot. L'un représente une Romaine à mi-corps, sa coëffe rebattue sur les yeux, et l'autre a pour sujet une jeune fille chez qui un chevalier à l'ordre de Christ veut s'introduire déguisé en marchand de petit métier. Une vieille servante en lui tirant le manteau découvre à sa maîtresse la supercherie et celle-ci le congédie avec le geste napolitain."[4] The whereabouts of the second picture mentioned by de Lalande are unknown.

The piquancy of the Neapolitan gesture for Greuze's French contemporaries can be imagined from these lines in the comtesse de Genlis's *Dictionnaire critique et raisonné des étiquettes de la Cour,* which was published in 1818 but accurately records pre-Revolutionary manners: *"Les femmes ne gesticuloient point autrefois; on trouvoit que leur maintien devoit toujours être calme, et que des gestes en parlant ôtoient la douceur et la modestie."*[5]

With its pendant, *The Neapolitan Gesture* shares the feature of naive children observing disreputable behavior among their elders but failing to grasp its significance. Their obverse, the old woman and the dog, recognize and denounce the imposture. A drawing for the old servant is included in this exhibition (No. 13), and studies of the male figure and of the dog are in the Hermitage.[6] A wash drawing of three of the figures appeared in the Présidente de Bandeville sale, Paris, December 3–10, 1787, lot 85, sold for 30 francs to Desmarest. A chalk drawing of the model for the crouching boy, signed *"Greuze f. Roma,"* appeared in the Georges Bourgarel sale, Paris, November 13–15, 1922, lot 93. A version of the head of the other child is in the Iveagh Bequest at Kenwood.

The Neapolitan Gesture is of interest in that it includes about as much of a landscape as Greuze ever painted in his early years. The artist's lack of interest in landscape troubled Natoire at the very time Greuze was executing *The Neapolitan Gesture,* for in a letter to Marigny dated February 22, 1757, the *Directeur* of the Académie wrote: *"Il vient de finir le pendant d'un tableau pour M. l'abbé Gougenot, où il y a beaucoup de méritte. Ce sera presque son dernier ouvrage de Rome. Je souhaitterois que, dans son genre, il y joignit la partie du paysage; cela donneroit de la variété à ses tableaux."*[7]

1 Moitte's engraving of the picture, exhibited as No. 201 in the Salon of 1763, bears the inscription *"Tiré du cabinet de M. l'abbé Gougenot, Cons^{er} au Grand Conseil, honoraire amateur de l'Académie Royale de Peinture et de Sculpture."*
2 Greuze frequently dismissed his models once they had assembled, pleading lack of inspiration and leaving the abbé Gougenot to pay them. See Gougenot des Mousseaux, "Notice sur l'abbé Gougenot," *Revue universelle des arts,* I, 1855, p. 441
3 "It is a Portuguese, disguised as a match-seller, who wishes to make his way into a house in order to see a young lady. The servant suspects some imposture, pulls his cloak and exposes the Order of

Christ (which Greuze calls *his dignity*). The Portuguese is abashed, and the girl, who is present, mocks him in the Neapolitan manner, that is to say by placing her fingers under her chin. It was to emphasize this gesture, which is very pretty, that Greuze made his picture." Abbé J.-J. Barthélémy, *Voyage en Italie,* Paris, 1801, p. 216
4 "One remarks among the Neapolitans a particular gesture which is most agreeable; it is done by passing the back of the fingers rapidly under the chin; it expresses negation, like our gesture of turning the head to right and left, but it is much more gracious: it gives a woman an opportunity to show off a beautiful hand or make a fine diamond sparkle; it is also used in Rome, where they have borrowed

it from the Neapolitans, who got it, they say, from the Orientals; but it is little used in other parts of Italy. M. Greuze found this gesture so agreeable, so piquant, that he employed it in two pictures he did in Rome for M. Gougenot. One represents a Roman woman in half-length, her headdress lowered over her eyes, and the other has as its subject a girl into whose house a chevalier of the Order of Christ wants to make his way disguised as a pedlar. An old servant woman, pulling at his coat, reveals the hoax to her mistress and the latter sends him off with the Neapolitan gesture." J.-J. Le Français de Lalande, *Voyage d'un françois en Italie,* Venice—Paris, 1769, VI, p. 342

5 "Ladies in former times never gesticulated; it was felt that their bearing should always be calm, and that gestures while speaking deprived them of gentleness and modesty." Madame la comtesse de Genlis, *Dictionnaire critique et raisonné des étiquettes de la Cour,* Paris, 1818, I, p. 240, "Gestes"
6 Monod-Hautecoeur, Nos. 17, 52
7 "He has just finished the pendant of a picture for M. l'abbé Gougenot, which has much merit to it. This will be practically his last work from Rome. I wish that, in his genre, he would add an element of landscape; it would give variety to his pictures." A. Lecoy de la Marche, ed., *L'Académie de France à Rome: Correspondance inédite de ses directeurs,* Paris, 1874, p. 276

15 Boy with Lessonbook
(*Un Ecolier qui étudie sa leçon*)
Oil, on canvas, 24⅛ x 18⅞ in. (61.8 x 48.0 cm)
Edinburgh, National Galleries of Scotland

Collections: chevalier de Damery;[1] sale of the estate of
Jean-François de Troy, Paris, April 9, 1764, lot 154; Clos
sale, Paris, November 18–19, 1812, lot 13, sold for 754
francs; John Smith, London, 1816; Allen Ramsey, London;
his son, Major-General Ramsey, London, 1837; his cousin,
Lord Murray of Henderland; Lady Murray; bequeathed
by her to the museum in 1861

    Exhibitions: Salon of 1757, No. 119
    Bibliography: Brookner, pp. 60, 98, Pl. I; Fried, p. 148,
fig. 6; Martin-Masson, No. 965; National Gallery of
Scotland, *Catalogue of Paintings and Sculpture*, Edinburgh,
1957, pp. 113–14; Smith, No. 138; Wright, p. 82
    Engraving: C. Levasseur, 1761

As subtle in content as in execution, the *Boy with Lesson-
book* depicts the process of memorization. Though Greuze
apparently executed this portrait of an unknown child in
Italy,[2] its distinct Dutch quality is reminiscent of
Rembrandt's treatment of a similar subject in his portrait
of *Titus at His Desk* (Rotterdam, Museum Boymans-van

Beuningen). It may have been the somber palette of the
present work that led Renou to say of Greuze's entries in
the Salon of 1757, "*Il prodigue trop de tons noirs.*"[3]
    The boy's pensive expression, the tilt of his head and
the unusual coiffure, with the hair pulled up into a central
braid, strongly recall Saly's marble *Bust of a Young Girl*,
first exhibited in the Salon of 1750 and known in many
versions. The subject of that bust has been identified by
Levey as the daughter of Jean-François de Troy, *Directeur*
of the Académie de France in Rome until his death in
1752.[4] As Saly had presumably executed, or at least begun,
the bust during his stay at the Académie from 1740 until
1748, it is quite conceivable that during his own sojourn
there Greuze came to know a version of the marble or a
study for it. Coincidentally, though the sale of de Troy's
estate, among other properties, in 1764 included no bust
by Saly, the present portrait, which must have been
executed well after de Troy's death, did appear in that sale.

1 Levasseur's engraving of the
picture, dated 1761, describes it as
belonging to "M. Damery,
Lieutenant aux gardes françaises."
For de Damery, see No. 40
2 According to P. Rémy in the
catalogue of the de Troy sale
3 "He lavishes too much on dark

tones." M. Renou, *Observations sur
la physique et les arts*, Paris, 1757,
pp. 15–16
4 M. Levey, "A New Identity for
Saly's 'Bust of a Young Girl,' "
Burlington Magazine, February,
1965, p. 91

16 Portrait of Louis Gougenot, abbé de Chezal-Benoît

Oil, on oval canvas, 23³⁄₁₆ x 20⁷⁄₁₆ in. (59.0 x 52.0 cm)
Dijon, Musée des Beaux-Arts

Collections: Louis Gougenot, abbé de Chezal-Benoît, Paris;
his grandnephew, chevalier Gougenot des Mousseaux,
Paris, 1855; Metzer sale, Paris, 1857, lot 94 (?); anonymous
sale, Paris, November 22, 1972, lot 42, acquired by
the museum

Exhibitions: Salon of 1757, No. 119 (?); Brussels, Palais
des Beaux-Arts, De Watteau à David, 1975, No. 23

Bibliography: Gougenot des Mousseaux, "Notice sur
l'abbé Gougenot," *Revue universelle des arts*, I, 1855, pp.
439–48; Martin-Masson, No. 1131; P. Quarré, "J.-B.
Greuze et J.-B. Lallemand," *XXVè Congrès de l'Association
Bourguignonne des Sociétés savantes*, Tournus, 1954, pp. 21–22,
and "Acquisitions pour le Musée: Portrait de l'abbé
Gougenot par Greuze," *Bulletin de la Société des Amis du
Musée de Dijon*, 1970–72, pp. 95–96; "La Chronique des arts,"
Gazette des Beaux-Arts, February, 1974, Supplement, p. 17,
No. 50

Engraving: N.-G. Dupuis

One of Greuze's earliest portraits, this likeness of Louis
Gougenot may be the "*Portrait de M*** en ovale*" exhibited
in the Salon of 1757. The artist had just returned from
Italy, where he had travelled as Gougenot's invited
companion. The dramatic lighting, the oval format and
the absence of hands, décor or accessories recall the
portraits of Van Dyck, whose work Greuze knew well from
engravings and whose name was frequently mentioned in
connection with his own.[1] Greuze's portrait of Louis de
Silvestre (fig. 10), for example, exhibited in 1755, was
described as "*dans le goût de Vandec*,"[2] and the abbé's
grandnephew, who states that the present portrait was
executed in 1757, described it as "*peint à la manière de
Van Dyck*."[3] This may be the "*portrait peint sur toile, dans
son cadre de bois sculpté et doré*" mentioned in the inventory
of Louis Gougenot's possessions drawn up after his death.[4]

That Greuze succeeded in capturing the personal qualities
of his subject is indicated by this passage in Gougenot's
obituary: "*La décence, la douceur, la modestie et la bienfaisance
constituaient son caractère, et ses vertus étaient peintes sur son
visage*."[5] The flesh tints in the portrait suggest that Gougenot resembled his father, whom he described as "*haut
en couleurs*."[6]

Louis Gougenot (1719–1767) was born into a distinguished
family associated with the house of Condé. Trained for
the magistrature, he became a member of the Grand Conseil
de France and commendatory abbot of the abbey of
Saint-Benoît. From an early age he was deeply interested
in the arts. He wrote biographies of Galloche, Oudry,
Le Lorrain and Coustou, advised Pigalle (who most
likely introduced him to Greuze) on the iconography
of the Maréchal de Saxe monument and published
anonymously in 1748 a *Lettre sur la peinture, la sculpture
et l'architecture à M****. During his Italian trip with
Greuze, Gougenot kept a journal with the intention of
writing a guidebook, but it was J.-J. Le Français de
Lalande, an astronomer, who eventually published this
material in his own *Voyage d'un françois en Italie* (1769),
which remained the most popular French guide to Italy
until the mid-nineteenth century. In his journal Gougenot
recalled inviting Greuze to accompany him: "*A peine
mes préparatifs furent-ils faits que j'ai eu le désagrément de voir
mon confrère se dédire; l'entreprise l'effraya. Sur le point donc de
rompre tous mes projets pour ce contre temps, je proposai à M.
Greuze jeune peintre de Bambochades qui venoit d'être reçu avec
applaudissement à l'Académie de m'accompagner en le défrayant
tout pendant le voyage. Il reçut cette offre comme une suite de
bonne fortune*."[7] On January 10, 1756, the Académie rewarded
Gougenot for his generosity towards Greuze by electing
him an honorary member. Greuze, however, had little to
do with his benefactor after he returned to Paris.[8]

The fact that the subject of Greuze's entry No. 119 in
the Salon of 1757 was not identified would have been
characteristic of Louis Gougenot, whose major publication
appeared anonymously, whose travel journal was pirated
and whose pursuit of solitude was noted by his contemporaries. In Montparnasse he lived quietly in a house he
called his *masure* (shanty), surrounded by his collections.

A bronze portrait bust of Gougenot executed by Pigalle
for the abbé's tomb in the Eglise des Cordeliers, Paris, was
removed from that church during the Revolution and has
not been traced. It is recorded, however, in a painting by
Alexandre Roslin exhibited as No. 45 in the Salon of 1769.[9]

1 Wille was to record Greuze's interest in Van Dyck in a journal entry dated February 21, 1762: "*Il y a quelques jours que M. Greuze, mon ami, me vint voir. Il trouva chez moi les cent portraits de Van Dyck, bonnes épreuves, bien reliés, dorés sur tranche et, comme je remarquai que le tout lui faisoit plaisir, je lui en fis présent; cela lui en fait encore davantage.*" ("It was several days ago that M. Greuze, my friend, came to see me. He found at my place the hundred portraits of Van Dyck, good proofs, well bound, gilt-edged, and, as I noticed that the set delighted him, I made him a gift of it; that pleased him even more.") Wille, I, pp. 188–89

2 "in the taste of Van Dyck." L. Gougenot, "Album de voyage en Italie," ms., Paris, collection of the baronne de Soucy, I, p. 141
3 "painted in the manner of Van Dyck." Gougenot des Mousseaux, "Notice sur l'abbé Gougenot," *Revue universelle des arts*, I, 1855, p. 441
4 "portrait painted on canvas, in a frame of carved and gilded wood." J. Guiffrey, "Scellés et inventaires d'artistes: Louis Gougenot, Honoraire de l'Académie de Peinture," *Nouvelles Archives de l'art français*, 1884, p. 406
5 "Decency, gentleness, modesty and benevolence formed his character, and his virtues were painted on his

face." M. Salé, "Nécrologe de l'abbé Gougenot, amateur," *Revue universelle des arts*, XII, 1860, p. 177
6 "of a ruddy complexion." Quoted in S. Rocheblave, "Jean-Baptiste Pigalle et son art," *Revue de l'art ancien et moderne*, 1902, p. 274
7 "My preparations were barely complete when I had the annoyance of seeing my colleague back out; the venture frightened him. On the point therefore of breaking off all my plans because of this untoward event, I proposed to M. Greuze, the young painter of Genre scenes who had just been enthusiastically received into the Académie, to accompany me entirely at my expense during the trip. He welcomed this offer as a con-

tinuation of good fortune." Gougenot, *op. cit.*, I, pp, 138–39
8 "*chéri, aimé et estimé de tous ceux qui le connurent, il* [Gougenot] *n'éprouva d'oubli que de la part de Greuze, qui, cependant, le trouva toujours aussi indulgent qu'empressé de lui être utile.*" ("cherished, loved and esteemed by all who knew him, he [Gougenot] was neglected only by Greuze, who, however, always found him as indulgent as he was eager to be useful to him.") Gougenot des Mousseaux, *op. cit.*, p. 442
9 France, private collection. See: London, Heim Gallery, French Portraits in Paintings and Sculpture, exhib. cat., 1969, No. 36

17 Portrait of George Gougenot de Croissy

Oil, on canvas, 31⅞ x 25³⁄₁₆ in. (81.0 x 64.0 cm)
Signed and dated: *J. B. Greuze 175[?]*
Brussels, Musées royaux des Beaux-Arts de Belgique

Collections: baron de Soucy, Paris, 1888; his sale, Paris, December 14, 1937, lot C; Paul Mikhaïloff, Paris; purchased from him by the museum in 1951

Exhibitions: Paris, Hôtel de Chimay, Exposition de l'art français sous Louis XIV et sous Louis XV, 1888, No. 12

Bibliography: P. Bautier, "Le Portrait de George Gougenot de Croissy par Greuze au Musée de Bruxelles," *Bulletin des Musées Royaux des Beaux-Arts,* 1953, pp. 27–31; A. de Champeaux, "Exposition de l'art français sous Louis XIV et sous Louis XV," *Gazette des Beaux-Arts,* July, 1888, p. 35; R. A. d'Hulst, *Le Musée de Bruxelles,* Paris, 1965, pp. 144–45; Musées Royaux des Beaux-Arts, *Catalogue de la peinture ancienne,* Brussels, 1953, p. 58

George Gougenot (1721–1784), younger brother of Greuze's patron Louis Gougenot (see No. 16), succeeded their father, George (d. 1748), as *conseiller-secrétaire* to the King.[1]

In contrast to the total simplicity of his brother's portrait, this one suggests the more rarefied atmosphere of the court and of Paris, where Greuze probably painted it after his return from Rome. The subject's literary interests are suggested by the clearly legible title of the open book beneath his hand—an edition of Addison and Steele's *The Spectator* published in London in 1753. In 1756 George Gougenot published anonymously his own *Etat présent de la Pennsylvanie.* It was he who inadvertently permitted de Lalande to incorporate his brother's travel journal in de Lalande's *Voyage en Italie,* as its author noted: "*Je n'aurais osé, dans cet ouvrage porter des jugements sur les oeuvres de peinture et de sculpture qui sont en Italie, si je n'eusse eu communication d'un manuscrit qui m'a mis à la portée de compléter ma description à cet égard . . . et ce n'est pas sans peine que j'ai obtenu de M. Gougenot de Croissy la communication d'un manuscrit si précieux.*"[2]

The spectacular rendition of lace in this and other early portraits by Greuze is a demonstration of the principle the artist expressed to the young portraitist Joseph Ducreux: "*Nempastés jamais vos dentelles ni vos gazes.*"[3] Comparaison with portraits by Greuze's teacher Natoire suggests that it was from him that Greuze learned this aspect of his technique.

An identical chair with lavender upholstery appears in the pendant portrait of Madame Gougenot de Croissy by Greuze included in this exhibition (No. 18).

1 Pigalle's portrait bust of the elder George Gougenot, which was executed for the family's funeral chapel in the Eglise des Cordeliers, Paris, is now in The National Gallery of Victoria, Australia.
2 "I should not have dared in this work to pass judgment on the works of painting and sculpture found in Italy had I not had access to a manuscript that enabled me to complete my descriptions in this respect . . . and it was not without difficulty that I obtained from M. Gougenot de Croissy access to so precious a manuscript." Quoted in in Gougenot des Mousseaux, "Notice sur l'abbé Gougenot," *Revue universelle des arts,* I, 1855, pp. 442–43
3 "Never let your laces or your gauzes get pasty." Quoted in Goncourt, I, p. 298, n. 1

18 Portrait of Marie-Angélique de Varenne, Madame George Gougenot de Croissy

Oil, on canvas, 31½ x 24¾ in. (80 0 x 63.0 cm)
New Orleans Museum of Art

Collections: baron de Soucy, Paris, 1888; his sale, Paris, December 14, 1937, lot B, bought in;[1] his daughter, comtesse Joachim de Dreux-Brézé, Paris, 1953; her son, comte Charles Evrard de Dreux-Brézé, Paris, 1958; Galerie Cailleux, Paris, 1968; private collection, New York; Dr. Klaus Virch, Kiel; acquired from him by the museum in 1976

Exhibitions: Paris, Hôtel de Chimay, Exposition de l'art français sous Louis XIV et sous Louis XV, 1888

Bibliography: P. Bautier, "Le Portrait de George Gougenot de Croissy par Greuze au Musée de Bruxelles," *Bulletin des Musées Royaux des Beaux-Arts,* 1953, p. 30, Pl. I; A. de Champeaux, "Exposition de l'art français sous Louis XIV et sous Louis XV," *Gazette des Beaux-Arts,* July, 1888, p. 35; R. A. d'Hulst, *Le Museé de Bruxelles,* Paris, 1965, p. 144

This portrait of Madame Gougenot, executed probably in 1757, forms the pendant to Greuze's portrait of her husband (No. 17), from which it was separated in 1937. Born Marie-Angélique de Varenne in 1737, the subject was the daughter of Marie-Jacques Verany de Varenne, *écuyer* and *conseiller-secrétaire* to the King, an associate of Gougenot's father. Madame Gougenot was the sister-in-law of Greuze's patron Louis Gougenot (No. 16).

Undoubtedly proud of the skill in depicting lace he demonstrates in this portrait, Greuze, as Yvonne Cox has pointed out,[2] has represented Madame Gougenot in the act of "knotting"—that is, making a kind of lace edging using thread and an ornamental shuttle called a *navette.* Madame de Genlis described the appeal of this mid-eighteenth-century pastime: "*Jadis les femmes, pour avoir une contenance dans leurs visites et dans un cercle, tiroient de leurs sacs à ouvrage une jolie navette d'or, d'écaille ou d'ivoire, et faisoient des noeuds. Cet ouvrage en général ne servoit à rien; mais il étoit une espèce d'emblême qui exprimoit l'aversion que toute femme doit avoir pour une totale oisiveté; c'était l'enseigne du travail des doigts. Ce maintien avoit de la grâce; il caractérisoit particulièrement une femme.*"[3] In a 1717 issue of the *Spectator,* an edition of which Greuze included in his portrait of Madame Gougenot's husband, the advantages of knotting are described in terms applicable to this painting: "it shews a white Hand and a Diamond ring to great advantage and it leaves the Eyes at full liberty to be employed as before, as also the Thoughts and Tongue."[4] *Navettes* appear in contemporary portraits by Nattier and Tocqué, and one is seen in Giuseppe Baldrighi's portrait of Louis XV's daughter Louise-Elisabeth, painted in 1757 at her summer palace at Colorno (Parma, Galleria Nazionale). Greuze visited Colorno on November 9-10, 1755, in the company of Madame Gougenot's brother-in-law.[5]

1 The pendant of this portrait was lot C in the same sale.
2 Oral communication, June, 1976, referring to G. Townsend's excellent study, "Portrait by John Singleton Copley of a Lady 'Knotting,'" *Wadsworth Atheneum Bulletin,* Fall, 1966, pp. 12-23
3 "In former times, women, in order to have a proper bearing while making visits and in an intimate group, would draw from their workbags a pretty navette of gold, shell or ivory, and would make knots. This work in general served no purpose; but it was a sort of emblem that expressed the aversion every woman should have for total idleness; it was a token of work with the fingers. This deportment was graceful; it distinguished a woman in a particular way." Madame la comtesse de Genlis, *Dictionnaire critique et raisonné des étiquettes de la Cour,* Paris, 1818, II, p. 3, "*Navettes*"
4 Quoted in Townsend, *op. cit.,* p. 18
5 L. Gougenot, "Album de voyage en Italie," ms., Paris, collection of the baronne de Soucy, I, pp. 332-36

19   **Portrait of Abraham de Roquencourt**
Oil, on canvas, 32 x 26 in. (81.3 x 66.0 cm)
New York, Wildenstein and Co.

Collections: Roquencourt family, Neuchâtel
   Exhibitions: New York Union League Club, Eighteenth-
Century French Painting, 1931, No. 12; Toronto, Art
Gallery of Ontario, Eighteenth-Century Portraits, 1932,
No. 11; New York, Wildenstein and Co., The Great
Tradition of French Painting, 1939, No. 20

The subject of this sympathetic, sober portrait has
traditionally been identified as Abraham de Roquencourt,
about whom nothing is known. The books with which
he is shown indicate that he may have been a scholar or
writer. The intimacy of the format, the attention paid to
details of lace and hands, even the form of the chair
suggest a relationship with Greuze's Gougenot portraits
of 1757 (Nos. 16, 17, 18).

20 Portrait of Madeleine Barberie de Courteilles
(*Portrait de Mademoiselle de ***, sentant une rose*)
Oil, on oval canvas, 30½ x 24¾ in. (77.4 x 63.0 cm)
Brunswick, Herzog Anton Ulrich-Museum

Collections: Courteilles family, until 1848; comtesse Lehon,
Paris; her sale, Paris, April 3, 1861, lot 1, sold for 6,000
francs; Lord Foley, Ruxley Lodge, Claygate, Surrey; his
sale, Ruxley Lodge, October 11, 1919, lot 509; René
Gimpel, Paris; private collection, Geneva, until 1969;
Galerie Heim, Paris; acquired by the museum in 1975

   Exhibitions: Salon of 1759, No. 111; Geneva, Musée Rath,
Trésors des collections romandes, 1954, No. 38; London,
Heim Gallery, French Portraits in Painting and Sculpture,
1969, No. 32; New York, Metropolitan Museum of Art,
International Exhibition Under the Auspices of C.I.N.O.A.,
1974–75, No. 140

   Bibliography: Brookner, pp. 60, 100, Pl. II; Diderot,
Salons, I, pp. 53–54; R. Gimpel, *Diary of an Art Dealer*,
New York, 1966, p. 112, n. 5, p. 262; Martin-Masson,
Nos. 1084, 1281; "La Chronique des arts," *Gazette des
Beaux-Arts*, March, 1976, Supplement, p. 21, No. 74

It is difficult to believe that Diderot could have written of
Greuze's entries in the Salon of 1759, among which the
present portrait appeared, "*Les Greuze ne sont pas merveilleux
cette année. Le faire en est roide, et la couleur fade et blanchastre.
J'en étois tenté autrefois. Je ne m'en soucie plus.*"[1] In fact the
explosive brilliance in this portrait of the flowers set
against the varied whites recalls the reference to "*l'éclat
des couleurs*" employed by Diderot two years later in
speaking of the *Young Shepherd Holding a Flower* (No. 24).[2]
The present portrait resembles the pendant of the latter,
Simplicity, which was shown the same year as *Mademoiselle
de Courteilles*. Both represent demure girls holding flowers,
and both are oval.

   Aubert de la Chesnaye des Bois's *Dictionnaire de la
noblesse* of 1772 records a marquis de Courteilles, *conseiller
d'état* and *intendant des finances*, who may have been the
father of the subject of this portrait.[3] His position at
court was comparable to that of a number of Greuze's
patrons at that time.

   An engraving by F.-A. Moitte entitled *La Fleuriste* is
related to this painting but shows minor differences.[4]
According to an inscription on the print it was based on
a drawing belonging to the chevalier de Damery (see
No. 40).

1   "The Greuzes are not marvelous
this year. Their execution is stiff,
and the coloring insipid and chalky.
I used to be tempted by them. I
don't care for them any more."
Diderot, *Salons*, I, p. 68
2   "the burst of the colors." *Ibid.*,
p. 135
3   F.-A. Aubert de la Chesnaye des
Bois, *Dictionnaire généalogique,
héraldique, chronologique et historique*,
Paris, 1772, V, p. 244
4   Martin-Masson, No. 1039;
Portalis-Béraldi, III, p. 112

21   Portrait of Anne-Marie de Bricqueville de
Laluserne, marquise de Bezons (*Portrait de Madame
la Marquise de ***, accordant sa guitarre*)
Oil, on canvas, 37 x 30 in. (94.0 x 76.2 cm)
Inscribed: "ANNE MARIE DE BRICQUEVILLE DE LALUSERNE /
EPOUSE DE JACQUES BAZIN MARQUIS DE BESONS / TRES HAUT
ET TRES PUISSANT SEIGNEUR DES / MAISONS HU[?]IN
NEUVILL, ET AUTRES LIEUX, ET / LIEUTENANT GENERAL
DES ARMEES DU ROI"
Baltimore Museum of Art, Mary Frick Jacobs Collection

Collections: Dr. Soulier, Paris (?); Wildenstein et Cie., Paris,
by 1925;[1] Mary Frick Jacobs, Baltimore, acquired in 1925;
bequeathed by her to the museum in 1938
   Exhibitions: Salon of 1759, No. 109; Hartford, Wadsworth
Atheneum, Hommage to Mozart, 1956, No. 24; Baltimore
Museum of Art, Age of Elegance: The Rococo and Its
Effects, 1959, No. 14, and From El Greco to Pollack:
Early and Late Works by European and American Artists,
1968, No. 29
   Bibliography: Brookner, pp. 60, 99, Pl. 24; Diderot,
Salons, I, pp. 53, 54; G. Hoffman, "The Painter Greuze
and His Portrait of the Marquise de Besons," *Baltimore
Museum of Art News,* April, 1949, pp. 1–3; Martin-Masson,
No. 1277; E. Munhall, "Greuze's Portrait of Comtesse
Mollien, Study of a Motif," *Baltimore Museum of Art News,*
Fall, 1962, p. 17, n. 6; *The Collection of Mary Frick Jacobs,*
Baltimore, 1938, Pl. 19

The rather obtrusive eighteenth-century inscription on
this portrait, uncovered in 1954, identifies the subject as
Anne-Marie Bricqueville de Laluserne, wife of Jacques-
Gabriel Bazin de Bezons (1725–1782), an important military
figure under Louis XV. After participating as *maréchal de
camp* in the battles of Sunderausen and Minden at the time
his wife's portrait was being exhibited in the Salon of
1759, the marquis de Bezons was made *lieutenant général*
in 1762.[2]
   This portrait is related in its musical theme to *The
Fowler* of 1757 (No. 12) and to the portrait of Lalive de
Jully (No. 22), with which it was exhibited in 1759.
Diderot summarily dismissed Greuze's contributions to
the Salon that year (see No. 20), but another critic,
comparing Greuze's studies of heads to his other entries,
wrote, "*je lui donnerais volontiers la palme pour ses portraits.*"[3]
   Jerzy Golos has kindly pointed out that while Greuze
depicted the normal five double-courses of strings running
along the body of the guitar and their corresponding pairs
of pegs at the top of the instrument, the artist included
six pairs of strings at the bottom, below the subject's
right hand.[4]

1   "I called on him [Nathaniel
Wildenstein] with a rich American
to whom he showed the most
beautiful Greuze that I know, the
Countess of X playing the mandolin.
He asked him 1,650,000 francs for
it." R. Gimpel, *Diary of an Art
Dealer,* New York, 1966, pp. 263–
64, entry for June 20, 1925
2   See: E. Franceschini, *Dictionnaire
de biographie française,* Paris, 1951,
V, p. 1031; J.-B.-P.-J., chevalier de
Courcelles, *Dictionnaire historique et
biographique des généraux français
depuis le onzième siècle jusqu'en 1820,*
Paris, 1820–28, I, pp. 445–46
3   "I would gladly give him the
palm for his portraits." *Lettre
critique à un ami sur les ouvrages de
M.M. de l'Académie exposés au Sallon
du Louvre,* Paris, 1759, p. 27
4   Letter dated March 5, 1976

22 Portrait of Ange-Laurent de Lalive de Jully
(*Le Portrait de M. de *** jouant de la harpe*)
Oil, on canvas, 46 x 34⅞ in. (116.8 x 88.5 cm)
Washington, National Gallery of Art, Samuel H. Kress
Collection

Collections: Lalive de Jully, Paris, 1759; comtesse Edouard
de Fitz-James, Paris, 1778 (?); duc de Feltre, Paris, 1818
(?); comte Charles de Goyon, château de la Roche-Goyon,
1870 (?); comtesse de Goyon, 1874; comte Alexandre de
Laborde, Paris, 1927; sold by him in 1937 to Duveen
Brothers, New York; given to the museum by Samuel H.
Kress and The Kress Foundation in 1944

   Exhibitions: Salon of 1759, No. 108; Paris, Union
Centrale des Beaux-Arts, Exposition au profit de la
colonisation de l'Algérie par les Alsaciens-Lorrains, 1874,
No. 207; Paris, Exposition Universelle, Portraits nationaux
du XVIIIè siècle, 1878, No. 701; Paris, Louvre, Exposition
de tableaux au profit de l'oeuvre des orphelins d'Alsace-
Lorraine, 1885, No. 242; Paris, Musée Carnavalet, Les
Grands Salons littéraires, 1927, No. 173; Paris, Société
des Amateurs d'Art, L'Art français, 1931, No. 193;
Copenhagen, Palais de Charlottenborg, L'Art français au
XVIIIè siècle, 1935, No. 86; New York World's Fair, Five
Centuries of History Mirrored in Five Centuries of French
Art, 1939, No. 227

   Bibliography: Brookner, pp. 99–100, Pl. 23; Diderot,
Salons, I, pp. 53–54, II, p. 36; S. Eriksen, "Lalive de
Jully's Furniture 'à la grecque,' " *Burlington Magazine,*
August, 1961, pp. 340–47, and *Early Neo-Classicism in
France,* London, 1974, pp. 195–97, 311–12, 377–79; F.
Kimball, "The Beginnings of the *Style Pompadour,*" *Gazette
des Beaux-Arts,* July, 1954, pp. 62–64; P. Mantz, "Exposition
Universelle: Les Portraits historiques au Trocadéro,"
Gazette des Beaux-Arts, December, 1878, pp. 879–80;
Martin-Masson, Nos. 1184, 1185; National Gallery of
Art, *Paintings and Sculpture from the Samuel H. Kress
Collection,* Washington, 1959, p. 361, and *Summary Catalogue
of European Paintings and Sculpture,* Washington, 1965,
p. 63, No. 773

This portrait has gained notice in recent years as a visual
record of what is perhaps the earliest known neoclassical
furniture in France, Lalive de Jully's celebrated suite
à la grecque dated by Eriksen to about 1756–57.[1] Designed
by L.-J. Le Lorrain, it was praised by the comte de
Caylus but ridiculed by Cochin. The ebony-veneered
writing table with gilt-bronze mounts visible through the
harp is now in the Musée Condé at Chantilly, along
with a matching filing cabinet; the chair and harp have not
re-emerged. Greuze must have executed the portrait
sometime after returning from Italy in the summer of
1757 and before the opening of the Salon in late September
of 1759.

As in his portrait of Watelet (No. 35), Greuze here
represents his subject casually garbed in a dressing gown

and actively pursuing his artistic interests, evidence of
which surrounds him. Baron Grimm's description of
Lalive, written in 1770, fits Greuze's image of the man:
"*riche d'ailleurs et d'une figure intéressante, un peu dévot, un
peu musicien, un peu graveur.*"[2] It was Grimm who spoke
also of Lalive's tragic ending: "*il est tombé dans un état de
mélancolie qui a affecté sa tête et l'a séquestré de la société.*"[3]

Ange-Laurent de Lalive de Jully (1725–1779) inherited a
fortune in 1751 from his father, the *fermier-général* Lalive
de Bellegarde. Five years later he purchased the post of
introducteur des ambassadeurs à la Cour de France, roughly
equivalent to that of chief of protocol, a position he
occupied until about 1767. After the death of his first
wife in 1752 he abandoned what his sister-in-law Madame
d'Epinay described as a dissipated life and became an avid
collector. By 1754, when he was elected an honorary
member of the Académie, his collection was well known.
In 1764, after moving from the house in the rue Saint-
Honoré where Greuze had painted him in his *cabinet
flamand,* Lalive published a guide to his collection, which
was open to anyone interested. Apart from his Italian
and Flemish paintings, he concentrated on acquiring
paintings and sculpture by contemporary French artists,
especially Greuze.

In his *Catalogue historique* Lalive listed the ten paintings
by Greuze he then owned, including this portrait, which
hung in the first room facing the garden. He described it
thus: "*Un tableau de Greuze: représentant le portrait de M. ***
jouant de la harpe. Ce tableau est d'une belle couleur, et d'une
parfaite ressemblance, et de la plus grande finesse pour l'exécution:
les étoffes y sont rendues avec la légerté et la vérité de la nature.*"[4]
The portrait hung between a *Virgin* by Blanchard and
Lemoyne's study for his painting of *Fecundity* in the
Salon de la Paix at Versailles.

The sculpture at the right in the portrait cannot be
identified with certainty but is probably one of the
figures of a *Vestal* or a *Sibyl* "*dans le style antique*" that
Lalive lists in the *Catalogue historique,* mentioning examples
by Berruer, Caffiéri, Legros and Pajou. As such it would
allude to the collector's interest in contemporary
archaeological discoveries and in the stylistic revival of
classical forms. Lalive shared these interests with the
comte de Caylus, Gougenot, the abbé Barthélémy and
others—a group that Diderot scorned as "*antiquaires.*"
Diderot even wrote of the mental illness that overcame
Lalive with little sympathy—"*votre bon ami M. de La Live
n'est pas devenu imbécile, mais fou*"[5]—and he probably
disapproved of Greuze's associations with such company.

In addition to the present portrait Greuze executed a
small study for it included in this exhibition (No. 6) and
a portrait of Lalive in pastel shown as No. 122 in the
Salon of 1765. Known only through Augustin de
Saint-Aubin's engraving, the pastel depicts Lalive poised
over the open pages of *Les Hommes illustres de France,* a
work he had planned as a sequel to Charles Perrault's
book of the same title and for which he executed a set of
portrait engravings. It was never published.

1 S. Eriksen, *Early Neo-Classicism in France*, London, 1974, p. 311

2 "wealthy, moreover, and interesting looking, a bit of a devout, a bit of a musician, a bit of an engraver." Baron F.-M. Grimm, *Correspondance littéraire, philosophique et critique*, Paris, 1877–82, VIII, p. 465

3 "he has fallen into a state of melancholy which has affected his head and has isolated him from society." *Ibid*.

4 "A painting by Greuze: representing the portrait of M. *** playing the harp. This painting is of a beautiful coloring, and of a perfect resemblance, and of the greatest finesse in its execution: the fabrics in it are rendered with lightness and truth to nature." A.-L. de Lalive de Jully, *Catalogue historique du cabinet de peinture et sculpture françoise de M. de Lalive*, Paris, 1764, p. 55

5 "Your good friend M. de La Live has not become simply foolish, but mad." Quoted in Eriksen, *op. cit.*, p. 195

**23 Silence! (*Un tableau représentant le Repos,
caractérisé par une Femme qui impose silence à son
fils, en lui montrant ses autres enfans qui dorment*)**
Oil, on canvas, 24¾ x 20 in. (62.8 x 50.8 cm)
London, Her Majesty Queen Elizabeth II

Collections: Jean de Jullienne, Paris, 1759 (not listed in his
sale, Paris, March 30–May 22, 1767);[1] de Montulé; his
sale, Paris, December 20–23, 1783, lot 81, sold for 2,100
or 2,400 livres to Verrier; marquis de Vaudreuil; his sale,
Paris, November 26, 1787, lot 96; Stanley sale, London,
June 7, 1815, bought in at £ 180; purchased in Paris,
1817, by Lord Yarmouth, third Marquess of Hertford, for
George IV, and recorded at Carlton House on January 9,
1818 (payment of £ 138 made to Lord Yarmouth on March
7, 1818); Buckingham Palace since 1843

Exhibitions: Salon of 1759, No. 103; R. A., 1946–47,
No. 429; R. A., 1954–55, No. 186; The Queen's Gallery,
George IV and the Arts of France, 1966, No. 56; R. A.,
1968, No. 305

Bibliography: R. Bishop, *Paintings of The Royal Collection*,
London, 1937, p. 145, repr. facing p. 139; Brookner, pp.
60, 100, Pl. 20; L. Cust, *The Royal Collection of Paintings at
Buckingham Palace and Windsor Castle*, London, 1905, I,
n.p., and *Catalogue of Paintings and Drawings in Buckingham
Palace*, London, 1909, p. 202; Diderot, *Salons*, I, pp. 52–53,
68; Fried, p. 163, fig. 14; Goncourt, I, pp. 339, 351;
Martin-Masson, No. 213; Smith, No. 57

Engravings: L. Cars and C. Donat-Jardinier; C. Corbutt;
J.-E. Haïd; Z. Zetze

In this unusual variant on the nursing theme, Greuze
effectively illustrates the conflicting wills of an imposing
young mother and her dishevelled son, eager to blow his
small horn and indifferent to the slumber of his infant
brothers. It is probably he who has broken the drum that
hangs from the chair at right. Greuze's *The Spoiled Child*
in the Hermitage, exhibited as No. 111 in the Salon of
1765, resembles the present picture sufficiently in size, setting
and subject matter to suggest that it may have been
conceived as a contrasting pendant to it, the present scene
representing a disciplining mother, the other an indulgent
one.

Lent by the prestigious collector Jean de Jullienne to
the Salon of 1759, *Silence!* was the artist's leading entry
that year. Although Diderot dismissed Greuze's Salon
works, the anonymous critic of the *Petites Affiches de Paris*
mentioned "*différens morceaux de M. Greuse, entre autres un
tableau plein d'esprit, qui représente le repos.*"[2] In 1787 *Silence!*
was described in the catalogue of the de Vaudreuil sale as
having "*fait le plus grand honneur à l'artiste.*"[3]

That Greuze practiced the advice he gave to Joseph
Ducreux—"*Faites des études avant que de peindre en dessinant
surtout*"[4]—is attested to by the several drawings he did for
the figures in this composition. Only one remains in the
Hermitage of the group of four acquired by the Grand
Duke Paul Petrovitch in 1782.[5] A drawing for the head of
the sleeping child at right is in the collection of M. J.
Jamet, France. A study for the legs of the boy at left belongs
to Germain Seligman, New York.

A reversed copy of *Silence!* formerly in the museum at
Bonn, from which it was sold in 1935, was done after one
of the engravings of the picture.

1 The inscription on L. Cars'
engraving of the picture states
"*Tiré du cabinet de Monsieur de
Jullienne.*"
2 "different pieces by M. Greuze,
among others a picture full of spirit
which represents repose." *Petites
Affiches de Paris*, Paris, 1759, p. 3
3 "done the greatest honor to
the artist."

4 "Make studies before painting,
especially by drawing." Quoted in
Goncourt, I, p. 385, n. 1
5 Monod-Hautecoeur, No. 28; cf.
Nos. 29, 41, 71. Drawing No. 41
was lot 112 in the Boerner sale,
Leipzig, April 29, 1931, sold for
1,100 marks to Gilbert Lévy, and
lot 547 in the René Fribourg sale,
London, October 16, 1963.

24 **Young Shepherd Holding a Flower** (*Un jeune Berger qui tente le sort pour sçavoir s'il est aimé de sa Bergère*)

Oil, on oval canvas, 28⅜ x 23⅜ in. (72.0 x 59.5 cm)
Paris, Musée du Petit Palais

Collections: marquise de Pompadour, Versailles, 1761 (d. 1764); her brother, marquis de Marigny; his sale, Paris, March 18, 1782, lot 43, sold with pendant for 2,399 livres 19 sols "*à Robit, pour le Roi de France*" [sic];[1] comte Hyacinthe François Joseph d'Espinoy, Paris; his sale, Paris, January 14–19 and February 4–9, 1850, lot 935, with pendant, sold for 615 francs to Ward; baronne Edouard de Rothschild, Paris; acquired by the museum in 1975

    Exhibitions: Salon of 1761, No. 101
    Bibliography: Martin-Masson, No. 481; Smith, No. 25

The *Young Shepherd Holding a Flower* and its pendant, *Simplicity* (Walter Morrison Picture Settlement, Sudeley Castle, Winchcombe, Cheltenham, Gloucestershire), were commissioned from Greuze during his Italian sojourn by the marquis de Marigny, who intended them for his sister, the marquise de Pompadour. Marigny, who had been impressed by pictures Greuze had sent back from Rome, instructed Natoire in a letter dated November 28, 1756, to assist Greuze financially by giving him lodging and working space in the Académie, at the same time commissioning the two pictures on these generous terms: "*je luy laisse la liberté de son génie pour choisir le sujet qu'il voudra. Ces deux tableaux sont destinés à être placés dans l'appartement de Madame de Pompadour au château de Versailles. . . . Il seront veus de toutte la cour, et il pourroit en naistre de gros avantages pour luy, s'ils sont trouvés bons.*"[2] On December 22, 1756, Natoire sent Marigny the disappointing news that since the artist's health would not permit him to remain long in Rome,

Greuze was requesting permission to delay the execution of the commission until after he had returned to Paris.[3] Marigny graciously accepted Greuze's refusal in a letter of January 13, 1757,[4] anticipating the artist's immediate return. However, Greuze did not reach Paris until that summer. He eventually painted *Simplicity* in time for it to be exhibited in 1759, but the *Young Shepherd* was shown at the Salon only in 1761.

The *Young Shepherd* depicts a boy about to blow on a dandelion in the traditional gamble of learning whether his love is reciprocated; in its pendant, a girl is represented pulling off the petals of a daisy in a complementary gesture. As close in subject and manner to Madame de Pompadour's favorite painter, Boucher, as anything Greuze ever painted, this shepherd is all the same not one of what Diderot called the "*paysans chimériques*"—the fanciful peasants—of Boucher.[5] The realism and wistful sentiment Greuze brought to his subject, combined with the delayed execution of this important commission, may explain the lack of any subsequent commissions or purchases from the Royal favorite.

Diderot caught the echo of Boucher in this painting when he saw it in the Salon of 1761: "*Ce Berger, qui tient un chardon* [sic] *à la main, et qui tente le sort pour savoir s'il est aimé de sa bergère, ne signifie pas grand'chose. A l'élégance du vétement, à l'éclat des couleurs, on le prendrait presque pour un morceau de Boucher. Et puis, si on ne savait pas le sujet, on ne le devinerait jamais.*"[6]

In his review of the Salon, the abbé de la Porte mentioned Madame de Pompadour as owner of the *Young Shepherd Holding a Flower* and identified it as pendant to the *Simplicity* exhibited in 1759. In comparison, de la Porte felt, "*Il ne cède point au premier par le mérite de l'art mais peut-être par les grâces du caractère de simplicité, plus touchantes dans un sexe que dans un autre.*"[7]

1 "to Robit, for the King of France." So inscribed in the annotated copy of the sale catalogue in the Frick Art Reference Library, New York
2 "I allow him the liberty of his genius to choose the subject he wishes. These two pictures are destined to be placed in the apartment of Madame de Pompadour at the château of

Versailles. . . . They will be seen by all the court, and great advantages could come of it for him, if they are found good." A. de Montaiglon and J. Guiffrey, eds. *Correspondance des directeurs de l'Académie de France à Rome avec les Surintendants des Bâtiments*, Paris, 1901, II, Lettre 5202, p. 165
3 *Ibid.*, Lettre 5207, p. 168
4 *Ibid.*, Lettre 5211, p. 170

5 Diderot, *Salons*, I, p. 143
6 "This *Shepherd*, who holds a thistle [sic] in his hand, and who tempts destiny to learn whether he is loved by his shepherdess, does not mean a great deal. By the elegance of the costume, by the burst of the colors, one would almost take it for a piece by Boucher. Moreover, if one did not know the subject, one would never

guess it." *Ibid.*, p. 135
7 "It yields not at all to the first by the merits of its art but perhaps by the graces of the character of simplicity, more touching in one sex than in another." Abbé J. de la Porte, "Observations d'une Société d'amateurs sur les tableaux exposés au Salon cette année, 1761," *L'Observateur littéraire*, 1761, p. 52

25 Two Male Heads after Rubens' *Marriage by Proxy*

Red chalk, on white paper, 11½ x 17¼ in. (29.2 x 43.8 cm)
New York, Mr. Emile E. Wolf

Collections: acquired in London in 1965

A rare testimony to Greuze's study of Rubens' Medici Series (Louvre), this drawing records the features of the officiating bishop and an attendant figure in the canvas depicting Marie de Medici's marriage by proxy to Henri IV. Wille (No. 39) noted in his diary that on July 22, 1760, he and Greuze had examined the Medici Series, which was then still installed in the Palais du Luxembourg: "*M. Greuze et moi avons été dans la galerie de Rubens au Luxembourg, qu'on nous ouvrit exprès. Nous montâmes sur l'échelle pour voir de près les tableaux faits par ce grand homme, et considérâmes la manière de peindre et de colorier ses ouvrages, etc., digne de remarque.*"[1]
   Greuze's friend the abbé Gougenot (No. 16), who had long urged the public display of the Royal art collections and the Medici Series in particular, wrote of the latter in 1750, noting in reference to the figures in the *Marriage by Proxy* that "*ce sont presque tous portraits.*"[2] In his manuscript "Critique sur la peinture, la sculpture, la gravure et l'architecture" of 1750 he further stated, "*On reconnoist derrière le Grand Duc, deux seigneurs françois dont l'un est Roger de St. Lary, duc de Bellegarde, Pair et Grand Ecuyier de France, et l'autre Nicolas Brulart de Sillery depuis Chancellier de France, qui avoit négocié ce mariage.*"[3] In Greuze's drawing the duc de Bellegarde is the figure to the right; the bishop is Cardinal Pietro Aldobrandini, nephew of Pope Clement VIII. Greuze has juxtaposed the two figures, omitting that of the Grand Duke of Tuscany, who appears between them in Rubens' painting.[4]
   The *Marriage by Proxy* was copied by a number of French artists, ranging from Laurent de La Hyre to Fantin-Latour.

1 "M. Greuze and I have been in the Rubens gallery at the Luxembourg, which was opened specially for us. We climbed a ladder to view up close the pictures done by that great man, and pondered what was remarkable about the manner of painting and of coloring his works, etc." Wille, I, p. 139
2 "they are almost all portraits." L. Gougenot, ed. L. Laren, "L'Exposition des tableaux du Roy au Luxembourg en 1750," *Bulletin de la Société de l'Histoire de l'Art français*, 1909, p. 189

3 "One recognizes behind the Grand Duke two French lords, one of whom is Roger de St. Lary, duc de Bellegarde, Peer and Master of the Horse of France, and the other Nicolas Brulart de Sillery, later Chancellor of France, who had negociated the marriage." Paris, Bibliothèque Nationale, Cabinet des Estampes, Ya ²55
4 For a historical and iconographical discussion of the Rubens painting, see J. Thuillier and J. Foucart, *Rubens' Life of Marie de Medici*, New York, 1967, pp. 77-78

26 Portrait of François Babuti (*M. Babuti*)
Oil, on oval canvas, 23½ x 19 in. (59.7 x 48.2 cm)
Paris, M. Michel David-Weill

Collections: Mrs. Lyne Stephens, London; her sale, London,
May 9–17, 1895, lot 374; Rodolphe Kann, Paris; his sale,
Paris, 1907, No. 148; Madame Roussel, Paris; her sale, Paris,
March 25–28, 1912, lot 11, sold for 109,000 francs; David
David-Weill, Neuilly; Pierre David-Weill, Paris

Exhibitions: Salon of 1761, No. 97; Paris, Gazette des
Beaux-Arts, *Le Siècle de Louis XV vu par les artistes*, 1934,
No. 174; R. A., 1968, No. 306

Bibliography: W. von Bode, *Catalogue de la collection
Rodolphe Kann: Tableaux*, Paris, 1907, II, No. 148, p. 58,
repr. facing p. 58; Brookner, pp. 60, 62, 100, 101, Pl. 27;
Diderot, *Salons*, I, pp. 53, 54, 68, 97, 98, 134, Pl. 55; H.
Frantz, "La Collection Roussel," *L'Art décoratif*, April 20,
1912, p. 256; L. Hautecoeur, "Greuze, portraitiste," *L'Art
et les artistes*, February, 1924, pp. 170, 171; G. Henriot,
Collection David Weill: Peinture, Paris, 1926, I, pp. 171–73,
repr. p. 175; Martin-Masson, No. 1055; E. Michel, "La
Galerie de M. Rodolphe Kann ," *Gazette des Beaux-Arts*,
June, 1911, p. 504; C. Strienski, "Le Salon de 1761 d'après
le catalogue illustré par Gabriel de Saint-Aubin," *Gazette
des Beaux-Arts*, September, 1903, pp. 210, 212, 214; J.
Thuillier and A. Châtelet, *French Painting from Le Nain to
Fragonard*, Geneva, 1964, p. 224, repr. p. 222; *L'Illustration*,
February 2, 1922, cover ill.

In reference to this painting Greuze has recently been
called "the best portrait painter of his generation."[1] The
natural sympathy the artist brought to portrayals of the
aged was undoubtedly heightened here by the fact that in
this work he was painting the father of the woman he had
recently married.

François Babuti was a bookseller whose shop Diderot
said was on the quai des Augustins[2] but Greuze located in
the rue Saint-Jacques,[3] the same address given in the artist's
marriage contract. According to that document Babuti
came from a middle-class family in Annecy[4] and had married
first a Mademoiselle Berthier in 1715 and second a
Mademoiselle Marie-Anne Réal, who was the mother of
Greuze's wife. Babuti died in 1769, leaving his life annuity
to his daughter and son-in-law.

Despite repeated assertions to the contrary, there is no
evidence that this is the portrait of "*M. Babuti, libraire*"
exhibited as No. 113 in the Salon of 1759. On the other
hand, its presence in the Salon of 1761 is attested to both
by Saint-Aubin's sketch of the portrait in his Salon *livret*[5]
and by Diderot's vivid description of it: "*celui de Babuti,
beau-père du peintre, est de toute beauté. Et ces yeux éraillés et
larmoyants, et cette chevelure grisâtre, et ces chairs, et ces détails
de vieillesse qui sont infinis au bas du visage et autour du cou.
Greuze les a tous rendus; et cependant sa peinture est large.*"[6]
The abbé Joseph de la Porte was similarly enthusiastic:
"*Mais celui de M. Babuty, son beau-père, sera considéré comme un
vrai chef-d'oeuvre, et peut-être comme une utile leçon, dans la
manière de bien traiter une tête. Ce n'est pas seulement par les
caricatures que gravent les années, qu'il a donné à ce portrait la
force de l'effet, et la vérité du caractère; mais c'est par des passages,
dans les teintes des carnations dérobés à la nature même, avec cette
finesse que lui est uniquement réservée.*"[7] The anonymous critic
of the *Petites Affiches de Paris* mentioned merely "*d'excellens
portraits de Greuze.*"[8]

The Swedish engraver Floding described the portrait to
the comte de Tessin in a letter dated November 23, 1761:
"*Le portrait de son beau-père M* Babuti, libraire, étoit un chef-
d'oeuvre pour l'exécution, excepté qu'il tiroit un peu sur le gris
violet pour la couleur, ce qu'on lui reproche assez ordinairement.*"[9]

The present portrait, a self-portrait and a portrait of his
wife "*en vestale*" (as a vestal virgin) were exhibited by
Greuze as a trio of family portraits in the Salon of 1761.
According to the catalogue they were all the same size.[10]
Greuze also executed a portrait of his brother-in-law, which
is now lost. It too was oval, and of roughly the same
dimensions as the other three.[11]

A miniature reproducing the present portrait is in the
collection of the comte de Milly, Berzé-le-Châtel (Saône-
et-Loire).

1 J. Thuillier and A. Châtelet, *French Painting from Le Nain to Fragonard*, Geneva, 1964, p. 224
2 "*Je l'ai bien aimée, moi, quand j'étois jeune, et qu'elle s'appeloit mademoiselle Babuti. Elle occupoit une petite boutique de libraire sur le quai des Augustins.*" ("I was very fond of her myself, when I was young and she was called mademoiselle Babuti. She worked in a little bookshop on the quai des Augustins.") Diderot, *Salons*, II, p. 152
3 "*Peu de jours après être arrivé de Rome, je ne sai par quelle fatalité, je passay dans la rue Saint-Jacques (à Paris) j'apperçu Mademoiselle Babuty dans son couloir: elle étoit la fille d'un Libraire. . . .*" ("A few days after arriving from Rome, I know not

by what fatal luck, I walked down the rue Saint-Jacques (in Paris), I noticed Mademoiselle Babuty in her passageway; she was the daughter of a bookseller. . . .") J. Boilly, ed., "Mémoire de Greuze contre sa femme," *Archives de l'art français*, II, 1852–53, pp. 154–55
4 "*fils d'un bourgeois de la ville d'Annecy.*" G. Wildenstein, "Quelques Documents sur Greuze," *Gazette des Beaux-Arts*, October, 1960, pp. 227–28
5 Dacier, *Saint-Aubin*, VI, p. 64
6 "that of *Babuti*, father-in-law of the painter, is of great beauty. Those red-rimmed, tearful eyes, and that graying hair, and those flesh tones, and those details of old age which are infinite in the lower part of the face and around the neck,

Greuze had rendered them all; and yet his painting is broadly handled." Diderot, *op. cit.*, I, p. 134
7 "But that of M. *Babuty*, his father-in-law, will be considered a true masterpiece, and perhaps a useful lesson in the manner of properly treating a head. It is not only through the distortions with which the years leave their mark that he has given this portrait its powerful effect, and its truth of character, but it is through certain passages in the flesh tints stolen from nature herself, with that finesse uniquely reserved to him." Abbé J. de la Porte, "Observations d'une Société d'amateurs sur les tableaux exposés au Salon cette année, 1761," *L'Observateur littéraire*, 1761, p. 61

8 "some excellent portraits by Greuze." *Petites Affiches de Paris*, August 31, 1761, p. 4
9 "The portrait of his father-in-law Mr Babuti, the bookseller, was a masterpiece of execution, except that it tended a bit toward grayish-violet in its coloring, a criticism rather frequently made of him." M. G. W. Lundberg, "Le Graveur suédois Pierre-Gustave Floding à Paris et sa correspondance," *Archives de l'art français*, XVII, 1932, p. 291
10 "*ces trois tableaux sont de même grandeur.*" Diderot, *op. cit.*, I, p. 98
11 Jules Burat sale, Paris, April 28–29, 1855, lot 79 (65.0 x 50.0 cm); E. May sale, Paris, June 4, 1890, lot 102 (62.0 x 52.0 cm). As Seznec has suggested, this may be the portrait Greuze exhibited in 1759 (Diderot, *op. cit.*, I, p. 54).

27 Head of an Elderly Woman (Study for *The Stepmother*)

Red chalk, on white paper, 16¼ x 12⅞ in. (41.3 x 32.7 cm)
New York, The Metropolitan Museum of Art, Rogers Fund

Collections: Jules Porgès, Paris; comtesse de Fitz-James, Paris; Baron Gutman, Berlin; William H. Schab Gallery, New York; acquired by the museum in 1949

   Bibliography: Martin-Masson, No. 121; Portalis-Béraldi, II, p. 691; J. Renouvier, *Histoire de l'art pendant la Révolution*, Paris, 1863, p. 519

This drawing is a study for the head of the grandmother in Greuze's lost painting *The Stepmother*. A compositional sketch for the final work appeared in the Mailand sale, Paris, April 4–19, 1881, lot 73, and studies for other characters are in the Louvre, the Hermitage and the Musée Greuze at Tournus.

   Jean-Charles Le Vasseur engraved the composition twice. The first print must have appeared in the mid-1760s, for at that time there circulated in Paris a caricature dedicated to the "*très-haute, très-plaisante et très-ridicule dame, femme de J.-B. Greuze,*"[1] that included a sketchy representation of *The Stepmother*, along with one of Flipart's engraving of Greuze's *Self-Portrait* of about 1763 (No. 36). The caption drew attention to Madame Greuze's participation in her husband's dealings with engravers, as well as to her wanton behavior. The second, and larger, print was mentioned by Greuze himself in a letter relating to *The Stepmother* published in the *Journal de Paris* on April 13, 1781. In it he proudly recounts the evolution of the subject and differentiates the roles of the various characters, including the elderly woman depicted in this drawing:

"*Permettez, messieurs, que je profite de la voie de votre journal pour donner une note historique de l'estampe que je dois mettre au jour le 28 du présent mois et que j'ai fait graver par M. le Vasseur. Elle a pour titre la* Belle-Mère. *Il y avait longtemps que j'avais envie de tracer ce caractère, mais à chaque esquisse l'expression de la belle-mère me paraissait toujours insuffisante. Un jour, en passant sur le Pont-Neuf, je vis deux femmes qui se parlaient avec beaucoup de véhémence; l'une d'elles répandit des larmes et s'écriait: Quelle belle-mère! Qui, elle lui donne du pain, mais elle lui brise les dents avec le pain. Ce fut un coup de lumière pour moi; je retournai à la maison et je traçai le plan de mon tableau, qui est de cinq figures: la belle-mère, la fille de la défuncte, la grand'mère de l'orpheline, la fille de la belle-mère et un enfant de trois ans. Je suppose que c'est l'heure du dîner et que la jeune infortunée va se mettre à table comme les autres; alors la belle-mère prend un morceau de pain sur la table, et, la retenant par son tablier, elle lui en donne par le visage. J'ai tâché de peindre dans ce moment le caractère de haine réfléchie qui vient ordinairement d'une heine invétérée. La jeune fille cherche à l'éviter et semble lui dire: Pourquoi me frappez moi? Je ne vous fait point de mal. Son expression est la modestie et la crainte. Sa grand'mère est à l'autre bout de la table; pénétrée de la plus vive douleur, elle élève vers le ciel ses yeux et ses mains tremblantes, et semble dire: 'Ah, ma fille, où es-tu? Que de malheurs, que d'amertume!' La fille de la belle-mère, peu sensible au sort de sa soeur, rit en voyant le désespoir de cette femme respectable, et avertit sa mère en la tournant en ridicule. Le petit enfant, qui n'a pas encore le coeur corrompu, tend ses bras reconnaissants vers sa soeur, qui prend soin de lui. Enfin, j'ai voulu peindre une femme qui maltraite un enfant qui ne lui appartient pas et qui, par un double crime, a corrompu le coeur de sa propre fille.*"[2]

1 "most high, most amusing and most ridiculous lady, the wife of J.-B. Greuze." Impression in the Bibliothèque Nationale, Cabinet des Estampes. See: Paris, Bibliothèque Nationale, Diderot, 1963–64, exhib. cat., No. 297
2 "Permit me, gentlemen, to avail myself of your journal in order to provide a historical note concerning the print that I intend to publish on the 28th of this month and that I had engraved by M. le Vasseur. It is entitled the *Stepmother*. I had long wanted to portray this character, but in each sketch the expression of the stepmother seemed insufficient. One day, crossing the Pont-Neuf, I saw two women talking with great vehemence; one of them broke into tears and was crying out: What a stepmother! Yes, she gives her bread, but she breaks her teeth with the bread. It was a flash of inspiration for me; I returned home and laid out my picture, which includes five figures: the stepmother, the daughter of the deceased woman, the orphan's grandmother, the stepmother's daughter and a child of three. I imagine that it is dinner time and that the young unfortunate is about to sit at the table as the other have; then the stepmother takes a piece of bread from the table, and, holding her by her apron, thrusts it in her face. I tried to paint in this instant the character of deliberate hatred that usually is the product of constant hatred. The girl tries to avoid her and seems to say to her: Why strike *me?* I do you no wrong. Her expression is modest and fearful. Her grandmother is at the other end of the table; grieved to the very heart, she raises toward heaven her eyes and her trembling hands, and seems to say: 'Ah, my daughter, where are you? What misery, what bitterness!' The stepmother's daughter, insensitive to her sister's lot, laughs on seeing the despair of that respectable woman, and diverts her mother's attention in order to ridicule her. The little child, whose heart is not yet corrupted, holds out his grateful arms toward his sister, who looks after him. In short, I wanted to depict a woman who mistreats a child that does not belong to her and who, in a double crime, has corrupted the heart of her own daughter." Quoted in Goncourt, I, p. 302

28 The Improper Proposal (*Les Offres malhonnêtes*)
Brush, gray and brown ink wash, over pencil on white
paper, 13⅜ x 10½ in. (34.0 x 26.7 cm)
Inscribed on verso: *a S.A.S. au chateau de Chantilly / J.
B. Greuze*
New York, Mrs. Donald S. Stralem

Collections: C.-H. Watelet, Paris; his sale, Paris, December
6, 1786, lot 203; Louis-Henri-Joseph, prince de Condé,
Chantilly (?); Eugène Tondu, Paris; his sale, Paris, May
10–13, 1865, lot 257 (?); Baudoin, Paris; his sale, Paris,
June 22, 1938, lot 8
   Exhibitions: R. A., 1968, No. 325
   Bibliography: Brookner, p. 98; Martin-Masson, Nos.
293, 383; Munhall, 1965, pp. 85–87, fig. 7, p. 88; Smith,
No. 135

In this drawing, executed probably in the early 1760s,
Greuze treats the popular subject of "the unlikely couple,"[1]
a theme frequently painted by Northern artists in the
sixteenth and seventeenth centuries who exploited, as

Greuze does, the contrast between an absurd old man and a
winsome girl he attempts to seduce with a bag of money.
   Claude-Henri Watelet, whose portrait by Greuze is
included in this exhibition (No. 35), executed an engraving
in his Rembrandtesque manner after this drawing, which
he owned. The inscription on the verso of the drawing
suggests that it was at some time sent to a prince de Condé,
possibly after Watelet's sale.
   The same theme reappears in the fragmentary painting
of *The Surprised Housekeeper* (No. 29) and, somewhat modified,
in *The Confused Girl* (Paris, Musée Jacquemart-André), a
composition that includes only the girl and the old woman
leaning through the window. The Ingouf brothers
engraved the latter work in 1773.[2]
   A drawing of the old man and the girl in reverse, a
study for *The Improper Proposal*, was formerly in the
Hermitage;[3] two studies for the old woman's head remain
in that museum.[4] The old man and the details of the chair,
the walking stick and the hat in the left foreground
reappear in Greuze's drawing *The Paralytic* in The National
Gallery of Canada, Ottawa.

1 On the theme of the "*ungleichliche
liebespaar*," see A. Pigler,
Barockthemen, Budapest, 1956, II,
pp. 544–47
2 Portalis-Béraldi, II, p. 454

3 Monod-Hautecoeur, No. 22;
sale, C. G. Boerner, Leipzig, May
4, 1932, lot 45, Pl. VIII, sold to
comte de Vito Jerdinando, Rome
4 Monod-Hautecoeur, Nos. 127,
136

29 The Surprised Housekeeper

Oil, on canvas, 19¹¹⁄₁₆ x 11 in. (50.0 x 28.0 cm)
Marseille, Musée Grobet-Labadié

Collections: Chiff, Paris; his sale, Paris, April 13, 1867, lot
28; Marquiset, Paris; his sale, Paris, April 28–29, 1890, lot
21, sold for 300 francs; Mathey, Paris; sold by him for 700
francs to Monsieur and Madame Grobet-Labadié in 1905

   Exhibitions: New York, M. Knoedler and Co., Masters of
the Loaded Brush, 1967, No. 67

   Bibliography: Munhall, 1966, pp. 85–87, fig. 1; D. Posner,
"Baroque and Rococo Oil Sketches," *Burlington Magazine*,
June, 1967, p. 363; J. Vergnet-Ruiz and M. Laclotte, *Les
Petits et Grands Musées de France*, Paris, 1962, p. 238

This oil, either a fragment of a larger picture or a partial
compositional study, is related to Greuze's drawing *The
Improper Proposal* (No. 28), which depicts the attempted
seduction of a servant by an old man. Here Greuze repeats
the foreground kitchen paraphernalia of the drawing as
well as the startled cat, but he heightens the drama through
the girl's frightened expression and contorted posture and
through the placement of the seducer's hands ominously
enclosing her instead of merely clutching a bag of money.

   The rarity of such sketches and the fragmentary character
of this one account for the hesitant attribution it has been
given in the past.

   The so-called *Portrait of the Artist's Wife* in the National-
museum, Stockholm,[1] closely resembles the upper figure of
the girl in this sketch, as does the *Head of a Girl Wearing a
Bonnet* in the Musée des Beaux-Arts, Besançon.[2]

1 *Catalogue descriptif des collections
de peinture au Musée National de
Stockholm*, Stockholm, 1928, No.
2107; Munhall, 1966, fig. 3
2 No. D 2726; Munhall, *op. cit.*,
fig. 5

30 Compositional Study for *A Marriage Contract*

Brush, black and brown ink wash, over pencil, on white
paper, 13¾ x 19½ in. (35.0 x 49.5 cm)
Paris, Musée du Petit Palais

Collections: marquis Jean-Joseph de La Borde, Paris (?); his
sale, Paris, May 16, 1783, lot 38 (?); Vaudreuil, Paris; his
sale, Paris, November 26, 1787, lot 162, sold with pendant
for 800 francs to Lebrun; Jean-Baptiste-Laurent Boyer de
Fonscolombe, Aix-en-Provence; his sale, Paris, January 18,
1790, lot 189; baron Roger, Paris; his sale, Paris, December
23–24, 1842, lot 131, sold for 1,050 francs; Auguste Simon,
Paris; his sale, Paris, March 10–15, 1862, lot 30, sold for
660 francs to Clément; Eugène Dutuit, Rouen (Lugt 709);
bequeathed by him to the museum in 1902

Exhibitions: Paris, Ecole des Beaux-Arts, Dessins des
maîtres anciens, 1879, No. 569; Zurich, Kunsthaus, Chefs-
d'oeuvre du Petit Palais, 1947, No. 75

Bibliography: H. Lapauze, *Catalogue sommaire des collections
Dutuit,* Paris, 1907, No. 968, p. 186; Martin-Masson, No.
114

This compositional study for *A Marriage Contract* of 1761
(No. 34) includes the essential details of the final painting,
with the notable exceptions of the figure mounting the
staircase, a different cupboard door, the absence of a cloth
hanging from the cupboard's middle shelf and certain variations of expression among the figures. The fact that none of
these elements appears in an unfinished version of this
drawing in the Musée des Beaux-Arts, Le Havre, suggests
that the latter may be a copy by an unknown hand after
Greuze's painting.[1]

Greuze executed a large number of compositional and
figure studies for *A Marriage Contract.* It was by means of
such drawings that be achieved the remarkable fluidity of
his final composition. As Diderot noted of the painting,
*"La composition m'en a paru très-belle. . . . Il y a douze figures;
chacune est à sa place, et fait ce qu'elle doit. Comme elles s'en
enchaînent toutes! comme elles vont en ondoyant et en pyramidant!"*[2]

1 Musée des Beaux-Arts,
*Catalogue des dessins du XVIè au
XVIIIè siècles,* Le Havre, 1957, No.
AD 57
2 "Its composition seemed to me
very beautiful. . . . There are twelve
figures; each is in its proper place,
and does what it should do. How
they are all linked together! how
they move along rippling and
rising in a pyramid!" Diderot,
Salons, I, p. 141

31 Head of an Old Man (Study for *A Marriage Contract*)
Red and black chalk, gray ink wash, on white paper,
21⅞ x 15½ in. (55.6 x 39.4 cm)
New Haven, Yale University Art Gallery, Everett V. Meeks
Fund

Collections: Morrison, Basildon Park, 1914; Prince
Merchersky, Paris; Mathias Komor, New York; acquired
from him by the museum in 1961

Exhibitions: London, Grosvenor Gallery, Third National
Loan Exhibition, 1914–15, No. 110; Sarasota, Ringling Art
Museum, Master Drawings, 1967; Cambridge, Fogg
Museum of Art, Paintings, Drawings and Sculpture from
the Yale University Art Gallery, 1967; Notre Dame, Art
Gallery, University of Notre Dame, Eighteenth Century
France, 1972, No. 39

Bibliography: E. Haverkamp-Begemann and A.-M. S.
Logan, *European Drawings and Watercolors in the Yale
University Art Gallery*, New Haven—London, 1970, I, No.
53, pp. 30–31, II, Pl. 37; Martin-Masson, No. 1679

This drawing is a study for the head of the father of the
bride in *A Marriage Contract* of 1761 (No. 34). It represents
the same old model who posed for *Filial Piety*
(Hermitage), a painting that Greuze exhibited in 1765 but
for which he was making preliminary studies in 1761. The
present drawing may be the one Wille (No. 39) recorded
purchasing from the artist on July 17, 1761: "*J'ay acheté de
M. Greuze une grande tête de vieillard dessinée sur papier blanc aux
crayons noir et rouge. C'est la tête du père de l'*Accord du
mariage, *tableau qu'il fait actuellement. Elle m'a coûté trois
louis d'or.*"[1]

A drawing of the same model, a study for *Filial Piety*, is
also in the Hermitage.[2] A drawing related to the latter is in
the Cafmeyer collection, Paris, and another was sold in
London, July 13, 1972, lot 13 (formerly David-Weill
collection, Neuilly, and Cranbrook Academy of Art,
Bloomfield Hills, Michigan).

The unusual degree of empathy Greuze brought to
expressive subjects such as this was noted by Diderot in
connection with a contemporary drawing for *Filial Piety*
shown in the Salon of 1761: "*Le vieillard est dans son
fauteuil. . . . sa tête, celle de son fils et celle de sa femme sont
d'une beauté rare. Greuze a beaucoup d'esprit et de goût. Lorsqu'il
travaille, il est tout à son ouvrage; il s'affecte profondément: il
porte dans le monde le caractère du sujet qu'il traite dans son
atelier, triste ou gai, folâtre ou sérieux, galant ou réservé, selon la
chose qui a occupé le matin son pinceau et son imagination.*"[3]

1 "I have bought from M. Greuze
a large head of an old man drawn
in black and red chalk on white
paper. It is the head of the father
in *The Marriage Agreement*, a
picture he is now working on. It
cost me three gold louis." Wille,
I, p. 173
2 Monod-Hautecoeur, No. 137,
Pl. LVI
3 "The old man is in his armchair
. . . . his head, that of his son and
that of his wife are of a rare beauty.
Greuze has a great deal of spirit
and taste. When he is working, he
is completely bound up in his work;
he is deeply moved himself; he
brings into the world the character
of the subject he is treating in his
studio, sad or gay, playful or
serious, gallant or reserved,
according to whatever has engaged
that morning his brush and his
imagination." Diderot, *Salons*, I
p. 135

32 Head of a Girl with Eyes Downcast

(Study for *A Marriage Contract*)
Brush, gray ink wash, red chalk, pencil, on white paper,
15 9/16 x 11 13/16 in. (39.5 x 30.1 cm)
New York, private collection

Collections: Saint Petersburg, Academy of Fine Arts (Lugt S 2699 a); Leningrad, Hermitage; sale, Boerner, Leipzig, April 29, 1931, lot 105, sold for 950 marks to Mincieux; sale, Geneva, June 15, 1960, lot 204; Slatkin Gallery, New York; Louis Silver, Chicago

   Bibliography: Monod-Hautecoeur, No. 103, Pl. XL

In Greuze's painting *A Marriage Contract* (No. 34) and in his compositional study for it (No. 30) the bride, for whom this drawing is a study, tips her head slightly in an affectionate gesture toward a younger sister weeping on her right shoulder. The effect is rather more coquettish than the contemplative one seen in this sheet. A study for the full figure of the bride, engraved by Beauvarlet when it was in the de Damery collection, is in the Musée Vivant-Denon, Chalon-sur-Saône.[1] In neither that study nor the present drawing does the girl have flowers tucked into her bodice as she does in the painting.

1 Martin-Masson, No. 388; L. Armand-Calliat, *Musée Vivant-Denon: Catalogue de la Section des Beaux-Arts,* Chalon-sur-Saône, 1963, No. 256, Pl. XXIII

33 Young Man Standing (Study for *A Marriage Contract*)
Black, red and white chalk, stumped, on buff paper,
20 x 11⅜ in. (50.7 x 29.0 cm)
Inscribed on back of mount: *Etude du paralytique* [sic]
Chicago, Art Institute of Chicago, The Helen Regenstein
Collection

Collections: Saint Petersburg, Academy of Fine Arts (Lugt
S 2699 a); Leningrad, Hermitage; sale, Boerner, Leipzig,
May 4, 1932, lot 48, bought in; anonymous sale, London,
March 26, 1968, lot 77, sold to John P. Hardy; acquired
by the museum from the Paul Drey Gallery, New York,
in 1968
  Exhibitions: Saint Petersburg, Academy of Fine Arts,
1903; Leningrad, Hermitage, 1926, No. 209 in catalogue
by Dobroklonsky
Bibliography: Monod-Hautecoeur, No. 48; *Mir Iskousstwa*,
1903, p. 233, No. 12

This figure of a young man is a study for the groom in
A Marriage Contract (No. 34). In the painting, he holds the
wedding dowry in his outstretched left hand and his
bride's arm is wrapped around his right arm. His
proportions are less elongated in the final work, and his
right hand is posed differently.
  When *A Marriage Contract* was exhibited in the Salon of
1761, the figure of the groom was singled out by several
critics. The abbé Joseph de la Porte noted: "*on entend ce
qu'il* [the father] *dit au jeune homme à qui il remet le sac
d'argent, et qui l'écoute debout avec une attention respectueuse.*"[1]
Diderot described the figure thus: "*Le fiancé est d'une figure
tout à fait agréable . . . il est un peu penché vers son beau-père;
il prête attention à son discours, il en a l'air pénétré; il est fait
au tour, et vêtu à merveille, sans sortir de son état.*"[2] Baron
Grimm added to Diderot's description, "*Son gendre est
pénétré de reconnaissance; il est fort touché; il voudrait remercier.*"[3]
  Another study for this figure, formerly in the Léonce
Rabillon collection, is now in a private collection,
Baltimore. A study for the groom's head was formerly in
the Hermitage,[4] and another one, presumably comparable
to the studies for the father and the bride included in this
exhibition (Nos. 31, 32), appeared in the Lucien Bonaparte
sale, Paris, March 17–20, 1834, lot 62.

1 "one can hear what he [the
father] is saying to the young man
to whom he hands the bag of
money, and who listens to him
standing with respectful attention."
Abbé J. de la Porte, "Observations
d'une Société d'amateurs sur les
tableaux exposés au Salon cette
année, 1761," *L'Observateur
littéraire*, 1761, pp. 48–49
2 "The fiancé is of an altogether
agreeable appearance. . . . he leans
a bit toward his father-in-law; he
pays attention to his discourse, he
seems moved by it; he is well built,
and dressed excellently, but not
beyond his station." Diderot,
Salons, I, p. 142
3 "His son-in-law is full of
gratitude; he is deeply touched;
he would like to express his thanks."
Ibid., p. 145
4 Monod-Hautecoeur, No. 75,
Pl. XXX

34 A Marriage Contract (*Un Mariage, et l'instant où le père de l'Accordée délivre la dot à son gendre*)
Oil, on canvas, 36¼ x 46 1/16 in. (92.0 x 117.0 cm)
Paris, Musée du Louvre

Collections: purchased for 39,000 livres in 1761 by the marquis de Marigny; his sale, Paris, March 18, 1782, lot 391, sold for 16,650 livres to Joullain for Louis XVI

Exhibitions: Salon of 1761, No. 100; Copenhagen, Palais de Charlottenborg, L'Art français du XVIIIè siècle, 1935, No. 81; Vienna, Oberes Belvedere, Kunst und Geist Frankreichs im 18. Jahrhundert, 1966, No. 34; Paris, Hôtel de la Monnaie, Louis XV, 1974, No. 109

Bibliography: Brookner, pp. 52, 62–63, 102–04, 106–08, Pl. 29; Duchesne, *Museum of Painting and Sculpture*, London, 1831, p. 407; F. Engerand, *Catalogue des tableaux du Roy, contenant les nouvelles acquisitions faites par l'ordere de M. le comte d'Angiviller, déposées au Cabinet du pavillon haut au Louvre*, Paris, [c. 1785], No. 1900; Hautecoeur, pp. 40–42, Pl. V; W. Kemp, "Das Bild der Menge (1789–1830)," *Städel-Jahrbuch*, IV, 1973, pp. 257–58, fig. 5; J. Locquin, *La Peinture d'histoire en France de 1747 à 1785*, Paris, 1912, pp. 17, 68, 275; Martin-Masson, No. 114; Munhall, 1964, pp. 8–10, fig. 9; Rosenberg, Reynaud and Compin, I, No. 316; R. Rosenblum, *Transformations in Late Eighteenth Century Art*, Princeton, 1967, pp. 51–53; Smith, No. 16; Valori, pp. 368–69

Engraving: J.-J. Flipart, 1770[1]

Painted only two years after Greuze's own marriage in the church of Saint-Médard, Paris, *A Marriage Contract* depicts the ceremony of *promesses de mariage*, the registration of a civil marriage contract before a notary. Protestants in mid-eighteenth-century France considered this a complete marriage; for Catholics it was only the complement to the sacramental ceremony performed by a priest. This picture surprised and pleased its first public with its strongly narrative character, its wealth of realistic detail employed in the depiction of a rustic scene and its appeal to emotional identification.

A letter from Cochin to the marquis de Marigny, *Directeur des Bâtiments du Roi*, dated September 17, 1761, provides a specific date for the completion of the painting: "*M. Greuze achève aujourd'huy le tableau qu'il fait pour votre cabinet; il l'aura encore chés lui demain et après-demain. J'ay l'honneur de vous en instruire, affin que si vous aviés quelque curiosité de le voir avant qu'il fût exposé au Salon, vous puissiez la satisfaire. Aussitôt qu'il sera séché, il le fera porter au Salon.*"[2] This letter also clearly contradicts the frequently repeated assertion that *A Marriage Contract* was executed for Randon de Boisset and acquired by Marigny from him. Furthermore, the Salon catalogue of 1761 states

that the painting already belonged to the marquis de Marigny, and the abbé Joseph de la Porte wrote in the same year that "*Ce morceau précieux appartient au mécène même qui préside sur les arts.*"[3] When Flipart's engraving of *A Marriage Contract* was exhibited in 1771, the Salon *livret* indicated the same ownership for the picture.

A Marriage Contract was the only painting from the sale that followed Marigny's death to be acquired by the King. Cochin advised d'Angiviller, the new *Directeur des Bâtiments du Roi* (fig. 14), on its acquisition, stating that it was "*le plus beau qu'il a fait dans ce genre,*" and he was seconded by Pierre, who called it "*Le plus beau tableau de M. Greuze, très bon et même beau.*"[4] Both expressed some concern, however, that the painting's glazes had already worn off.

Mariette described the picture in his *Abécédario* as "*justement regardé comme le chef d'oeuvre de ce peintre*" and added, "*Je souhaite me tromper, mais je crois que ce peintre ne fera jamais rien de plus accompli.*"[5]

Though it was shown only during the last two weeks of the Salon, *A Marriage Contract* was the sensation of the exhibition. Diderot had difficulty in seeing the picture because of the crowds: "*Enfin je l'ai vu, ce tableau de notre ami Greuze; mais ce n'a pas été sans peine; il continue d'attirer la foule.*"[6] His lengthy discussion of it in his "*Récapitulation*" of the exhibition concentrated on the realistic details of the subject and on the depiction of emotions. Nor did he fail to note in passing the parallel between the hen and her brood and the mother with hers: "*Voilà un petit trait de poésie tout à fait ingénieux.*"[7] He concluded that the picture was "*certainement ce que Greuze a fait de mieux*" and that the artist's choice of subject "*marque de la sensibilité et de bonnes moeurs.*"[8]

The abbé de la Porte commented that "*son pinceau sçait ennoblir le genre rustique, sans en altérer la vérité.*"[9] As the picture demands, he interpreted the significance of each character by analyzing his appearance and expression, from the old father, "*d'une physionomie ouverte, avec toute la noblesse de son état,*" to the future bride, of whom he remarked that "*la pudeur et la présence des parens retiennent la main, prête à se poser sur celle du futur, qu'elle désire mais qu'elle n'ose toucher,*" and even to the jealous older sister at far left, whose expression conveys a "*mélange de dépit, de regret et de jalousie.*"[10]

The Swedish engraver Floding made a subtle comparison between Greuze's skillfull delineation of emotions and the example set by a great predecessor in this domain: "*J'ose dire que ce grand homme surpasse de beaucoup le célèbre Le Brun pour l'expression générale non variée, au lieu que l'expression de Greuze est d'une grande variété et bien sentie dans le tout en général, comme dans les figures en particulier.*"[11]

Gabriel de Saint-Aubin executed a characteristically precise drawing of *A Marriage Contract* in his Salon *livret*, with the enigmatic note: "*M. de Lécluse, souvenir.*"[12]

Greuze's success with the picture extended beyond the limits of the Salon. Before the year was out, the players of the Italian Comedy had represented *A Marriage Contract* as a *tableau vivant* in *Les Noces d'Arlequin*[13] and the abbé Aubert had composed a moral tale entitled *L'Accordée de village*, in which the scene Greuze depicted is observed and minutely described by a free-thinking financier "*qui avoit vu dans le monde beaucoup de mariages brillans et malheureux.*"[14]

For this major painting Greuze executed a quantity of preparatory drawings, ranging from general compositional designs to studies of individual figures and heads. In addition to the compositional study included in this exhibition (No. 30) and the drawing at the Musée des Beaux-Arts, Le Havre, discussed with it, there existed a watercolor study for *A Marriage Contract* that appeared in the de Jullienne sale, Paris, March 30–May 22, 1767, lot 979, in the Grimod de la Reynière sale, Paris, August 21, 1797, lot 55, and in the Revil sale, Paris, March 29,

1842, lot 113. A watercolor-and-gouache compositional study, with a boy and dog in place of the little girl feeding the chickens, appeared in the Meunié sale, Paris, December 14, 1935, lot 22. Martin lists another study in the comte de V*** sale, Paris, December, 1858.

A study for the figure of the bride is in the Musée Vivant-Denon, Chalon-sur-Saône.[15] Studies for her head include one in this exhibition (No. 32), another listed by Martin as in the E. Marcille collection, Paris, in 1860 and a pastel that appeared in the Lalive de Jully sale, Paris, March 5, 1770, lot 137, in the Randon de Boisset sale, Paris, February 27—March 25, 1777, lot 215 (sold with a pendant bust of the girl in *The Broken Pitcher* for 2,360 livres to Brogniard), and possibly in the "G" sale, Paris, December 31—January 2, 1853, lot 41.

For the groom Greuze executed a drawing of the full figure included in this exhibition (No. 33) and at least two studies of the head, one formerly in the Hermitage[16] and another that appeared in the Lucien Bonaparte sale, Paris, March 17–20, 1834, lot 62. A half-length study for the mother appeared in a sale in Paris, June 10, 1963,

Fig. 15 *A Marriage Contract* (detail)

lot 3, and a head of the father is included in this exhibition (No. 31). A study for the head of the notary appeared in the Defer-Dumesnil sale, Paris, May 10–12, 1900, lot 153, and a study of his full figure, facing right, is in a private collection, Paris. A study for the head of the jealous sister at far left is in the Philadelphia Museum of Art. A canvas depicting a boy with his head raised, closely related to the figure behind the mother, is in the Akademie der bildenden Künste, Vienna.

The lasting popularity of Greuze's *A Marriage Contract* is attested to by the innumerable copies executed after it, both as complete compositions and as individual figures. Worth recording are one of the complete work by Greuze's pupil Philiberte Ledoux (see No. 103) in the Musée des Beaux-Arts, Quimper, and lost copies painted in 1856 and 1863 by Fantin-Latour, whom Duranty called *"le plus remarquable de tous les copistes."* [17] Within a decade after *A Marriage Contract* was completed, the goldsmith Roucel executed a snuffbox mounted with miniatures after works by Greuze, with one plaque reproducing this painting. [18] Prints reproducing the painting in various media were executed throughout the nineteenth century.

1 E. Dacier, *La Gravure de genre et de moeurs*, Paris, 1925, pp. 77–78; Portalis-Béraldi, II, p. 199
2 "Today M. *Greuze* completes the picture he is doing for your collection; he will still have it at his studio tomorrow and the day after. I have the honor of informing you of this, so that if you should have any curiosity to see it before it is exhibited at the Salon, you can satisfy it. As soon as it is dry, he will have it taken to the Salon." M. Furcy-Raynaud, ed., "Correspondance de M. de Marigny," *Archives de l'art français*, 1903, XIX, Lettre 271, p. 203; see also Diderot, *Salons*, I, p. 99
3 "This precious piece belongs to the very Maecenas who presides over the arts." Abbé J. de la Porte, "Observations d'une Société d'amateurs sur les tableaux exposés au Salon cette année, 1761," *L'Observateur littéraire*, 1761, p. 52
4 "the most beautiful he has done in this genre." "M. Greuze's most beautiful picture, very good and even beautiful." J. Guiffrey and L. Courajod, "Documents sur la vente de la collection du Mⁱˢ de Ménars (1782)," *Nouvelles Archives de l'art français*, 1873, p. 391
5 "justly considered this painter's masterpiece." "I hope I am mistaken, but I believe this painter will never do anything more accomplished." P.-J. Mariette,

Abécédario, ed. P. de Chennevières and A. de Montaiglon, Paris, 1853–54, II, p. 330
6 "At last I have seen it, this picture by our friend Greuze; but it was not without difficulty; it continues to attract the crowd." Diderot, *op. cit.*, I, p. 141
7 "There is a thoroughly ingenious little stroke of poetry." *Ibid.*, p. 143
8 "certainly the best thing Greuze has done." "shows sensibility and high principles." *Ibid.*, p. 144
9 "his brush knows how to ennoble the rustic genre, without altering its truth." De la Porte, *op. cit.*, p. 47
10 "of an open countenance, with all the nobility of his station." "modesty and the presence of her parents restrain her hand, ready to rest itself on that of her future husband, whom she desires but dares not touch." "mixture of resentment, regret and jealousy." *Ibid.*, pp. 48–50
11 "I dare say that this great man far surpasses the celebrated Lebrun in the area of general, unvaried expression, for expression with Greuze is of great variety and heartfelt throughout the general whole as much as in the individual figures." M. G. W. Lundberg, "Le Graveur suédois Floding à Paris et sa correspondance," *Archives de l'art français*, XVII, p. 292

12 M. T. Cartwright, "Gabriel de Saint-Aubin, an Illustrator and Interpreter of Diderot's Art Criticism," *Gazette des Beaux-Arts*, April, 1969, p. 220, fig. 7, p. 221; Dacier, *Saint-Aubin*, VI, p. 64; C. Strienski, "Le Salon de 1761 d'après le catalogue illustré par Gabriel de Saint-Aubin," *Gazette des Beaux-Arts*, September, 1903, pp. 210, 213–14
13 J.-A. Jullien, [known as Desmoulmiers], *Histoire anecdotique et raisonnée du théâtre italien depuis son rétablissement en France jusqu'à l'année 1769*, Paris, 1769, VII, pp. 15–16
14 "who had seen in society many marriages both brilliant and unhappy." Abbé J.-L. Aubert, "L'Accordée de village, Conte moral," *Année littéraire*, VI, 1761, p. 214
15 Martin-Masson, No. 388; L. Armand-Calliat, *Musée Vivant-De-non: Catalogue de la Section des Beaux-Arts*, Chalon-sur-Saône, 1963, No. 256, Pl. XXIII
16 Monod-Hautecoeur, No. 75, Pl. XXX
17 "the most remarkable of all copyists." T. Reff, "Copyists in the Louvre," *Art Bulletin*, December, 1964, p. 555
18 *Album de l'exposition rétrospective d'objets d'art de 1904 à Saint-Pétersbourg*, Saint Petersburg, 1908, p. 209, fig. 99, p. 217

35 Portrait of Claude-Henri Watelet (*Le Portrait de M. Watelet, Receveur Général des Finances*)
Oil, on canvas, 10⁷⁄₁₆ x 8¼ in. (26.5 x 21.0 cm)
Paris, private collection

Collections: C.-H. Watelet, Paris (?); J. Doucet, Paris; his sale, Paris, June 6, 1912, lot 157; Lucien Guiraud, Paris; Sir Robert Abdy, London, acquired before 1970
  Bibliography: G. Allen, "Fin de siècle dans un atelier," *Connaissance des arts*, August, 1970, p. 63; Brookner, p. 101; Diderot, *Salons*, I, p. 183, II, p. 36; M. Henriet, "Un Amateur d'art au XVIIIè siècle: L'Académicien Watelet," *Gazette des Beaux-Arts*, September–October, 1922, pp. 173–94; P. Hofer, *A Visit to Rome in 1764*, Cambridge, 1956; Martin-Masson, Nos. 1258–60; J. Mathey, "Greuze et Fragonard copistes de Rubens," *Bulletin de la Société de l'Histoire de l'Art français*, 1933, p. 184; Portalis-Béraldi, III, p. 648; Smith, No. 134
  Engraving: C.-H. Watelet, 1765 (fig. 16)

The Salon *livrets* of 1763 and 1765 both list portraits of Watelet among Greuze's entries, as No. 131 and No. 116 respectively. According to Mathon de la Cour, the portrait of 1763 never actually appeared in the Salon,[1] presumably because Watelet's departure for Rome prevented the artist from completing it. The portrait of 1765 evidently was a different canvas, as the dimensions given for it in the *livret* are larger than those listed for the 1763 painting, which in turn far exceed those of the present canvas. The small size of the present portrait and the fact that the 1765 version was described as showing Watelet examining a bronze reduction of the Medici *Venus* suggest that this is

Fig. 16 Portrait of Claude-Henri
Watelet, etching by Watelet after
Greuze, Paris, Bibliothèque
Nationale, Cabinet des Estampes

yet a third likeness, executed perhaps after Watelet's
return from Italy in 1764.

Greuze apparently intended this version to form a painted
pastiche of Rembrandt's etched portrait of *Jan Six*, which
it so closely resembles. As such it testifies to Greuze's
knowledge of Rembrandt and offers as well iconographical
parallels between the two artists' relationships with their
subjects. In this regard Brookner quotes as follows an
inscription found on an etched reproduction of this
portrait done by Watelet himself: "This print was engraved
by M. Watelet . . . after a drawing by the celebrated
Greuze, the idea being to give a pendant to the rare and
beautiful print called *The Burgomaster Jan Six*. He was the
friend and benefactor of Rembrandt, M. Watelet is also
the friend of the artist after whom he has himself engraved
this print which is both his portrait and as it were another
Six who was also the friend of the Arts and Literature."[2]
The problem posed by this inscription as quoted is that it
states the print was based on a drawing and not no
a painting.

Claude-Henri Watelet (1718–1786) belonged to that
wealthy, talented circle of amateur artists and collectors
who contributed to Greuze's initial success. Having
inherited in 1740 the lucrative sinecure of *Receveur général
des finances*, Watelet developed his artistic talents and
emerged as a prolific engraver, a poet, translator and
playright, a violinist and an aesthetician. He became a
membre libre of the Académie in 1747, and following the
publication in 1760 of his poem *L'Art de peindre* he was
received into the Académie Française. Known as a
collector of Rembrandt's prints, he produced the year
before his death a collection of his own prints imitating
the Dutch master's, entitled *Rymbranesques*. Among
Parisian collectors such as Boucher, Silvestre and Mariette,
the portrait of *Jan Six* held a special place. Gersaint's
catalogue of Rembrandt's oeuvre published in 1751 cited
its rarity and mentioned an example owned by the abbé de
Fleury, Canon of Notre-Dame.[3] Sixteen years later Basan's
Dictionnaire des graveurs again spoke of its rarity: "*Divers
portraits admirables, entr'autres, celui du Bourguemestre Six qui
est le plus rare de tous, et dont les premières épreuves sont avant
le nom de Rembrandt.*"[4]

The present portrait captures Watelet's distinctive
physiognomy, which is also recorded in his own engraving
after Cochin's profile portrait of him,[5] and its details
recall the subject's artistic and musical interests. The bust
on the table most likely represents Marguerite Le Comte,
Watelet's perennial companion in his picturesque house at
Argenteuil called Le Moulin Joli. Her features were recorded
by Greuze in a portrait now in the collection of baron
Edmond de Rothschild, Pregny. That work too was
engraved by Watelet.

While Diderot wrote brusquely of both the 1765
portrait and its subject—"*Il est terne, il a l'air d'être embu;
il est maussade. C'est l'homme, retournez la toile*"[6]—most of
Watelet's contemporaries spoke of him with great affection
and consideration.

1 "*Le public a regretté vivement
celui de M. Watelet, qui n'a pas été
exposé.*" ("The public deeply missed
that of M. Watelet, which was
not exhibited.") Mathon de la
Cour, *Lettres à Madame *** sur les
peintures, les sculptures et les gravures
exposées dans le Sallon du Louvre en
1763*, Paris, 1763, p. 62
2 Brookner, p. 101
3 E.-F. Gersaint, *Catalogue
raisonné de toutes les pièces qui
forment l'Oeuvre de Rembrandt,
composé par feu M. Gersaint et mis
au jour par les Srs Helle et Glomy*,
Paris, 1751, p. 217

4 "Various admirable portraits,
among others that of the Burgomaster Six, which is the rarest of
all, and of which the first proofs
are before Rembrandt's signature."
F. Basan, *Dictionnaire des graveurs
anciens et modernes*, Paris, 1767,
II, p. 412
5 Reproduced in M. Henriet,
"Un Amateur d'art au XVIIIè
siècle: L'Académicien Watelet,"
Gazette des Beaux-Arts, September-
October, 1922, p. 174
6 "It is dull, the colors appear to
have dried in; it is sullen. That is
the man, turn the canvas to the
wall." Diderot, *Salons*, II, p. 152

1 "J. B. Greuze Painted/ by
himself at the age/ of 31 years/
given by Mme. Trognon/ December
30, 1854." "Given by M. Henriquel-
Dupont/ October 18, 1887"
2 Portalis-Béraldi, II, p. 201,
citing in addition a trial proof of
the print *"retouchée"* by Greuze;
C. Le Blanc, *Manuel de l'amateur
d'estampes*, Paris, [1854-89],
II, p. 240, No. 17
3 Wille, I, p. 142
4 "as for the coiffure . . . in the
form of a pigeon wing and with
spirals . . . like Caesar's belt, he
loves to relate to you what
determined him to adopt it. It is he
who tells the tale. I was young then,
amorous as one is at that age and
very much loved by a charming
woman who had arranged a tryst
with me at her levée. Like
Alexander on the eve of a victory
I slept the sleep of my future
happiness, I was late getting up
and appeared for my appointment
informally dressed . . . and without
having thought of fixing my hair
. . . what, little rascal, said she,
her own hair in curlers, come
here, I want to attend to your
hair, with a delicate hand she. . . .
The disorder of the scene was all
apparent . . . now go see in the
mirror how you like yourself, said
Madame, I see that the hand of the
Graces has today presided over my
form. I swear by your charms never
to have it otherwise in my life, for
fifty years I have kept my word."
Michel Nitot [called Charles
Dufresne], "Cahiers," ms., Paris,
Musée des Arts Décoratifs,
Bibliothèque, VIII, pp. 49-50
5 "The first visit I received, as
I was arising the next day, was
that of Greuze, whom I found
unchanged. One might even have
said that he had not let his hair
down; his curls were floating
around either side of his head
just as at my departure." M.-L.-E.
Vigée-Lebrun, *Souvenirs*, Paris,
n.d., II, p. 106
6 C. Oulmont, "Sur un hommage
à Greuze," *Gazette des Beaux-Arts*,
October–December, 1918, pp.
381-84, repr. facing p. 382

36 Portrait of the Artist

Brush, India ink wash, on white paper, 6¼ x 5¼ in.
(15.7 x 13.4 cm)
Inscribed on an old label from the back of a former frame:
*"J. B. Greuze Peint / par lui-même à l'âge / de 31 ans /
donné par Mme. Trognon / le 30 décembre 1854"* and, in
another hand, *"Donné par M. Henriquel-Dupont / le 18
octobre 1887"*[1]
Oxford, Ashmolean Museum, Lent by the Visitors of the
Ashmolean Museum

Collections: Trilha sale, Paris; G. Duplessis, Paris; Madame
Trognon, Paris, 1854; Henriquel-Dupont, Paris, 1887;
A. Fauchier-Magnan, Paris; his sale, London, December 4,
1935, lot 22; Colnaghi, London; T. H. Cobb, London;
K. T. Parker, Oxford; presented by him to the museum
in 1947

Exhibitions: R. A., 1968, No. 332
Bibliography: Ashmolean Museum, *Annual Report*, Oxford,
1947, p. 44; Martin-Masson, No. 1150; Smith, No. 1
Engraving: J.-J. Flipart, 1763;[2] C.-E. Gaucher, 1782

This small drawing was the source of the best-known
image of Greuze during his lifetime: J.-J. Flipart's engraved
portrait, dated 1763.

The severe classical quality of the drawing relates it to
several other profile portraits done by Greuze, including
one of Diderot (No. 50), which was engraved by Gaucher
in 1766, one of Catherine II, which was based on the
portrait bust Houdon exhibited in the Salon of 1773 and
was itself copied by Gaucher in 1782, and one of the
Scottish engraver Sir Robert Strange, which was engraved
by the subject. Greuze's drawing of the latter (whereabouts
unknown) was made probably in 1760, when Wille

mentioned receiving a visit from Strange, who was then on his way to Italy for a prolonged sojourn.[3]

In contrast to the simple coiffures he gave the Diderot and Strange portraits, Greuze lavished considerable attention on his own elaborately dressed and powdered curls. The engraver Charles Dufresne in his "Cahiers" recounts the origin of Greuze's very personal manner of dressing his hair: "*quand à la coëffure . . . en aile de pigeon et à spires . . . comme la ceinture de César, il aime à vous raconter ce qui le détermina à l'adopter. C'est lui qui raconte. J'étois jeune alors amoureux comme on l'est à cet âge et très aimé d'une femme charmante qui m'avait donné rendez-vous à son lever. Comme Alexandre la veille d'une victoire je dormais du sommeil de mon bonheur futur, je tardois à me lever et me rendis au rendez-vous en négligé . . . et sans avoir pensé à me coiffer . . . comment petit espiègle que dit elle, les cheveux aussi sous la papillotte, approchez vous je veux me charger de votre coëffure, d'une main délicate elle. . . . Le désordre de la scène présida autour . . . allez vous voir à présent dans le miroir comment vous trouvez vous, dit Madame, je vois que la main des Graces a présidé autour aujourd'huy a ma figure. Je jure par vos charmes de m'en avoir jamais d'autres de ma vie, il y a cinquante ans que j'ai . . . tenu parole.*"[4] That Greuze was faithful to his word is attested to by Madame Vigée-Lebrun, who recorded Greuze's visit to her immediately after her return to Paris in January, 1802: "*La première visite que je reçus, le lendemain, à mon lever, fut celle de Greuze, que je ne trouvai pas changé. On eût dit même qu'il ne s'étoit point décoiffé: ses boucles de cheveux flottaient autour de chaque côté de sa tête comme à mon départ.*"[5]

A copy of this drawing, with coat and jabot added, was included by an unknown miniaturist in a series of portraits of eighteenth-century French artists in The Frick Collection, New York. In a drawing formerly in the vicomte de Clinchamp collection, Prud'hon decorated an imaginary tomb of Greuze with a profile head based on Flipart's engraving.[6]

Two other self-portraits are included in this exhibition (Nos. 95, 114).

37 Portrait of Henri-Constance de Lort de Sérignan de Valras, Bishop of Mâcon

Oil, on canvas, 57⅛ x 45¼ in. (145.0 x 115.0 cm)
Mâcon, Musée Municipal des Ursulines

Collections: Monseigneur Gabriel François Moreau, Bishop of Mâcon, 1794; seized during the Revolution; Pic, Mâcon; his sale, Mâcon, 1840, sold for 2,400 francs to Ronot; Ronot, Mâcon; bequeathed by his daughter to the museum in 1880

Exhibitions: Paris, Exposition Universelle, Exposition Centennale de l'art français, 1900;[1] Toledo Museum of Art, Art Institute of Chicago and Ottawa, National Gallery of Canada, The Age of Louis XV: French Painting from 1710 to 1774, 1975–76, No. 43, Pl. 96

Bibliography: Brookner, pp. 104–05, Pl. 32; L. Lex, "Gabriel François Moreau, évêque de Mâcon (1763–1790)," *Réunion des Sociétés des Beaux-Arts des Départements*, XXII, 1898, pp. 606–39

Greuze must have executed this remarkable portrait of Monseigneur de Valras, Bishop of Mâcon, shortly before the latter's death in 1763. Since there is no record that the artist visited Mâcon, a town near his native Tournus, between 1755 and, presumably, 1769, he probably painted the portrait in Paris. It subsequently belonged to Valras' successor, Monseigneur Moreau. In an inventory of the latter's possessions, made when they were seized by the Revolutionary government in 1794, it was listed as: "*Tableau peint à l'huile, portrait de l'évêque Valeras, tête [sic] par Greuse, 4 pieds 6 pouces de haut, 3 pieds 6 pouces de large, bordure dorée de 6 pouces, nº 95.*"[2] The present frame, with its ecclesiastical ornaments, appears to be the one mentioned in the inventory.

Henri-Constance de Lort de Sérignan de Valras was Bishop of Mâcon from 1732 until 1763. It was perhaps he who commissioned from Greuze his early painting of *Saint Francis*, done for the Couvent des Récollets at Tournus and now in the Madeleine there, or perhaps he came to know Greuze from having seen that work.

When compared with contemporary representations of ecclesiastics such as Roslin's *Portrait of the Abbé Terray* (Versailles), which hung alongside it in the Age of Louis XV exhibition of 1975–76, Greuze's painting at first appears understated. But closer scrutiny reveals the quiet brilliance of this subtle portrayal of an austere individual, the sure draughtsmanship apparent in the hands, the cross and the writing implements and the bravura rendering of lace and moire. Brookner is probably correct in relating this work to Van Dyck's portrait of Margareta Snyders (New York, Frick Collection), which it resembles in scale and pose and which Greuze could have seen in the collection of the duc d'Orléans; the Van Dyck is listed in inventories of the Duke's pictures drawn up in 1752 and 1785.

Alongside a copy of the Holy Bible on the table at extreme left is a volume on the spine of which are legible the letters OPERA ST AUG, in reference to the works of St. Augustine. The most complete edition of his writings was prepared by the Maurines of the congregation of Saint-Maur, near Mâcon, and published in Paris between 1679 and 1700.

1   G. Lafenestre, "Les Arts à l'exposition universelle de 1900, La Peinture ancienne," *Gazette des Beaux-Arts*, December, 1900, p. 559

2   "Picture painted in oil, portrait of bishop Valeras, head [*sic*] by Greuze, 4 feet 6 inches high, 3 feet 6 inches wide, gilded frame of 6 inches, no. 95." Quoted in P. Rosenberg, *The Age of Louis XV: French Painting from 1710 to 1774*, Chicago, 1975, p. 49

38 Presumed Portrait of Louis-Philippe, duc d'Orléans

Red and black chalk, stumped, over pencil, 20⁷⁄₁₆ x 12⁷⁄₈ in. (51.9 x 32.6 cm)
Paris, Musée du Louvre, Cabinet des Dessins

Collections: Paignon Dijonval, Paris, 1810; Pierre Defer, Paris; purchased from him by the museum in 1842 for 60 francs

Exhibitions: R. A., 1932, No. 828; Paris, Gazette des Beaux-Arts, Le Dessin français dans les collections du XVIIIè siécle, 1935, No. 312; Paris, Palais Galliéra, Exposition du costume, 1937; Paris, Musée Carnavalet, La Révolution française, 1939; Paris, Musée des Arts Décoratifs, Les Goncourt et leur temps, 1946, No. 385; Art Institute of Chicago, Minneapolis Institute of Arts, Detroit Institute of Arts and San Francisco, Palace of the Legion of Honor, French Drawings: Masterpieces from Seven Centuries, 1955–56, No. 70; Paris, Cabinet des Dessins du Musée du Louvre, Pastels et miniatures des XVIIè et XVIIIè siècles, 1963

Bibliography: M. Bénard, *Cabinet de M. Paignon Dijonval*, Paris, 1810, No. 3691; Bouchot-Saupique, No. 13, Pl. VII; Goncourt, I, pp. 346–47; Guiffrey-Marcel, No. 4568; Martin-Masson, No. 1268; Reiset, No. 769; D. Sutton, *French Drawings of the XVIII Century*, London, 1949, p. 42, No. XIX

Engraving: J. de Goncourt

This superb drawing, one of Greuze's masterpieces as both draughtsman and portraitist, has traditionally been thought to represent Louis-Philippe, duc d'Orléans (1725–1785), father of Louis-Philippe Joseph, known as Philippe Egalité. However, no name was given for the subject in the Paignon Dijonval catalogue of 1810 (No. 3691, "*portrait d'homme*"), and Edmond de Goncourt expressed disbelief in the traditional identification.

Comparison with the equally brilliant painted portrait of Charles-Claude de la Billarderie, comte d'Angiviller (1730–1809), in the Metropolitan Museum of Art, New York (fig. 14), exhibited in the Salon of 1763, suggests a possible alternative identification. Both portraits show a long, jowly face with high forehead, a similar portly figure and a similar coat with elaborate frogging. The period 1763–65 was for Greuze particularly rich in portraits.

39 Portrait of Johann Georg Wille
(*Le Portrait de M. Wille, Graveur du Roi*)
Oil, on canvas, 23¼ x 19¼ in. (59.0 x 49.0 cm)
Signed and dated: *J. B. Greuze 1763*
Paris, Institut de France, Musée Jacquemart-André

Collections: J. G. Wille, Paris, 1763–1808; chevalier de
Sitivan, Paris; his sale, Paris, April 19–20, 1830, lot 79;
anonymous sale, Paris, March 21, 1840, lot 56; François
Delessert, Paris, 1846; his sale, Paris, March 15–18, 1869,
lot 28, sold for 29,000 francs to Edouard André

Exhibitions: Salon of 1765, No. 117; Paris, Salon of
1846, La Peinture française depuis la fin du dix-huitième
siècle; Paris, Union Centrale des Beaux-Arts, Exposition
au profit de la colonization de l'Algérie par les Alsaciens-
Lorrains, 1874, No. 126; Paris, Portraits d'un siècle, 1883,
No. 113; Berlin, Akademie der Künste, Ausstellung von
Werken französicher Kunst, 1910, No. 60; Paris, Palais
National des Arts, Chefs-d'oeuvre de l'art français, 1937,
No. 166; R. A., 1954–55, No. 180; New York, Wildenstein
and Co., Treasures of the Musée Jacquemart-André, 1956,
No. 38; Albi, Musée Henri de Toulouse-Lautrec, Chefs-
d'oeuvre du Musée Jacquemart-André, 1959, No. 35;
Paris, Bibliothèque Nationale, Diderot, 1963–64, No. 324;
R. A., 1968, No. 309; Paris, Hôtel de la Monnaie,
Louis XV, 1974, No. 110

Bibliography: Brookner, pp. 40–41, 60, 63, 64, 90, 92,
Pl. 28; Diderot, *Salons*, II, pp. 35, 36, 153; L. Hautecoeur,
"Greuze, Portraitiste," *L'Art et les artistes*, February,
1924, pp. 170–71; G. Lafenestre, "La Peinture au Musée
Jacquemart-André, III, " *Gazette des Beaux-Arts*, February,
1914, pp. 100–11; G. Lafenestre et al., *Le Musée Jacquemart-
André*, Paris, 1914, pp. 58–60; Martin-Masson, Nos. 1262,
1264; T. Thoré, *Le Salon de 1846*, Paris, 1846, p. 4; Wille,
I, pp. 238, 239, 240, 241–42, 300

Engraving: J. G. von Müller, 1776

Executed in six sittings, this portrait was recognized
immediately as one of Greuze's finest achievements. Time
has not changed that appraisal. Wille proudly described
it in his journal, saying: "*Effectivement, mon portrait est bien
la meilleure chose que ce grand peintre a peut-être fait jusqu'à
présent.*"[1]

On November 11, 1763, Greuze received twenty-five
gold louis from a Russian businessman named Bacherach
whose portrait he had just completed. To thank Wille,
who had arranged this important commission, Greuze
undertook to paint his friend's portrait. Having invited
Wille for morning coffee, Greuze began his work with a
full day's session on November 19. The surprised Wille
noted in his journal that "*l'ébauche en fut faite d'une manière
admirable et digne d'un Rubens ou d'un Van Dyck.*"[2]
After the second sitting, on November 21, Wille was
confident over the outcome of his portrait, "*qui sera
admirablement bien fait, car il en est content lui-même.*"[3]
The head must have been nearly completed then, for at a
third, prolonged session on November 29 Greuze did not

feel well enough to work on the head and concentrated
on the clothing. Apparently he continued with the costume
on December 1, on December 4—the day Wille noted that
the portrait was finished—and again on December 6. Wille
brought his servant to claim the portrait on December 10,
and it was received enthusiastically by his family. He
returned to Greuze's studio that evening, bringing Madame
Greuze a silver bowl with lid for which he had paid
200 livres.[4]

The portrait figured among Greuze's entries at the next
Salon, that of 1765, and elicited universal praise. Diderot
was rhapsodic: "*Très-beau portrait. C'est l'air brusque et dur
de Wille; c'est sa roide encolure; c'est son oeil petit, ardent,
effaré; ce sont ses joues couperosées. Comme cela est coiffé! que le
dessin est beau! que la touche est fière! quelles vérités et variétés
de tons! et le velours, et le jabot, et les manchettes [sic] d'une
exécution! J'aurois plaisir à voir ce portrait à côté d'un Rubens,
d'un Rembrant ou d'un Vandick. J'aurois plaisir à sentir ce
qu'il y auroit à perdre ou à gagner pour notre peintre. Quand on a
vu ce Wille, on tourne le dos aux portraits des autres, et même
à ceux de Greuze.*"[5] Bachaumont noted that "*M. Greuze se
soutient avec le plus grand succès,*"[6] and the anonymous
critic of the *Année littéraire* admired Greuze's "*pinceau
heurté, facile et plein de fierté.*"[7] Mathon de la Cour remarked,
"*Les portraits de M. Wille et de M. Caffiéri sont traités avec
le feu, avec lequel on devroit toujours peindre les artistes.*"[8]

Johann Georg Wille (1715–1808), born in Biebertal,
Hesse, arrived in Paris in 1736 and became a pivotal figure
in the European art world, respected not only as an engraver
and a teacher but also as a dealer in paintings, drawings,
prints and medals. He became an associate member of the
Académie in 1755, the same year as Greuze, and took an
active interest in its affairs all his life. Wille also belonged
to many provincial and foreign academies and was an
official engraver to Frederick the Great and to the King of
Denmark. The journal he kept from 1759 to 1793 records
his varied activities and testifies to the deep and lasting
friendship he felt for Greuze, who supervised the artistic
education of his son, Pierre-Alexandre (1748–1821).
Greuze's portrait captures Wille's simple, forthright
character and suggests as well his enjoyment of gastronomy
and fashion. In connection with the important element
of the brocade waistcoat in the portrait, it is appropriate
to recall one of Wille's youthful follies: having received
unexpected funds from his father during his early days in
Paris, Wille immediately spent the money on an elaborate
dinner, some medals, a sword, a gold-rimmed hat and
"*une veste de soie à fleurs fond d'argent de fabrique de Lyon.*"[9]

On September 14, 1766, Wille recorded that his former
pupil Halm had made a drawing after Greuze's portrait for
a M. Huber.[10] A signed and dated replica of Wille's portrait
appeared in the A. Polovtzoff sale, Paris, December 2–4,
1909, lot 137, sold for 83,500 francs, and was subsequently
in the Prat-Noilly collection, Marseille, until 1933. A
copy of lesser quality, formerly in the Lacaze collection,
is in the Musée Rolin at Autun.

1 "Truly, my portrait is indeed the best thing that this great painter has perhaps done up until the present." Wille, I, p. 242
2 "the sketch for it was done in an admirable manner worthy of a Rubens or a Van Dyck." *Ibid.*, p. 238
3 "which will be admirably well done, for he is satisfied with it himself." *Ibid.*
4 *Ibid.*, p. 242
5 "Very beautiful portrait. This is Wille's bluff, harsh air; this is his stiff neck; this is his eye, small, intense, startled; these are his blotched cheeks. How his hair is done! how beautifully drawn! how proud is the handling! what truths and varieties of tones! and the velvet, and the ruffle, and the cuffs [*sic*] of such execution! I should take pleasure in seeing this portrait alongside a Rubens, a Rembrandt or a Van Dyck. I should take pleasure in feeling what it would thereby lose or gain for our painter. When one has seen this Wille, one turns his back to the portraits of the others, and even to those of Greuze." Diderot, *Salons*, II, p. 153
6 "M. Greuze maintains himself with the greatest success." P. de Bachaumont, "Jugement de Bachaumont sur cette exposition," 1765, ms., Paris, Bibliothèque Nationale, Cabinet des Estampes, Fond Deloynes, p.2
7 "brush which is contrasty, facile and full of pride." Quoted in Diderot, *Salons*, II, p. 36
8 "The portraits of M. Wille and M. Caffiéri are treated with the fire with which artists should always be painted." Mathon de la Cour, *Troisième Lettre à Monsieur ****, 1765, pp. 9–10
9 "a waistcoat made of Lyon silk with flowers on a silver ground." Wille, I, p. 80
10 *Ibid.*, I, p. 331

40 Presumed Portrait of the chevalier de Damery

Oil, on canvas, 25½ x 21½ in. (64.8 x 54.6 cm)
Boston, Mr. David Ames, Mr. Oliver F. Ames and Mrs. Peter S. Thompson

Collections: Boittelle, Paris; his sale, Paris, April 24–25, 1866, lot 61, sold for 2,980 francs; S.A.I. la princesse Mathilde, Paris; her sale, Paris, May 17–21, 1904, lot 34
   Bibliography: Martin-Masson, No. 1278

The subject of this dashing portrait has long evaded identification. But since the decoration so carefully depicted on his coat is that of the Military Order of Saint-Louis,[1] it is tempting to recognize in these sympathetic features the chevalier de Damery, a military man and an important collector who was a friend of Wille (No. 39) and whose name appears frequently on engravings executed after drawings by Greuze which he owned.

In 1760 the appraiser and framer Glomy identified de Damery in his "Journal des ouvrages" (Paris, Institut Néerlandais, Fondation Custodia) in a brief notation: *"Le chevalier d'Ameri, lieutenant de grenadiers aux gardes françaises."*[2] He was later named *lieutenant-colonel.* The *Almanach des artistes* of 1777 was more explicit: *"M. de Dammery, Chevalier de l'Ordre Royal et Militaire de St.-Louis, rue Copeau, près la Pitié, possède une nombreuse Collection de Tableaux et de Dessins."*[3]

It is Wille, however, who supplies the most information concerning this gentleman, for whom he had a particular affection. He refers to de Damery in his *Journal* for the first time on April 16, 1760, then frequently until 1770, after which there is a long silence concerning him until December 12, 1788, when Wille sadly mentions a long-outstanding debt de Damery owed him: *"Ce bon M.*

de Damery a eu bien des malheurs, sans cela il m'auroit payé depuis longtemps; il est très-honnête homme."[4] In various other passages he writes of de Damery, an *"officier aux gardes"* and a *"grand amateur des beaux-arts,"*[5] that he frequently lent paintings and drawings to engravers to reproduce, that he had Wille handle his finances when he was out of Paris and that from his country house near Epernay he sent Wille *"un tonneau de cent bouteilles de vin de Champagne."*[6] Lugt supposed that de Damery died in 1803, the year of the sale of what remained of his collection.

The strong similarities between this portrait and that of Wille and the record of an encounter between de Damery and Greuze in 1765 suggest that the two works must be nearly contemporary. The encounter was recorded in Wille's *Journal* on April 10, 1765: *"J'allai dîner chez M. le chevalier de Damery, avec M. Chevillet. M. le chevalier de la Tour-d'Aigues y étoit aussi. Après le repas nous allâmes tous, avec madame de Damery, au Luxembourg. Après que cette dame fut retournée à son logis, nous allâmes, nous autres hommes, chez M. Greuze, de là chez M. Huquier, marchand d'estampes."*[7]

It is known that de Damery owned at least twenty drawings by Greuze,[8] among them a study for the figure of the bride in *A Marriage Contract* (see No. 32) and a lost drawing of *The Return From the Wet Nurse* (see No. 42). Nearly all were early, highly finished genre scenes, small in size and intimate in their subjects. Several appeared in sales in the late 1770s, when de Damery was having financial difficulties. Edmond de Goncourt evoked de Damery as a collector in his *Maison d'un artiste: "possesseur d'une collection considérable de tableaux et de dessins,* [he] *fut un homme d'un goût sûr, un choisisseur délicat et raffiné. Je signale sa marque aux amateurs: elle n'est jamais sur un dessin médiocre."*[9]

1 See V. Mericka, *Orders and Decorations*, London, 1967, p. 12, Pl. 59
2 Quoted in F. Lugt, *Marques de collections*, Amsterdam, 1921, p. 531
3 "M. de Dammery, Chevalier of the Royal and Military Order of St.-Louis, rue Copeau, near the Pitié, possesses a large Collection of Paintings and Drawings." *Ibid.*
4 "This good M. de Damery has had many misfortunes, otherwise he would have paid me long ago; he is a very honest man." Wille, II, p. 193
5 "officer in the guards." "great lover of the fine arts." *Ibid.*, I, p. 134
6 "a barrel of a hundred bottles of Champagne wine." *Ibid.*, p. 310

7 "I went to dine at M. the chevalier de Damery's, with M. Chevillet. M. the chevalier de la Tour-d'Aigues was there too. After dinner we all went, with Madame de Damery, to the Luxembourg. After the lady was returned home, we men went on to M. Greuze's, from there to the house of M. Huquier, the print dealer." *Ibid.*, pp. 285–86
8 Among them Martin-Masson Nos. 287, 289, 302, 327, 329, 333, 336, 354, 356, 370, 372, 387, 388, 490, 1038, 1598
9 "owner of a considerable collection of paintings and drawings, [he] was a man of sure taste, a fastidious and refined 'choser.' I signal his mark to collectors; it is never on a mediocre drawing." E. de Goncourt, *La Maison d'un artiste*, Paris, 1881, I, p. 96

41 The Departure for the Wet Nurse
(Le Départ en nourrice)

Brush, gray ink wash, over pencil, on white paper, 12¹³⁄₁₆ x 10¹³⁄₁₆ in. (32.5 x 27.5 cm)
Signed: *Greuze;* on the verso, a faint sketch of the composition in pencil
Los Angeles, The Norton Simon Foundation

Collections: Randon de Boisset, Paris; his sale, Paris, February 27–March 25, 1777, lot 374, sold with pendant for 1,500 livres to Desmarest; Vassal de Saint-Hubert, Paris; his sales, Paris, March 29, 1779, lot 163, sold with pendant for 600 livres (or bought in?), and Paris, April 24–May 1, 1783, lot 160, with pendant; B. Houthakker Galleries, Amsterdam, 1936–52, with pendant; H. E. ten Cate, Almelo, the Netherlands, 1955, with pendant; C. G. Boerner, Düsseldorf, 1964, with pendant; Paul Drey Gallery, New York, with pendant; sale, London, June 27, 1974, lot 47, with pendant

Exhibitions: Amsterdam, Rijksmuseum, Tentoonstelling van Oude Kunst, 1936, No. 183; Amsterdam, B. Houthakker Galleries, Dessins anciens, français, hollandais, italiens, 1952, No. 32

Bibliography: Goncourt, I, p. 352; D. Hannema, *Catalogue of the H. E. ten Cate Collection*, Rotterdam, 1955, I, p. 133, No. 238, repr., II, Pl. 127; Martin-Masson, Nos. 132, 195, 355

Engravings: J.-B. Simonet; C.-H. Watelet[1]

With this drawing and its pendant (No. 42) Greuze takes up the subject of nursing, one which was much debated by his contemporaries. In *The Departure for the Wet Nurse* a mother embraces her child, who is about to be placed into a basket attached to a donkey's saddle and taken off with the wet nurse who already holds him.

The drawing illustrates the customary mid-eighteenth-century practice of sending infants to the country to be tended by a wet nurse. Wille (No. 39) records that Greuze and his wife followed this procedure with their daughter Anne-Geneviève, who was born in April of 1762 and was still with her wet nurse on September 19, 1763: "*M. Greuze me vint voir de très-grand matin, et me proposa de l'accompagner, en compagnie de Madame Greuze et M. Doyen, peintre, à Champigny, pour voir leur enfant, qui y est en nourrice. Je consentis d'autant plus volontiers qu'il est mon ami particulier, et, comme nous avions un bon carrosse de remise, nous étions de retour sur les six heures du soir.*"[2]

As in the case of its pendant, this drawing relates to

Greuze's *Bazile et Thibault*, an iconographical scenario he wrote for a series of pictures he planned to paint depicting the lives of two youths who received radically different educations, somewhat in the manner of Hogarth's *The Idle and Industrious Apprentices*. The second episode in the scenario, concerning the birth of Thibault, the bad child, takes place around the mother's bed, but Greuze's text includes a reference to the grandmother and the wet nurse's husband much as the grandmother and the wet nurse herself appear at right in the present drawing: "*Sa grand'mère tient les mains du nourricier et semble l'engager d'une manière très pathétique à prendre soin de son petit-fils.*"[3]

Diderot's *Encyclopédie*, though it recommends in other passages that mothers should nurse their own children, describes in an article entitled "*Nourice*" the ideal qualities of a wet nurse such as Greuze has represented here: "*Les conditions nécessaires à une bonne nourice se tirent ordinairement de son âge, du tems qu'elle est accouchée, de la constitution de son corps, particulièrement de ses mamelles, de la nature de son lait, et enfin de ses moeurs. . . . outre les moeurs qu'elle soit vigilante, sage, prudente, douce, joyeuse, gaie, sobre, et modérée dans son penchant à l'amour.*"[4]

In composition and format this drawing strongly resembles a painting formerly attributed to Rembrandt entitled *The Good Samaritan* (London, Wallace Collection),[5] a subject Rembrandt did treat in an etching dated 1633. Greuze could have known the painting when it was in the de Jullienne collection, from which it was sold in 1767.

Greuze also executed a drawing of this subject in a horizontal format. Formerly in the Hermitage,[6] it appeared in a sale at C. G. Boerner, Leipzig, May 4, 1932, lot 44, sold to Kaiser. It lacks the animated bustle of the present sheet, and its composition is dominated by a more classical architecture. Another related drawing is in the Cabinet des Dessins at the Louvre (No. 26954; Guiffrey-Marcel, No. 4539).

Contrary to the opinion of Martin and others, the present drawing was not the *Départ de Barcelonnette* exhibited as No. 164 in the Salon of 1769. From the *Avant-Coureur*'s precise description of the latter it could only have been a variation of the Savoyard subject included in this exhibition (No. 54). Another recurring error, again following Martin, is that the present drawing appeared in a Paignon Dijonval sale in 1810. There was no such sale, but M. Bénard's *Cabinet de M. Paignon Dijonval*, Paris, 1810, lists under No. 3685 a related subject engraved by Binet as *Le Ménage ambulant*.

1 Portalis-Béraldi, III, p. 557

2 "M. Greuze came to see me
very early in the morning and
suggested that I accompany him,
along with Madame Greuze and
M. Doyen, the painter, to
Champigny, to see their child who
is there with a wet nurse. I agreed
all the more willingly since he is
my special friend, and as we had
a good hired coach we were back
around six in the evening." Wille,
I, p. 230

3 "His grandmother holds the
hands of the wet nurse's husband
and seems to urge him in a most
touching manner to take care of

her grandson." Quoted in
Brookner, p. 156

4 "The conditions necessary for
a good wet nurse derive ordinarily
from her age, when she gave birth,
her physical condition, particularly
that of her breasts, the nature of
her milk, and finally her morals
. . . . beyond morals, let her be
vigilant, wise, prudent, gentle,
joyful, lively, sober, and moderate
in her inclination toward love."
Diderot, Encyclopédie, XI, pp. 360–61

5 Wallace Collection Catalogues,
Pictures and Drawings, London,
1968, pp. 262–64

6 Monod-Hautecoeur, No. 26,
Pl. IV

42 The Return from the Wet Nurse
(*Le Retour de nourrice*)

Brush, gray ink wash, over pencil, on white paper,
11¾ x 10³⁄₁₆ in. (29.9 x 25.9 cm)
Los Angeles, The Norton Simon Foundation

Collections: same as No. 41

Exhibitions: Amsterdam, Rijksmuseum, Tentoonstelling
van Oude Kunst, 1936, No. 184; Amsterdam, B. Houthakker
Galleries, Dessins anciens, français, hollandais, italiens,
1952, No. 33

Bibliography: Goncourt, I, p. 352; D. Hannema, *Catalogue
of the H. E. ten Cate Collection*, Rotterdam, 1955, I, p. 133,
No. 239, repr., II, Pl. 128; Martin-Masson, Nos. 195, 355

This drawing, the pendant to *The Departure for the Wet
Nurse* (No. 41), illustrates the return of the child from his
stay with the nurse, whose skirts he clutches as he recoils
in fear from the curious regards of the young, old and
canine members of his own family. His father carries his
crib, draped in a blanket. Despite the undeniable humor
of this tumultuous scene, Greuze's intention here was to
illustrate the inevitable misplacing of affections that
results from the prolonged absence of an infant from its
family during its early life.

Like its pendant, this drawing corresponds closely to
Greuze's scenario for *Bazile et Thibault, ou les deux
éducations*, in this to case the fourth episode: "*Thibault de
retour de nourrice. Le jeune Thibault revient de nourrice avec
tous ses bagages; sa nourrice le présente à sa mère qui s'empresse
à le recevoir; alors le petit enfant se rejette avec effroi dans les
bras de la mère qu'il connaît, et, par cette action, fait des
reproches à sa mère pour son indifférence.*"[1]

Diderot's article on mothers in the *Encyclopédie* expounds
the advanced view of the day on the subject of mothers
nursing their own children, as reflected in Greuze's text:
"*Si les mères nourrissoient leurs enfants, il y a apparence qu'ils en
seroient plus forts et plus vigoureux: le lait de leur mère doit leur
convenir mieux que le lait d'une autre femme: car le foetus se
nourrit dans la matrice d'une liqueur laiteuse, qui est fort
semblable au lait qui se forme dans les mamelles: l'enfant est
donc déjà, pour ainsi dire, accoutumé au lait de sa mère, au
lieu que le lait d'une autre nourrice est une nourriture nouvelle
pour lui. . . . Indépendamment du rapport ordinaire du
tempérament de l'enfant à celui de la mère, celle-ci est bien plus
propre à prendre un tendre soin de son enfant, qu'une femme
empruntée qui n'est animée que par la récompense d'un loyer
mercenaire, souvent fort modique. Concluons que la mère d'un
enfant, quoique moins bonne nourrice, est encore préférable à une
étrangère.*"[2] And again: "*Le premier devoir d'une mère est
d'alaiter ses enfans.*"[3]

The history of this drawing and its relationship to its
pendant have been confused by the existence of another
drawing for *The Return from the Wet Nurse*, now lost, which
included a boy beating a drum at lower right in place of
the all-seeing cat and a more legible and imposing
representation of the man bearing the crib. In that work the
elegant decorative objects shown here on and above the
mantelpiece are lacking. The lost drawing was engraved
by François Hubert in 1767,[4] with the chevalier de Damery
(No. 40) identified as its owner, and by F.-P. Charpentier,[5]
with a dedication to Madame de Damery. It appeared in
the sale of Jacqmin, "*joaillier du Roi*," Paris, April 26-
May 22, 1773, lot 858, described as being in brown ink.
The date of Hubert's engraving seems an appropriate
terminus ante quem for the present drawings, which may
have been done as early as 1763 when the artist visited
his daughter "*en nourrice.*"

A study for the head of the timorous child is in
the Hermitage.[6]

1 "Thibault back from the wet
nurse. The young Thibault returns
from the wet nurse with all his
baggage; his nurse presents him
to his mother, who is eager to
receive him; then the small child
recoils with fright into the arms
of the mother whom he knows,
and, by that action, reproaches
his mother for her indifference."
Quoted in Brookner, p. 157
2 "If mothers would nurse their
children, it appears that they would
thereby be stronger and more
vigorous; the milk of their mother
should suit them better than the
milk of another woman; for the
fetus is nourished in the womb by
a milky liquid very similar to the
milk that forms in the breasts:
the child is thus already, so to
speak, accustomed to its mother's
milk, whereas the milk of another
nurse is a new nourishment for
it. . . . Independently of the ordinary
relationship of the child's
temperament to that of its mother,
the latter is much better fitted to
take tender care of her child than
a borrowed woman who is animated
only by the reward of a mercenary
fee, often quite small. Let us
conclude that the mother of a
child, though less good as a nurse,
is still preferable to a stranger."
Diderot, *Encyclopédie*, XI, p. 361
3 "The first duty of a mother is
to nurse her children." *Ibid.*, p. 380
4 Portalis-Béraldi, III, p. 438
5 *Ibid.*, I, pp. 362–63
6 Monod-Hautecoeur, No. 152,
Pl. LIX

43 The Motherly Reprimand

Pen and brush, gray and brown ink wash, on white paper,
squared, 18 x 13½ in. (45.6 x 34.4 cm)
Signed: *J. B. Greuze*
Williamstown, Massachusetts, Sterling and Francine Clark
Art Institute

Collections: Trouard, Paris; his sale, Paris, February 22-27,
1779, lot 182, sold for 229 francs to Haudry; Haudry,
Orléans; J.-A. Boussac, Paris; his sale, Paris, March 4,
1931, lot 52; Président Charles d'Heucqueville, Paris; his
sale, Paris, March 24-25, 1936, lot 36
    Exhibitions: Williamstown, Massachusetts, Sterling and
Francine Clark Art Institute, Drawings of the Sixteenth,
Seventeenth and Eighteenth Centuries, 1965, No. 37
    Bibliography: E. Haverkamp-Begemann, S. D. Lawder
and C. W. Talbot, Jr., *Drawings from The Clark Art Institute*,
New Haven—London, 1964, I, No. 37, pp. 39-40, II, Pl.
44; Martin-Masson, No. 136

Though this drawing was squared for transfer, no painting
of the subject is known. Greuze's representation here of a
mother scolding her child for giving food to a dog is
related in theme to *Silence!* of 1759 (No. 23) and to the
painting *The Spoiled Child* in the Hermitage. In the latter
work the mother, instead of scolding the child, observes
its action benignly, an attitude noted indignantly by the
critic Mathon de la Cour in writing of that painting when
it appeared in the Salon of 1765: *"On vient de lui donner
une soupe; au lieu de la manger, il en donne tout doucement les
cuillières à un chien. La mère rit et regarde cette gentillesse avec
une complaisance extrême."*[1] Diderot found the subject
"charmant" but the picture *"sans intérêt."*[2]
    Greuze's interest in contemporary theories of child
training are evident in these and other works (see for
example Nos. 41, 42) which suggest the importance of
correcting minor transgressions at an early age in order to
prevent graver faults later on.
    A drawing of the child and the dog is in the Louvre
(No. 26957).

[1] "He has just been given soup;
instead of eating it, he very calmly
gives spoonfuls of it to a dog.
The mother laughs and watches
this kindness with an extreme
complaisance." Mathon de la Cour,
Troisième Lettre à Monsieur ***,
1765, pp. 6-7
[2] "charming." "without
interest." Diderot, *Salons*, II, p. 149

44 Girl Weeping over Her Dead Bird
(Une Jeune Fille, qui pleure son oiseau mort)
Oil, on canvas, 20½ x 18 in. (52.0 x 45.6 cm)
Edinburgh, National Galleries of Scotland

Collections: M. de Lalive de la Briche, 1765; General Ramsey, 1860; Lady Murray, Henderland; bequeathed by her to the museum in 1861

Exhibitions: Salon of 1765, No. 110; R. A., 1968, No. 308

Bibliography: Brookner, pp. 64, 65, 106, Pl. III; Diderot, *Salons,* II, pp. 34-35, 145-48; Fried, p. 171, fig. 21; Martin-Masson, No. 703; National Gallery of Scotland, *Catalogue of Paintings and Sculpture,* Edinburgh, 1957, p. 113; Wright, p. 82

Engraving: J.-J. Flipart[1]

Greuze treated this pathetic subject three times: in an oval painting shown in the Salon of 1759 as *Une Jeune Fille qui pleure la mort de son oiseau,* probably the work now in the collection of Dr. Claus Virch, Kiel;[2] in the present picture exhibited in 1765; and in a version now in the Louvre exhibited in the Salon of 1800 as *Un enfant hésitant de toucher un oiseau dans la crainte qu'il ne soit mort.*[3] In the first treatment a young woman wearing a necklace holds a bird in one hand and rests her head on the other in a mannered gesture; in the third, a girl shown half-length raises her hands in trepidation before touching a bird lying on a table.

The late Andrew McLaren Young,[4] among others, has suggested that these pictures were inspired by Catullus' *Lugete, O Veneris Cupidinesque,* a poem Greuze could have known from Marolle's translation of 1653.[5] In Sisson's modern English translation, that poem reads as follows:

"Time for mourning, Loves and Cupids
And any man of wit and love,
The sparrow's dead, my girl's own sparrow
That she loved more than her eyes:
For it was sweeter and knew her better
Than any girl might know her mother;
The bird would not move from her lap!
But hopping here and hopping there
Chirped for its mistress, no one else.
Now it goes to the darkened pathway
Out of which, they say, none comes back.
But curses on you, cursed darkness,
Orcus, you eat everything up.
You have taken my little sparrow away.
Oh, badly done! Oh, poor little bird!
It's all your doing, my poor girl's eyes
Are heavy and red with weeping now."[6]

Greuze has provided an image to match this poem in evoking the shock a child experiences in its first confrontation with the mystery of death. However, Diderot, who mentioned the poet Gessner rather than Catullus as a literary parallel, went much farther in his *Salon* to say, *"Cet enfant pleure autre chose, vous dis-je."*[7] He perceived in this work the same symbolic reference to the loss of virginity that he found in another painting by Greuze, *The Broken Mirror* of 1763 (London, Wallace Collection). His celebrated text dealing with the present picture is organized around an imaginary conversation with the girl, who tells Diderot of a visit from her lover during her mother's absence and how in her distraction afterward she permitted her bird, a gift from her lover, to die of starvation. She weeps not only over its death but also over the possibility that this event presages abandonment by her lover. Yet for all his enthusiasm over this painting Diderot wrote of Falconet's *Friendship* exhibited the same year: *"Je jure que la fille de Greuze, qui pleure son serin, est à cent lieues ed ce pathétique."*[8]

The nuances Diderot saw in the picture were not apparent to most other critics in 1765, though they all admired the work. *"M. Greuze se soutient avec le plus grand succès,"* said Bachaumont,[9] and another writer noted that *"Tout le monde admire le vrai de ce tableau; le coloris te le dessein y sont bien exécutés."*[10] After Diderot it was Mathon de la Cour who was most enthusiastic over the picture, *"un chef d'oeuvre de naturel et d'expression."* Slightly baffled by what he for a moment saw as excessive sorrow over a mere bird but subsequently recognized as the characteristic attachment of a child to a pet at an age when *"la Nature commence à attendrir le coeur pour le préparer aux plus douces impressions,"* he recorded the phenomenal success of the painting: *"Il m'est impossible, Monsieur, de faire passer jusqu'à vous l'attendrissement extrême que m'a causé cette figure. Je n'ai jamais vû un coloris plus vrai, des larmes plus touchantes, une simplicité plus sublime. Les connoisseurs, les femmes, les petits maîtres, les pédans, les gens d'esprit, les ignorans et les sots, tous les spectateurs sont d'accord sur ce tableau. On croit voir la Nature; on partage la douleur de cette fille; on voudroit la consoler; j'ai passé plusieurs fois des heures entières à la considérer attentivement; je m'y suis enivré de cette tristesse douce et tendre, qui vaut mieux que la volupté: et je suis sorti pénétré d'une mélancolie délicieuse."*[11]

Among the other admirers of the picture at the Salon was the marquis de Marigny, called *"Poisson Mécène"* by Diderot, who recorded as follows Marigny's encounter with Greuze: *"Cela est beau, dit-il à l'artiste, qui lui répondit: Monsieur, je le sais; on me loue de reste; mais je manque d'ouvrage."*[12]

The exquisite facture of this painting, more like Greuze's earlier work than anything else shown in 1765, was appreciated by Diderot and evoked in his detailed description of the subject. Mathon de la Cour summarized

Greeze's manner in saying, *"Ce morceau précieux est fini avec le plus grand soin."*[13]

The popularity of the subject explains the existence of innumerable copies after the painting and after Flipart's engraving of it. There is, for instance, in the Wadsworth Atheneum at Hartford an eighteenth-century oval copy after Flipart with the engraving's dedication to the duchesse de Gramont painted as though carved into stone. In the Museum of Art and Archaeology, University of Missouri, Columbia, is a miniature signed "Anna Greuze" also executed after Flipart.

1 Portalis-Béraldi, II, p. 199; F. Basan, *Dictionnaire des graveurs anciens et modernes*, Paris, 1767, I, p. 204
2 Formerly in the Hapsburg collection, Vienna; Galerie Cailleux, Paris; sold in London, June 30, 1971, lot 31
3 Rosenberg, Reynaud and Compin, I, No. 330
4 Letter dated July 17, 1967
5 *Les Poésies de Catulle de Vérone*, trans. M. Marolle, Paris, 1653, pp. 5, 7
6 *Catullus*, trans. C. H. Sisson, London, 1966, p. 12
7 "That child is weeping over something else, I tell you." Diderot, *Salons*, II, p. 147
8 "I swear that the girl of Greuze, weeping over her canary, is a hundred leagues from the pathetic character of this." *Ibid.*, p. 219
9 "M. Greuze maintains himself with the greatest success." P. de Bachaumont, "Jugement de Bachaumont sur cette exposition," 1765, ms., Paris, Bibliothèque Nationale, Cabinet des Estampes, Fonds Deloynes, p. 2
10 "Everyone admires the truth of this picture; its coloring and drawing are well executed." *Critique des peintures et sculptures de Messieurs de l'Académie royale l'An 1765*, Paris, 1765, pp. 25-26
11 "a masterpiece of naturalness and expression." "Nature begins to soften the heart in order to prepare it for the gentlest impressions." "It is impossible, Monsieur, for me to convey to you the extreme compassion this figure aroused in me. I have never seen coloring more true, tears more touching, simplicity more sublime. Connoisseurs, women, dandies, pedants, intellectuals, ignoramuses and fools, all the viewers are in agreement over this picture. You think you are seeing Nature; you share this girl's suffering; you would like to console her; on several occasions I have spent entire hours examining it with care; I have intoxicated myself with that sweet and tender sadness which is worth more than sensual pleasure; and I have gone out filled with a delicious melancholy." Mathon de la Cour, *Troisième Lettre à Monsieur ***, 1765, pp. 3-5
12 "That is beautiful, said he to the artist, who replied to him: Monsieur, I know it; they praise me for it, furthermore; but I am out of work." Diderot, *op. cit.*, II, p. 148
13 "This precious piece is finished with the greatest care." Mathon de la Cour, *op. cit.*, p. 5

45 Study of a Dog

Pastel, on cream paper, 7⅞ x 10¾ in. (20.0 x 27.4 cm)
Dijon, Musée Magnin

Collections: Jules Boilly, Paris; his sale, Paris, March 19–20, 1869, lot 139, sold for 80 francs
   Exhibitions: Galerie Sambon, Paris, L'Art animalier à travers les âges, No. 269
   Bibliography: Martin-Masson, No. 1484; Musée Magnin, *Peintures et dessins de l'Ecole française,* Dijon, 1938, No. 468

This lively drawing is a study for *La Philosophie endormie,* a pastel exhibited in the Salon of 1765 and engraved by J.-M. Moreau *le jeune* and Aliamet.[1] In that witty portrait, whose present whereabouts are unknown, Madame Greuze is depicted asleep in a chair with the dog on her lap and her arm resting on a table beside volumes of Newton, Epicurus, Plato, Descartes and Copernicus. With his usual vigor Diderot described the dog as it appeared in the portrait, its mouth closed and its eyes fixed on the viewer: *"Le chien que la belle main caresse, est un épagneul à longs poils noirs, le museau et les pattes tachetées de feu. Il a les yeux pleins de vie. Si vous le regardez quelque temps, vous l'entendrez aboyer."*[2] Goncourt described the transformed animal as it appeared in the engraving: *"un carlin aux oreilles rognées, au mufle froncé, aux yeux en colère."*[3]

   The same dog appears in Greuze's *Child Playing with a Dog* (No. 55) and is seen again, this time wearing a collar with studs instead of a ribbon, in a drawing of Madame Greuze asleep on a chaise longue (Amsterdam, Rijksmuseum).

1 Portalis-Béraldi, III, p. 157; E. Bocher, *Jean-Michel Moreau le jeune,* Paris, 1882, p. 95, No. 251; M. J.-F. Mahérault, *L'Oeuvre de Moreau le jeune,* Paris, 1880, p. 109, No. 145; A. Moureau, *Les Moreau,* Paris, 1893, p. 19
2 "The dog the beautiful hand caresses is a spaniel with long black fur, his muzzle and paws spotted with brown. His eyes are full of life. If you look at him for a while, you will hear him bark." Diderot, *Salons,* II, p. 152
3 "a pug with clipped ears, his nose wrinkled, his eyes angry." Goncourt, I, p. 311

46 Seated Elderly Woman

(Study for *The Well-Beloved Mother*)
Red chalk, on cream paper, 14⅞ x 11⅜ in. (37.7 x 28.8 cm)
Paris, Musée du Louvre, Cabinet des Dessins

Collections: original collection of the Cabinet des Dessins,
Musée du Louvre

Exhibitions: San Francisco, California Palace of the
Legion of Honor, Rococo: Masterpieces of XVIII Century
French Art from the Museums of France, 1949, No. 22;
Tokyo, Kyoto and Fukuoka, Art français, 1954–55, No. 54;
Venice, Vienna and Zurich, Le XVIIIè siècle français,
1955, No. 120; Vienna, Oberes Belvedere, Kunst und Geist
Frankreichs im 18. Jahrhundert, 1966, No. 84, Pl. 50

Bibliography: Bouchot-Saupique, No. 5, Pl. VII; Brookner,
p. 111, Pl. 44; Guiffrey-Marcel, VI, p. 58, No. 4559;
Hautecoeur, Pl. XXIV; Martin-Masson, Nos. 169, 1520;
"Mémorial des Laborde," IX, "Inconographie," ms.,
Paris, Laborde family, p. 100

This drawing, one of Greuze's finest, is a study for the
central figure of the grandmother in the painting *The
Well-Beloved Mother* (fig. 4), formerly in the collection of
the marquis de Laborde, Paris.

In his catalogue of the Salon of 1769, in which the
painting was listed as No. 152 but according to Diderot[1]
and Bachaumont[2] was not exhibited, Gabriel de Saint-Aubin
noted: "*Voy. M. de La Borde.*"[3] Indeed, the painting, for
all its pseudo-genre trappings, is in fact a commissioned
portrait of the family of the marquis Jean-Joseph de
Laborde, a wealthy financier. The elderly woman portrayed
in the present drawing and in the painting was his

mother-in-law, Barbe-Louise, vicomtesse de Nettine
(1706–1775), who was also the mother-in-law of Greuze's
patron Lalive de Jully (see No. 22). Born Mademoiselle
Stoupy, she married the Belgian banker Matthias de
Nettine. After his death she received the title of vicomtesse
from the Empress Maria-Theresa, whose banker her father
had been and for whom she herself served as banker in
the Netherlands.[4]

In a study for the group of the mother and children in
The Well-Beloved Mother (Vienna, Albertina, No. 12761),
Madame de Nettine is represented with one arm over a
crib and the other resting on her knee. Greuze's study of
her right hand, raised and open in a gesture of excitement,
is in the collection of Gaston Palewski, Paris.[5] A portrait
drawing of Madame de Nettine considered to be a copy
after a lost drawing by Joseph Bernard is in the Yale
University Art Gallery, New Haven.[6] It is a mirror image
of a print attributed to Augustin de Saint-Aubin.

In describing a sketch of *The Well-Beloved Mother*
exhibited in 1765, Mathon de la Cour singled out the
figure of the grandmother: "*La grand'mère est touchée
jusqu'aux larmes de cette scène tendre.*"[7] In his Salon commentary
Diderot mocked an imaginary creator of the sketch,
saying: "*Et cette grand'mère, vous auriez songé à l'amener
là; vous en êtes bien sûr!*"[8] He went on to describe her
appearance: "*Sur le fond du salon, le dos tourné à une cheminée
couverte d'une glace, la grand'mère assise dans un fauteuil, et
bien grand'mérisée de tête et d'ajustemens, éclatant de rire de la
scène qui se passe.*"[9] Diderot's general remarks that year on
Greuze's draughtsmanship could have been written in
reference to this drawing: "*La plume du poète, le crayon du
dessinateur habile, ont l'air de courir et de se jouer.*"[10]

1 Diderot, *Salons*, VII, p. 104
2 Bachaumont, *Mémoires secrets*,
XIX, p. 113
3 Dacier, *Saint-Aubin*, II, p. 81
4 F. Courboin, *Histoire illustrée de
la gravure en France*, Paris, 1924,
II, p. 141; J.-P. Poisson, "Le
Notariat parisien à la fin du 18è
siècle," *Dix-huitième siècle*, No. 7,
1975, p. 109
5 See: Paris, Galerie Prouté,
Colmar, 1964, No. 42
6 E. Haverkamp-Begemann and
A.-M. S. Logan, *European Drawings
and Watercolors in the Yale University
Art Gallery*, New Haven, 1970, I,
No. 38; A. Wolf, *The Edward B.
Greene Collection of Engraved Portraits
and Portrait Drawings at Yale
University*, New Haven—London,
1952, No. 13, Pl. XXXV, fig. 3

7 "The grandmother is moved to
the point of tears by this tender
scene." Mathon de la Cour,
*Troisième Lettre à Monsieur ***,
1765, pp. 11–12
8 "And that grandmother, you
would have thought of putting her
there; you are quite sure of it!"
Diderot, *op. cit.*, II, p. 154
9 "At the rear of the room, her
back turned to a fireplace
surmounted by a mirror, the
grandmother seated in an armchair,
and very grandmotherly in
expression and attire, bursting into
laughter at the scene taking place."
Ibid., p. 155
10 "The pen of the poet, the
chalk of the skillful draughtsman,
seem to run along and frolic
together." *Ibid.*, p. 154

47 Seated Female Figure

Red chalk, on white paper, 12½ x 8⅞ in. (31.7 x 22.5 cm)
Hartford, Wadsworth Atheneum, Henry and Walter
Keney Fund

Collections: G. B. Lasquin, Paris (Lugt S 1139 a); his sale,
Paris, June 7–8, 1928, lot 83; Savile Gallery, London;
acquired by the museum in 1928

 Exhibitions: Hartford, Wadsworth Atheneum, Loan
Exhibition of Drawings, 1928, No. 8; Middletown,
Connecticut, Wesleyan University, 1930; Connecticut
Valley Schools Art Exhibition, 1937; Detroit Institute of
Arts, Sixty Drawings from the Wadsworth Atheneum,
1948; Hartford, Wadsworth Atheneum, In Retrospect—
Twenty-one Years of Museum Collecting, 1949, No. 55

This drawing is related in mood, in theme and probably
in time to *The Schoolmistress* (fig. 12), but it is most likely
a preparatory study for a composition with numerous
figures that was engraved by Devisse under the title *La
Mère sévère*.[1] In that work a child approaches his seated
mother expecting punishment for having stolen a jar of
preserves. The style of the woman's gown in the present
work is comparable to that worn by the mother in *The
Well-Beloved Mother* (fig. 4), of which Greuze exhibited a
drawing in 1765, and is noticeably more elegant than the
costumes represented in earlier scenes of maternal discipline
such as *Silence!* (No. 23).

1 Martin-Masson, No. 337;
Portalis-Béraldi, III, p. 731

48 The Ungrateful Son (*Le Fils ingrat*)

Brush, brown and gray ink wash, over pencil, on white
paper, 12⅝ x 16⁹⁄₁₆ in. (32.0 x 42.0 cm)
Lille, Musée des Beaux-Arts

Collections: marquis de Laborde, Paris, with pendant;
his sale, Paris, May 16, 1783, lot 40, sold for 220 livres
to Dulac; Houtelart, Lille, with pendant; donated by
him to the museum, with pendant, in 1864

Exhibitions: Salon of 1765, No. 124, with pendant (?);
London, Heim Gallery, From Poussin to Puvis de Chavannes:
A Loan Exhibition of French Drawings from the Collections
of the Musée des Beaux-Arts at Lille, 1974, No. 53,
with pendant

Bibliography: Brookner, pp. 64-65, 100, 108, Pl. 38;
Diderot, *Salons*, II, pp. 37, 136; L. Gonse, "Musée de
Lille: Musée Wicar," *Gazette des Beaux-Arts*, January, 1877,
p. 88; Martin-Masson, No. 167; Munhall, 1964, p. 15, 16,
fig. 11; H. Pluchart, *Musée Wicar: Notice des dessins, cartons,
pastels, miniatures et grisailles exposés*, Lille, 1889, No.
1430; R. Rosenblum, *Transformations in Late Eighteenth
Century Art*, Princeton, 1964, p. 37

This is Greuze's original rendition of *The Father's Curse:
The Ungrateful Son*, a subject he would treat subsequently
in a major painting of 1777 (No. 84). In the drawing, an
old man is depicted imploring his son not to abandon his
destitute family to join the army. Other members of the
family react to the young man's departure according to
their positions in the household. The major differences
between the drawing and the painting, which was done in
reverse, are the transformation of the father's tortured
entreaties here into a violent curse in the painting and
the replacement of the son's cavalier stance in the drawing
with a pose of astonishment and anger in the later work.

Although there are minor discrepancies in detail between
this drawing and Diderot's description of Greuze's sketch
entitled *The Ungrateful Son* exhibited in the Salon of 1765,
they are due probably to Diderot's writing about the
drawing from memory or fragmentary notes. For Diderot
the drawing was *"très belle."* *"Tout est entendu, ordonné,
caractérisé, clair dans cette esquisse."*[1] He described the
setting and all the figures at length, commenting on
their individual roles, characters and histories. The critic
Mathon de la Cour was equally fascinated by the
dramatic subject. His description stressed the rustic setting,
and he alone raised the possibility that the youngest
children might be the sons, not the brothers, of the
young man.[2]

A later version of this subject is in the Albertina, Vienna
(No. 15374). The composition is reversed, as in the
painting, but it retains such features of the original sketch
as the soldier's helmet and clenched sword and the
nonchalant gesture of the son. A study for the daughter
who *"s'efforce d'arrêter le vieillard en le faisant asseoir malgré
lui"*[3] was in the Groult collection, Paris. It includes the
father's large chair, which, as Diderot relates, was called
a *"confessional."*[4]

1 "very beautiful." "Everything
in this sketch is understood, ordered,
well characterized, clear." Diderot,
Salons, II, p. 157
2 "*tous les enfans pleurent, en
voyant que leur père va quitter la
maison paternelle.*" ("all the
children weep, on seeing that their
father is going to leave the family
house.") Mathon de la Cour,
Troisième Lettre à Monsieur ***,
1765, p. 11

3 "struggles to restrain the old
man by making him sit despite
himself." *Ibid.*
4 "*Sur le devant . . . un grand
confessional de cuir noir, où l'on peut
être commodément assis.*" ("In the
foreground . . . a large black
leather confessional, in which one
can be comfortably seated." Diderot,
op. cit., p. 136

49 The Punished Son (*Le Fils puni*)

Brush, gray and brown ink wash, over pencil, on white
paper, 12⅝ x 16⁹⁄₁₆ in. (32.0 x 42.0 cm)
Lille, Musée des Beaux-Arts

Collections: marquis de Laborde, Paris, with pendant;
his sale, Paris, May 16, 1783, lot 41, sold for 201 livres
to Paillet; Houtelart, Lille, with pendant; donated by
him to the museum, with pendant, in 1864

Exhibitions: Salon of 1765, No. 125, with pendant (?);
London, Heim Gallery, From Poussin to Puvis de
Chavannes: A Loan Exhibition of French Drawings from
the Collections of the Musée des Beaux-Arts at Lille,
1974, No. 54, with pendant

Bibliography: Brookner, pp. 64–65, 73, 100, 108, Pl. 39;
Diderot, *Salons*, II, pp. 37, 158–59; L. Gonse, "Musée
de Lille: Musée Wicar," *Gazette des Beaux-Arts*, January,
1877, p. 88; Martin-Masson, No. 167; Munhall, 1964, pp.
15, 16, fig. 10; H. Pluchart, *Musée Wicar: Notice des dessins,
cartons, pastels, miniatures et grisailles exposés*, Lille, 1889,
No. 1431

The pendant to *The Ungrateful Son* (No. 48), this drawing
depicts the crippled and wasted son returning home just
as his father has died. The family mourns the dead man
passionately. Greuze executed a major painting on the
same theme in 1778 (No. 88). It includes an additional
foreground figure and excludes details such as the window,
the candle and the holy-water vessel.

It is reasonable to assume that this was the drawing
Greuze exhibited as No. 125 in the Salon of 1765, which
Diderot preferred to its pendant.[1] He described the im-
poverished setting and analyzed each figure in terms of his
emotions and dramatic function, noting, for instance, that
the son "*a perdu la jambe dont il a repoussé sa mère, et il est
perclus du bras dont il a menacé son père.*"[2] For Diderot, "*Cela
est beau, très beau, sublime; tout, tout.*"[3] He felt that *The
Punished Son* and its pendant were "*des chefs-d'oeuvre de
composition: point d'attitudes tourmentées ni recherchées; les
actions vraies qui conviennent à la peinture.*"[4]

The violent element of the sketch appalled Mathon de la
Cour, who, after describing the drawing in detail, noted:
"*Ces deux scènes effrayantes sont rendues de la manière la plus
forte dans les esquisses. Je ne conseillerois jamais à M. Greuze
de les exécuter. On souffre trop à les voir. Elles empoisonnent
l'âme d'un sentiment si profond et si terrible, qu'on est forcé
d'en détourner les yeux.*"[5] Diderot, for different reasons, also
felt that Greuze might never execute paintings after these
drawings—let alone sell them: "*Avec tout cela, le goût est
si misérable, si petit, que peut-être ces deux esquisses ne seront
jamais peintes, et que si elles sont peintes, Boucher aura plutôt
vendu cinquante des ses indécentes et plates marionnettes que
Greuze ces deux sublimes tableaux.*"[6] As late as 1785 the
anonymous author of the *Discours sur l'origine, les progrès
et l'état actuel de la peinture en France* concurred with Mathon
de la Cour's feelings that the aim of moralistic painting
should be positive rather than negative: "*personne n'est
au-dessus de lui* [Greuze] *dans les sujets de société, le* Père de
famille, *la* Dame de paroisse, *la* Piété filiale *nous offrent des
leçons utiles, et pour ainsi dire, vivantes, mais le* Fils ingrat,
la Malédiction paternelle, *la* mauvaise Belle-Mère *font
naître des idées moins consolantes et peut-être vaudroit-il mieux
de ne pas supposer l'existence de pareils monstres.*"[7]

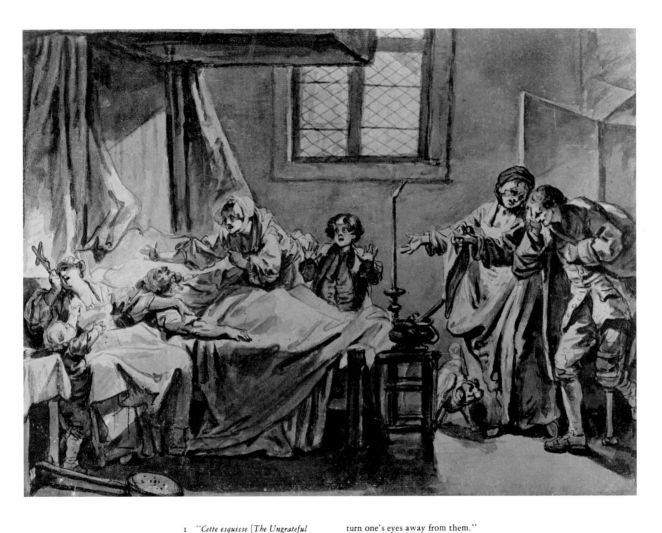

1 "*Cette esquisse* [*The Ungrateful Son*], *très belle, n'approche pourtant pas, à mon gré, de celle qui suit.*" ("This sketch [*The Ungrateful Son*], very beautiful, does not however approach, to my taste, the one that follows.") Diderot, *Salons*, II, p. 157
2 "has lost the leg with which he pushed away his mother, and he is crippled in the arm with which he threatened his father." *Ibid.*, p. 158
3 "That is beautiful, very beautiful, sublime; everything, everything." *Ibid.*
4 "masterpieces of composition: absolutely no over-elaborate or affected postures; real actions suitable to painting." *Ibid.*, pp. 158–59
5 "These two frightening scenes are conveyed in the strongest manner in the sketches. I would never advise M. Greuze to execute them. One suffers too much on seeing them. They poison the soul with a feeling so profound and terrible that one is forced to turn one's eyes away from them." Mathon de la Cour, *Troisième Lettre à Monsieur****, 1765, p. 13
6 "With all that, taste is so wretched, so trifling, that perhaps these two sketches will never be painted, and if they are painted, Boucher will sooner have sold fifty of his indecent and insipid marionnettes than Greuze these two sublime pictures." Diderot, *op. cit.*, p. 159
7 "no one is above him [Greuze] in subjects of society, The *Family Father*, the *Parish Lady*, *Filial Piety* offer us lessons that are useful and, so to speak, alive, but the *Ungrateful Son*, the *Father's Curse*, the *Evil Stepmother* give birth to less comforting ideas, and perhaps it would be better not to admit the existence of such monsters." *Discours sur l'origine, les progrès et l'état actuel de la peinture en France contenant des notices sur les principaux artistes de l'Académie pour servir d'introduction au Sallon*, Paris, 1785, pp. 24–25

50 Portrait of Denis Diderot

Black and white chalk, stumped, on warm brown paper,
14¼ x 11⅜ in. (36.1 x 28.3 cm)
Signed: *J. B. Greuze*; inscribed on an old label formerly
pasted to the back of the frame: *"Portrait de Diderot /
Dessiné par Greuze pour le Baron d'Holbach / donné par Mr.
d'Holbach fils à Mad^e de Vandeul, fille / de Diderot. / Après
la mort de Mad^e de Vandeul, il m'a été donné / par Monsr. de
Vandeul son fils, le 21 décembre 1824. / E. S."*
New York, The Pierpont Morgan Library, purchased as
the gift of John M. Crawford

Collections: Denis Diderot, Paris (?);[1] Paul-Henri Dietrich,
Baron d'Holbach, Paris (d. 1789); given by his son to
Madame de Vandeul, Diderot's daughter; given by her
son to "E. S." in 1824; François Marcille, Paris; his sale,
Paris, January 16–17, 1857, sold for 135 francs (?);[2]
Hippolyte Walferdin, Paris; his sale, Paris, April 3, 1880,
lot 76, sold for 200 francs; David David-Weill, Neuilly

Exhibitions: Paris, Salon of 1846, La Peinture française
depuis la fin du dix-huitième siècle;[3] New York, Wildenstein
and Co., French Eighteenth-Century Pastels, Water-Colors
and Drawings from the David-Weill Collection, 1938, No.
97, The French Revolution, 1943, No. 10, and French
Pastels and Drawings from Clouet to Degas, 1944, No. 43;
R. A., 1968, No. 321; Ann Arbor, University of Michigan
Museum of Art, The World of Voltaire, 1969, No. 47

Bibliography: F. B. Adams, Jr., *Ninth Report to The Fellows
of The Pierpont Morgan Library*, New York, 1959, pp. 108–09;
Diderot, *Oeuvres*, XX, pp. 116–17, and *Salons*, IV, p. 164;
G. Henriot, *Collection David Weill*, Paris, 1928, III, Pt. I,
pp. 209, 211; Martin-Masson, No. 1108; Portalis-Béraldi,
I, p. 159, II, pp. 64, 266; P. Rosenberg, "Quatre Nouveaux
Fragonard au Louvre," *Revue du Louvre*, No. 3, 1974,
pp. 186–87, fig. 7; Smith, No. 124; M. Tourneux, "Les
Portraits de Diderot," *L'Art*, 1878, XII, pp. 124–25;
Valori, p. 367, n. 1

Engravings: A. de Saint-Aubin, 1766; C.-E. Gaucher;[4]
G.-P. Benoît; N. Dupin *fils*; A.-B. Duhamel; Ryder

Executed in Greuze's studio probably in 1766, this portrait
records the features of the *philosophe* and art critic Denis
Diderot (1713–1784), who was for a while Greuze's most
outspoken and influential admirer.

In writing with some disappointment over his portrait
by Van Loo exhibited in the Salon of 1767 (Louvre),
Diderot described his appearance for posterity, making
specific reference to Greuze's drawing: *"J'avois un grand
front, des yeux très-vifs, d'assez grands traits, la tête tout-à-fait
du caractère d'un ancien orateur, une bonne-hommie qui touchait
de bien près à la bêtise, à la rusticité des anciens tems. Sans
l'exagération de tous les traits dans la gravure qu'on a faite
d'après le crayon de Greuze, je serais infiniment mieux. J'ai
un masque qui trompe l'artiste . . . ."*[5]

Employing the same severe profile view he had used a
few years earlier for his *Self-Portrait* (No. 36), Greuze
deliberately accentuated the antique qualities that Diderot
preferred to see in himself, attempting to record the writer's
features as he himself described them. The vogue for such
profile portraits, often engraved in medallion form reminiscent of ancient medals, had been launched by Charles-
Nicolas Cochin in the Salon of 1750. Cochin eventually
executed hundreds of them, many of which were engraved
by Augustin de Saint-Aubin. Trinquesse, Moreau *le
jeune* and various other members of the Saint-Aubin family
also produced such inconographic records of the period.[6]
In contrast to their attractive, delicate images, Greuze's
life-size profile portrait is more broadly drawn and,
characteristically, more powerful.

In his review of the Salon that preceded the execution
of this drawing (1765), Diderot had devoted more pages
to Greuze's entries than to those of any other artist,
admitting that *"Je suis peut-être un peu long."*[7] He called
Greuze *"votre peintre et le mien, le premier qui se soit avisé,
parmi nous, de donner des moeurs à l'art."*[8] Four years later
personal relations between Diderot and Greuze had
disintegrated to such a point that the *philosophe* stated in
his *Salon* entry, *"Je n'aime plus Greuze."*[9] He was also to
refer sardonically to the artist as *"feu mon ami Greuze."*[10]

A graying man of about fifty-three at the time Greuze
executed this drawing, Diderot saw published in 1766 the
last ten volumes of the monumental *Encyclopédie*, the work
he had undertaken with d'Alembert in 1747. Also in 1766
he received from Catherine II a fifty-year advance on the
pension she had offered him. Diderot began writing his
Salons, his critical reviews of the biennial exhibitions of the
Académie, in 1757. In 1765 he published his *Essai sur
la peinture*.

---

1 Writing in January of 1767,
Baron Grimm stated that Diderot
was given this drawing along with
the first proofs of Saint-Aubin's
engraving after it: *"Ce philosophe
étant il y a quelque temps chez Greuze,
celui-ci le fit asseoir et tira son profil.
Le philosophe s'attendait toujours à
recevoir du peintre ce profil en présent:
cependant ce profil avait disparu de
l'atelier de l'artiste sans arriver dans*

*le cabinet du philosophe. Enfin, un
beau matin, celui-ci reçoit le dessin,
et la planche gravée d'après ce dessin,
et les cent premières épreuves tirées.
Greuze a mis au bas de l'estampe
tout simplement* Diderot. *Elle a été
gravée par Saint-Aubin et c'est un
chef-d'oeuvre de gravure. C'est dommage
que la ressemblance et la physionomie
n'y soient point du tout. Un certain
barbouilleur de la place Dauphine,*

*nommé Garand, a fait pour moi un
profil cent fois plus ressemblant."*
("This *philosophe* having found
himself a while ago in the studio
of Greuze, the latter had him sit
and drew his profile. The *philosophe*
was expecting all the while to
receive this profile as a gift from
the painter; however the profile
had disappeared from the artist's
studio without arriving in the

philosophe's study. Finally, one
fine morning, the latter receives the
drawing, and the engraver's plate
made after the drawing, and the
first hundred proofs pulled from it.
Greuze put at the bottom of the
print simply *Diderot*. It was
engraved by Saint-Aubin and it is
a masterpiece of engraving. It is a
pity that the resemblance and the
physiognomy are not there at all. A

certain dauber in the place
Dauphine, Garand by name, did a
profile for me and the resemblance
is a hundred times better.'') Baron
F. Melchior von Grimm,
*Correspondance littéraire, philosophique
et critique*, ed. M. Tourneux, Paris,
VII, 1879, p. 202
2 According to Martin, No. 1108.
The drawing is not listed in the
catalogue of the sale of January
16–17, which was of paintings,
nor in the sale of Marcille's
drawings on March 4–7 of the
same year.
3 Thoré mentioned the drawing
in his review of the Salon
exhibition: *"un portrait de Diderot,
vu de profil, dessin assez faible, mais
précieux pour la ressemblance."* (''a
portrait of Diderot, seen in profile,
a rather weak drawing, but
precious for the likeness.'') T.
Thoré, *Le Salon de 1846*, Paris,
1846, p. 5
4 Lavater reproduced Gaucher's
engraving soon after its execution
in his *Physiognomische Fragmente zur
Befoerderung der Menschenkenntnis
und Menschenliebe*, Leipzig, 1775–78,
III, p. 300
5 ''I had a high forehead, very
lively eyes, rather large features, a
head totally in the character of an
ancient orator, a guilelessness that
nearly bordered on simplicity, on
the rusticity of ancient times.
Without the exaggeration of all
my features in the engraving that
has been made after Greuze's chalk
drawing, I would appear infinitely
better. I have a face that fools
artists. . . .'' Diderot, *Salons*,
III, p. 67
6 See for example: Paris, Galerie
Heim, Cent Dessins français du
Fitzwilliam Museum, Cambridge,
exhib. cat., 1976, Nos. 16, 70
7 ''Perhaps I go on a bit long.''
Diderot, *op. cit.*, II, p. 144
8 ''your painter and mine, the
first among us to take it upon
himself to instill moral principles
in art.'' *Ibid.*
9 ''I no longer like Greuze.''
Ibid., IV, p. 105
10 ''my late friend Greuze.''
Ibid., III, p. 197

51 The Death of a Father Mourned by His Children
(*La Mort d'un père regretté par ses enfants*)
Brush, India and brown ink wash, and pencil, on white
paper, 18⅞ x 26 in. (48.0 x 66.0 cm)
Strasbourg, private collection

Collections: van den Zande, Paris;[1] M. Dennel, Paris; his sale,
Paris, March 30, 1860, p. 4, sold for 1,000 francs; D. G.
d'Arozarena, Paris; his sale, Paris, May 29, 1861, lot 56,
sold for 500 francs to Vandeuil; Alfred Sensier, Paris; his
sale, Paris, December 14–15, 1877, lot 435; Hermann Voss
   Exhibitions: Salon of 1769, No. 160, with pendant
   Bibliography: Diderot, *Salons*, IV, p. 44; Martin-Masson,
No. 338

Greuze exhibited this drawing in the Salon of 1769, his
first Salon since 1765, along with its dramatic pendant
(No. 52). Diderot admired the present work but criticized
some of its details: *"Celui surtout de la Mort d'un père de
famille regretté de ses enfans est beau de composition, d'expression
et d'effet. Celui qui entend l'art le voit peint; mais qu'on m'ôte ce
chandelier d'église et ce bénitier avec le buis qui sert de
goupillon, ces accessoires sont faux; cet homme n'est pas mort et
le prêtre ne s'en est pas encore emparé."*[2] Daudet de Jossac, who
was shocked by its pendant, recalled Greuze's *Filial Piety*
of 1763 in praising the character of the present drawing:
*"et pour me guérir par le même feu qui m'a blessé, je quitte ce
vilain croquis pour aller voir celui de la mort du bon Père;
voilà un sujet digne, intéressant; je reconnois à ce dessin l'auteur
pathétique et sublime du Père paralytique servi par ses Enfans."*[3]
   In addition to detailed sketches of this drawing and its
pendant, Gabriel de Saint-Aubin made a minuscule note
in his Salon *livret* reading: *"Voy. celle de Germanicus du
Poussin."*[4] The association is apt, for Greuze's drawing
includes several elements quite possibly inspired by
Poussin's *Death of Germanicus* (Minneapolis Institute of
Arts), such as the curtained bed, the diversified crowd of
mourners, certain of their gestures, the sword-like
candlestick and the deep architectural opening to one side.
Greuze could have remembered Poussin's painting from
Rome, but it is more likely that he knew Guillaume
Chasteau's engraving of it, since Greuze's composition is
closer to the latter.

1 Provenance indicated by Martin
and in catalogues of the following
two sales
2 "Above all, the one of the Death
of a father mourned by his children
is beautiful in composition, in
expression and in effect. He who
understands art can see it as a
painting; but would someone take
away for me that church
candlestick and that holy-water
basin with the boxwood branch
that serves as a sprinkler,
those accessories are false; this man
is not dead and the priest has not
yet taken hold of him." Diderot,
Salons, IV, p. 108

3 "and to heal myself by the
same fire that wounded me, I
leave this nasty sketch to go see
that of the death of the good
Father; there is a worthy subject,
interesting; I recognize in this
drawing the touching and sublime
author of the paralytic Father
cared for by his Children."
[Daudet de Jossac], *Lettre sur les
peintures, gravures et sculptures qui
ont été exposées cette année au Louvre*,
Paris, 1769, pp. 28–29
4 "See that of Germanicus by
Poussin." Dacier, *Saint-Aubin*,
II, p. 82

52 The Death of a Cruel Father Abandoned by His Children (*La Mort d'un père dénaturé abandonné de ses enfans*)
Brush, India and brown ink wash, and pencil, on white paper, 18⁷⁄₁₆ x 25³⁄₁₆ in. (46.8 x 64.0 cm)'
Signed: *Greuze*
Tournus, Musée Greuze

Collections: Hippolyte Destailleurs, Paris (?); his sale, Paris, 1898, purchased by the museum[1]
   Exhibitions: Salon of 1769, No. 161, with pendant
   Bibliography: Diderot, *Salons*, IV, p. 44; Martin-Masson, No. 190

This drawing, the pendant to No. 51, with which it was exhibited in 1769, provoked a violent response from the critics. Though Diderot wrote that the artist "*s'est montré un homme de génie*"[2] with his drawings that year, most other commentators were appalled by the subject. Daudet de Jossac stated, "*Pendant que je suis occupé à reprocher le mauvais choix des sujets, il faut que tout d'une haleine, j'exprime mon mécontentement d'un dessin du même Auteur qu'il propose sans doute de traiter en grand. La Mort du Père dénaturé abandonné de ses enfans. . . . Quel sujet! . . . ce sujet me scandalise; je suis fâché qu'un François l'ait imaginé.*"[3] Fréron felt similarly: "*On voudroit aussi qu'il s'interdit les sujets atroces . . . le spectacle en est horrible . . . on n'y apperçoit qu'une barberie révoltante et sans exemple contre un mourant.*"[4] However, the anonymous critic of the *Avant-Coureur* appreciated Greuze's unique subject, and described it vividly: "*Ce dernier morceau est effrayant, le corps de ce malheureux mourant est à moitié jetté hors du lit; on lui enlève la bourse, et jusqu'au drap qui le couvre; le cierge placé au pied de son lit se brise, et la flamme le dévore en un instant.*"[5] De Camburat was able to express his reaction poetically:

> "*Quel crayon, pur, noble et léger*
> *Peint ce pere outragé d'une famille impie*
> *Terminant dans l'horreur une mourante vie?*"[6]

Greuze exaggerated the didactic value of his two moral scenes by depicting the villainous father expiring in a squalid garret while his counterpart lies in an elaborately canopied bed, and by representing in the former scene an agitated figure fleeing a stark interior and in the latter a crowd of mourners joined in grief and compassion.

1 According to Martin. However, there appears to have been no Destailleurs sale in 1898

2 "has shown himself a man of genius." Diderot, *Salons*, IV, p. 108

3 "While I am busy reproaching the bad choice of subjects, I must in the same breath express my discontent over a drawing by the same Author which he no doubt proposes to treat on a grand scale. *The Death of the cruel Father* abandoned by his children. . . . What a subject! . . . this subject scandalizes me; I am sorry that a Frenchman should have thought of it." [Daudet de Jossac], *Lettre sur les peintures, gravures et sculptures qui ont été exposées cette année au Louvre*, Paris, 1769, p. 29

4 "One would wish also that he prohibit himself atrocious subjects . . . the sight of it is horrible . . . one sees nothing in it but a revolting and unprecedented barbarity toward a dying man." E.-C. Fréron, "Lettre XIII: Exposition des peintures, sculptures et gravûres de Messieurs de l'Académie Royale," *L'Année littéraire*, Paris, 1769, pp. 310–11

5 "This last piece is frightening, the body of this wretched dying man is thrown half out of bed; someone is stealing his purse, and even the sheet that covers him; the candle placed at the foot of his bed breaks, and the flame will consume him in an instant." "Arts: Exposition des peintures, sculptures, gravures de M.M. de l'Académie Royale," *L'Avant-Coureur*, September 11, 1769, p. 396

6 "What pencil, pure, noble and light / Depicts this outraged father of a godless family / Ending in horror a dying life?" M. de Camburat, *L'Exposition des tableaux du Louvre, faite en l'année MDCCLXIX* Paris, 1769, No. 16

53 Old Man and Boy

Brush, gray ink wash, over pencil, on white paper,
13¹⁄₁₆ x 8³⁄₁₆ in. (33.2 x 22.4 cm)
Paris, Musée du Louvre, Cabinet des Dessins

Collections: A. Armand, Paris, 1879 (?); baron Roger
Portalis, Paris (Lugt 2232); his sales, Paris, March 14,
1887, lot 112, sold for 75 francs, and Paris, February 2,
1911, lot 113; given by Madame David Nillet to the
museum in 1933
  Exhibitions: Paris, Ecole des Beaux-Arts, Dessins de
maîtres anciens, 1879, No. 571 (?); Vienna, Oberes
Belvedere, Kunst und Geist Frankreichs im 18. Jahrhundert,
1966, No. 85; Paris, Louvre, Cabinet des Dessins, Dessins
français de 1750 à 1825: Le Néo-classicisme, 1972, No. 11
  Bibliography: Martin-Masson, No. 1491

In this variation on a theme Greuze treated more fully in
The Departure of a Young Savoyard (No. 54), the youth seems
to accept with some foreboding the assignment wearily
pointed out to him by the old man.
  In 1769 Greuze exhibited in the Salon a related drawing
with numerous figures entitled *"Départ de Barcelonnette."*
The critic of the *Avant-Coureur* described that composition,
in which the parent *"d'un petit Savoyard lui montre le chemin
de Paris,"* and concluded: *"Il y a beaucoup de vérité, de
mouvement et même de l'intérêt dans cette composition très-simple
en elle-même, mais très amusante par la manière dont l'artiste
l'a rendue."*[1]
  A date of around 1767 would seem appropriate for the
present drawing, especially considering the way in which
the poses recall those of Caracalla and Septimius Severus
in Greuze's reception piece already underway that year
(No. 70).

1 "of a young Savoyard points
out to him the road to Paris."
"There is much truth, movement
and even interest in this composition,
very simple in itself but very
diverting for the manner in which
the artist has rendered it." "Arts:
Exposition des peintures, sculptures,
gravures de M.M. de l'Académie
Royale," *L'Avant-Coureur,*
September 11, 1769, p. 396

54 The Departure of a Young Savoyard

Brush, black, gray and brown ink wash, over pencil,
13⅛ x 10¹⁵⁄₁₆ in. (33.3 x 27.8 cm)
Signed on verso: *J. B^{te} Greuze*
Amsterdam Historisch Museum

Collections: Meynier Saint-Fal, Paris (?); his sale, 1860, lot
22 (?); Fodor, Amsterdam; Stedelijk Museum, Amsterdam,
until 1975

Exhibitions: Amsterdam, Museum Fodor, Fodor 100
jaar, 1963, No. 75

Bibliography: Munhall, 1968, p. 94, fig. 11; R. A. Weigert,
"Les Dessins français conservés dans les principales collections
publiques de Hollande," *Bulletin de la Société de l'Histoire
de l'Art français,* 1933, p. 217; *Beschrikving der Schilderijen . . .
in Het Museum Fodor,* Amsterdam, 1863, p. 77

One of Greuze's many representations of the drama of
departure (compare No. 53), this drawing depicts a
Savoyard child setting forth from his home on an itinerant
career, a marmot box strapped over his shoulders and a
walking stick in his hand. A younger brother, not yet
pressed into service, continues his games at left. A large
standing figure had originally been indicated in the doorway.

In the mid-eighteenth century it was customary for male
inhabitants of Savoy to leave their homeland during the
winter to earn their livings abroad, principally by
providing amusements at street fairs and performing menial
tasks such as sweeping chimneys and selling water. Their
picturesque appearance fascinated French artists from
Watteau to Drouais, but it was characteristic of Greuze to
concentrate instead on the trauma of separation from family
and on the hardships these child laborers endured.

A related drawing, described in the catalogue of the
Mariette sale of 1775 as *"Une femme des montagnes de Savoie
montrant à jouer de la vielle à son fils,"*[1] is in the Albertina,
Vienna.

Greuze knew the area from which he drew these subjects,
for he and the abbé Gougenot (No. 16) had passed through
Chambéry and rural Savoy on their way to Italy. The
inclusion of rough masonry houses, the depiction of aged
persons left behind by the itinerant workers and the
recreation of the general ambiance of the mountain families
gave Greuze's drawings of Savoyards a documentary
realism lacking in his Parisian contemporaries'
representations of similar folk.

1 "A woman from the mountains
of Savoy showing her son how to
play the hurdy-gurdy"

55 Child Playing with a Dog
(Un Jeune Enfant qui joue avec un chien)
Oil, on canvas, 24¾ x 20¾ in. (62.9 x 52.7 cm)
London, private collection

Collections: duc de Choiseul, Paris, 1769; his sale, Paris, April 6–10, 1772, lot 136, sold for 7,200 livres; comtesse du Barry, Louveciennes; her sales, Paris, December 22, 1775, lot 20, bought in, and Paris, February 17, 1777, lot 51, sold for 7,201 livres to the marquis de Véri; marquis de Véri, Paris; his sale, Paris, December 12–14, 1785, lot 24, sold for 7,200 livres to Duclos-Dufresnoy; Duclos-Dufresnoy, Paris; his sale, Paris, August 28, 1795, lot 11, sold for 140,500 livres *assignats;* Montaleau, Paris; his sale, Paris, September 10, 1802, lot 46, sold for 8,016 livres; Robert de Saint-Victor, Paris; his sale, Paris, November 26, 1822, and January 7, 1823, lot 529; George Watson Taylor, London, 1824; his sale, London, July 24, 1832, lot 70, sold for £703 10s; Richard Manley Foster, Clewer Manor; his sale, London, 1876, lot 16, sold for £6,720 to Lord Dudley

Exhibitions: Salon of 1769, No. 155; London, British Institution, Pictures of the Italian, Spanish, Flemish, Dutch and English Schools, 1824, No. 84; London, John Cole Gallery, 1834; London, Abraham Roberti Gallery, 1836; R. A., 1871, No. 398; R. A., 1932, No. 318; R. A., 1968, No. 310

Bibliography: Bachaumont, *Mémoires secrets*, X, p. 49; Diderot, *Correspondance*, VII, pp. 103–04, and *Salons*, III, pp. 85, 107–08; Martin-Masson, No. 504; Portalis-Béraldi, II, pp. 535–37; G. Reitlinger, *The Economics of Taste*, London, 1961, p. 334; Smith, No. 21; Wright, p. 82

Engravings: C.-A. Porporati; R. de Launay; P.-C. Ingouf

John Smith's perceptive description of this picture explains its dramatic fascination. It is, he said, as though a bedroom door had suddenly been opened, arousing the mild fear and guilt of the child, who should have been sleeping, and the protective aggression of her pet: "A fine interesting child with brown hair and a chubby face: she is attired in her night clothes and cap, and appears to have just risen from her couch, and seated herself in a chair in order to caress a pet dog, which she holds in her arms; the little animal, flattered by such notice, is excited by the presence of some stranger, towards whom the eyes of the child are also directed."[1] Gabriel de Saint-Aubin's note in his Salon *livret*, "*C'est la fille de l'auteur*,"[2] further elucidates the intimacy of the picture and suggests that the model was the artist's third daughter, Louise-Gabrielle, who was born in early May of 1764. Her godparents were the artist's friend Wille (No. 39) and his wife, after whom she was named Louise.[3] The spaniel, of the type called in the eighteenth century simply *épagneul de la petite espèce* (small-sized spaniel), reappears in other works by Greuze,

most notably on the lap of Madame Greuze in *La Philosophie endormie* of about 1765, a preparatory study for which is included in this exhibition (No. 45).

Had Greuze been permitted to exhibit in the Salon of 1767, the *Child Playing with a Dog* would probably have appeared among his entries, for Diderot described it enthusiastically to Falconet in a letter dated August 15 of that year: "*Il y a encore de lui . . . La petite fille en chemise qui s'est saisie d'un petit chien noir qui cherche à se débarrasser de ses bras. Cela est beau, vraiment beau.*"[4]

Two years later this picture was Greuze's outstanding success in the Salon of 1769—which included also his controversial reception piece *Septimius Severus* (No. 70)—mainly because, for all its technical brilliance and psychological subtlety, it remained within the standard genre with which Greuze had been identified since 1755. Diderot lauded it as "*Le morceau le plus parfait qu'il y eût au Salon,*"[5] and Fréron noted that the picture was "*le plus universellement applaudi.*"[6] All agreed that Greuze's success with this picture should have taught the artist to abandon his aspirations after the more elevated genre of history painting. Daudet de Jossac spoke most intelligently of its painterly qualities: "*Tout ce que l'art peut imaginer de plus adroit et de plus mystérieux pour les tons se trouve dans la tête de cet enfant vêtu d'une camisole blanche . . . les ombres légères et transparentes, sans aucun noir, et tout cela si adroitement passé, qu'avec raison ce chef-d'oeuvre mérite une attention particulière et le suffrage général.*"[7]

Chardin, who was responsible for the hanging of the Salon of 1769, placed this picture between Greuze's *The Votive Offering to Cupid* (London, Wallace Collection) and *The Blown Kiss* (Pregny, baron Edmond de Rothschild). Diderot thought his intention was a malicious one of making this picture "*tuer deux autres,*"[8] but Chardin may simply have intended to group together three paintings which belonged at that time to the duc de Choiseul. All three appear in L. N. van Blarenberghe's miniature views of Choiseul's Paris residence on the celebrated "Choiseul" gold box of 1770–71 (Paris, baron Elie de Rothschild);[9] the *Child Playing with a Dog* is represented both in the *premier cabinet*, alongside the Rembrandt *Self-Portrait* of 1634 discussed in entry No. 5, and in the *cabinet à la lanterne*, over the fireplace.

There are versions of this picture in Milan (Civico Museo d'Arte Antica, Castello Sforzesco) and Toulon (Musée d'Art et d'Histoire). A copy attributed to Anne-Geneviève Greuze is in Berlin (Staatliche Museen, Dahlem), another, by Anne Dubois, is in Dijon (Musée des Beaux-Arts) and a third is in Rouen (Musée des Beaux-Arts). There also exist numerous copies after the engravings. A version was depicted in a watercolor representing the salon of the Empress Maria Fedorovna in the Winter Palace, St. Petersburg,[10] but its present whereabouts are unknown.

1   Smith, No. 21
2   "This is the artist's daughter."
Dacier, *Saint-Aubin*, II, p. 81
3   Wille, I, pp. 255-56
4   "Also by him is . . . *The little
girl in her nightgown* who has
taken hold of a little black dog
which is struggling out of her
arms. That is beautiful, truly
beautiful." Diderot, *Correspondance*,
VII, pp. 103-04
5   "The most perfect piece there

was in the Salon." Diderot, *Salons*,
III, p. 107
6   "the most universally
applauded." E.-C. Fréron, "Lettre
XIII: Exposition des peintures,
sculptures et gravures de Messieurs
de l'Académie Royale," *L'Année
littéraire*, Paris, 1769, p. 311
7   "All the most skillful and
mysterious tones that art can
imagine are found in the head of

this child dressed in a white
nightgown . . . light and transparent
shadows, quite devoid of black,
and all this so skillfully conveyed
that with good reason this
masterpiece deserves particular
attention and universal
approbation." [Daudet de Jossac],
*Sentimens sur les tableaux exposés au
Salon*, Paris, 1769, p. 21
8   "kill two others." Diderot,

Salons, IV, p. 108
9   See: F. J. B. Watson, *The
Choiseul Box*, London, 1963, pp.
12, 13; "The Choiseul Boxes,"
Appendix B in A. K. Snowman,
*Eighteenth Century Gold Boxes of
Europe*, London, 1966, pp. 149, 151
10 Reproduced in P. Jullian,
"Les Palais tels qu'on les habitait,"
Connaissance des arts, December,
1970, p. 99

56 River God (Study for *The Votive Offering to Cupid*)
Red chalk, on cream paper, 18⁷⁄₁₆ x 24⁷⁄₈ in. (46.8 x 63.2 cm)
New York, The Metropolitan Museum of Art, Joseph
Pulitzer Bequest

Collections: Galerie Cailleux, Paris; acquired by the museum
in 1960
   Exhibitions: Paris, Galerie Cailleux, Le Dessin français de
Watteau à Prud'hon, 1951, No. 185; Paris, Galerie
Charpentier, Figures nues d'école française, 1953, No. 9;
R. A., 1968, No. 319; New York, Metropolitan Museum of
Art, French Drawings and Prints of The Eighteenth
Century, 1972–73, No. 26
   Bibliography: J. Cailleux, "Jacob Van Loo, Greuze et
Porporati," *Bulletin des Musées et Monuments Lyonnais*, III,
No. 3, 1960, p. 292, n. 7; Metropolitan Museum of Art
Bulletin, October, 1961, pp. 47, 63–64; Wallace Collection
Catalogues, *Pictures and Drawings*, London, 1968, p. 136

This drawing was identified by Brookner in 1958 as a study
for the base of the stone statue in *The Votive Offering to
Cupid* (London, Wallace Collection; see fig. 17), a painting
which Greuze exhibited as No. 153 in the Salon of 1769[1]
but which Diderot mentioned as completed by the summer
of 1767.[2] Jacob Bean later associated the study with a drawing
by Louis de Boullogne the Younger in the Metropolitan
Museum of Art, New York, representing a similar figure
of a river god. Dean Walker has most recently suggested as
a common source for both drawings Michel Dorigny's
painting *Pan and Syrinx* in the Louvre,[3] which probably
provided as well the inspiration for the other figures
represented in the sculptural relief in Greuze's painting.
Nothing is known about the early history of Dorigny's
picture, which was acquired by the Louvre only in 1949,
except that it was engraved by the artist in 1666.[4]

1 "Cent Antiquaires parisiens,"
Connaissance des arts, May, 1958,
p. 55
2 Diderot, *Salons*, III, p. 225

3 Rosenberg, Reynaud and Compin,
I, No. 221
4 Information kindly communicated
by M. Sylvain Laveissière, February
26, 1976

57 Lot and His Daughters
Oil, on canvas, 28⅛ x 31½ in. (71.5 x 80.0 cm)
Strasbourg, private collection

Collections: Caroline Greuze, Paris; her sale, Paris, January
25–26, 1843, lot 4; Richard Wallace, Paris; his sale, Paris,
March 2–3, 1857, lot 46, sold for 900 francs; Charles
Sedelmeyer, Paris; his sale, Paris, April 22, 1896, lot 26,
sold for 1,980 francs to Lasquin; Dr. Hans Wendland,
Lugano; his sale, Berlin, April 15–16, 1931, lot 61;
Hermann Voss

   Bibliography: Brookner, p. 109; Martin-Masson, Nos. 14,
15; Wallace Collection Catalogues, *Pictures and Drawings*,
London, 1968, p. 139

This little-known but important picture appears to be
one of the several exercises in history painting Greuze
undertook prior to *Septimius Severus* (No. 70), in this case
treating the Biblical subject of Lot's incest with his
daughters (Genesis 19). The empty wine jugs whose contents
intoxicated Lot are visible in the foreground, and his
elder daughter, who slept with him the first night, lies by
his side. The younger daughter, who will follow the next
night, anxiously observes the scene of debauchery.

   The incestuous subject recalls the overtones of the
classical theme of the Roman Charity which Greuze was
treating at the same period (Nos. 59, 60). Both stories had
a loftier interest than lubricity, for Pero in the Roman
Charity risked her life to preserve her father's, and the
intention of Lot's daughters in sleeping with him in the
absence of any other man was to "in this way keep the
family alive through our father."

   Théophile Thoré incorrectly identified the subject of this
picture in the catalogue of the Caroline Greuze sale as
Noah and his daughters. In the same sale was a drawing for
the figure of Lot (lot 46), again misinterpreted by Thoré
as Noah.

   The striking similarities between the recumbent figure of
Lot in the present painting and the central figure in
Daumier's lithograph *La rue Transnonain, le 15 avril 1834*,
as well as other elements of the composition, suggest that
Daumier may have known the painting while it was still
in the collection of Greuze's daughter Caroline, a
fellow artist.

58 Female Nude with Arms Outstretched

Red chalk, on white paper, 11½ x 16⅝ in. (29.2 x 42.1 cm)
Paris, Fondation Custodia (Coll. F. Lugt), Institut
Néerlandais

Collections: Samuel Leith, Edinburgh (Lugt 1767); his sale,
Edinburgh, February 13–20, 1858; Hippolyte Walferdin,
Paris; his sale, Paris, April 12–16, 1880, lot 312; Louis-
Auguste, baron de Schwiter, Paris (Lugt 1768); his sale,
Paris, April 20–21, 1883, lot 61, sold for 88 francs; Albert
Besnard, Paris; his sale, Paris, May 31—June 1, 1934, lot
283, purchased by Frits Lugt (Lugt 1028)
    Exhibitions: Brussels, Palais des Beaux-Arts, Rotterdam,
Museum Boymans-van Beuningen and Paris, Orangerie
des Tuileries, Le Dessin français de Fouquet à Cézanne,
1949–50, No. 81; Paris, Institut Néerlandais and Amsterdam,
Rijksmuseum, Le Dessin français dans les collections
hollandaises, 1964, No. 92; Amsterdam, Rijksmuseum,
Franse Tekenkunst van de 18de Eeuw uit Nederlandse
Verzamelingen, 1974, No. 55
    Bibliography: G. Bauer, *Dessins français du XVIIIè siècle:
La Figure humaine,* Paris, 1959, Pl. 119; Martin-Masson,
No. 1311 (?); Mauclair, repr. p. 136

This fine drawing appears to be the earliest known study
for the several representations of Saint Mary of Egypt
executed by Greuze late in his career (see Nos. 110, 113).
A lost version of that subject showing the Saint with
blond hair was dated by Martin to 1760, but without
substantiation; the earliest record of that painting dates
only from the Duclos-Dufresnoy sale of 1795. The style of
the present sheet and even the appearance of the model
compare with other life drawings Greuze was executing
around 1768 (see fig. 18, Nos. 59, 64). Possibly he turned
to this study many years later as he evolved the subject of
the penitent sinner.
    On the back of the old mount of the present drawing are
three studies of feet in red chalk. While they resemble
those in Greuze's *Morning Prayer* (Montpellier, Musée
Fabre), they probably were drawn by Albert Besnard
(1849–1934), an artist who imitated the manner of
eighteenth-century draughtsmen and who once owned
this sheet.

59 Seated Female Nude

Red chalk, on cream paper, 17½ x 14½ in. (44.5 x 36.8 cm)
Signed: *J B G*
Cambridge, Massachusetts, Fogg Museum of Art, Harvard
University, Meta and Paul J. Sachs Collection

Collections: Caroline Greuze, Paris; her sale, Paris, January
25–26, 1843, lot 29, sold for 30 francs; Delbecq, Ghent;
his sale, Paris, January 20, 1845, lot 104, sold for 30 francs;
Emile Straus, Paris, 1886; his sale, Paris, June 3, 1929,
lot 72; sold by Birnbaum to Paul J. Sachs in 1929; entered
the Fogg Museum of Art in 1965

  Exhibitions: R. A., 1932, No. 781; Pittsburgh, Junior
League, Old Master Drawings, 1933–34, No. 15;
Copenhagen, Palais de Charlottenborg, L'Art français du
XVIIIè siècle, 1935, No. 396; Paris, Palais National des
Arts, Chefs-d'oeuvre de l'art français, 1937, No. 547; San
Francisco, Palace of Fine Arts, Golden Gate International
Exposition, 1940, No. 49; Hartford, Wadsworth Atheneum,
The Nude in Art, 1946, No. 28; New York, Century
Association, 1947; Detroit Institute of Arts and Richmond,
Virginia Museum of Fine Arts, French Drawings of Five
Centuries from the Collection of The Fogg Museum of Art,
1951–52, No. 19; Waterville, Maine, Colby College,
Drawings, 1956, No. 13; Rotterdam, Museum Boymans-van
Beuningen, Paris, Musée de l'Orangerie and New York,
Metropolitan Museum of Art, French Drawings from
American Collections, Clouet to Matisse, 1958–59, No. 60

  Bibliography: F. Boucher and P. Jacottet, *Le Dessin
français au XVIIIè siècle*, Lausanne, [1952], No. 79; W. R.
Deusch, *Die Aktzeichnung in der Europäischen Kunst*, Bonn,
1952, No. 63, Pl. 63, p. 103; Martin-Masson, Nos. 226,
1310; J. Mathey, "Greuze et Fragonard copistes de Rubens,"
Bulletin de la Société de l'Histoire de l'Art français, 1933, No.
2, pp. 183–87; A. Mongan and P. J. Sachs, *Drawings in The
Fogg Museum of Art*, Cambridge, 1940, I, No. 623, p. 331,
III, fig. 312; Munhall, 1965, pp. 26, 27; S. de Ricci, *Les
Dessins français*, Paris, 1937, Pl. XX; H. Tietze, *European
Master Drawings in The United States*, New York, [c. 1947],
pp. 210, 211; J. Watrous, *The Craft of Old-Master Drawings*,
Madison, Wisconsin, 1957, pp. 120–22; *L'Art*, XLI, 1886,
p. 230

This celebrated drawing dates from the crucial period in
Greuze's career around 1767, when he decided to present to
the Académie as his reception piece a subject appropriate
to history painting rather than one of the genre scenes
with which he had been associated. The gesture of the
woman pressing her breast suggests that the drawing was a
preliminary study for a representation of the classical
theme known as the Roman Charity, the popular subject
taken from Valerius Maximus of Pero breast-feeding her
imprisoned father Cimon after he had been sentenced to die
of starvation. Thoré made this association in cataloguing
the drawing in 1843.[1] It was repeated when the drawing
appeared in the Delbecq sale in 1845,[2] and in 1933 Mathey
related this sheet to Greuze's more complete representation
of the Roman Charity in the drawing from the Louvre
included in this exhibition (No. 60). With the subject of
the Roman Charity Greuze was able to transfer the theme
of the nursing woman, which he had represented
frequently in genre scenes, to the level of history painting.

  In addition to the Louvre drawing, there was formerly
in the Hermitage a related red chalk study of the same
model seen in profile, with her breasts exposed and her
crossed arms resting on a table.[3] A full-figure study of the
same model, seated and with her head again in sharp
profile, is in a Paris private collection. A counterproof of
the present drawing belongs to M. Baderou, Paris. Watrous
pointed out the unusual use in the present sheet of a
greasy red chalk, a medium more frequently encountered
in nineteenth-century works.

  Of the several paintings of the Roman Charity attributed
to Greuze that appeared in nineteenth-century sales,[4] the
only one known at present is a small oil in a Paris private
collection showing Cimon with his hands bound and
Pero holding a cloak to conceal her action.[5]

  Mathey noted the similarities between the Fogg and
Louvre drawings and Rubens' depiction of the same subject
in a painting now in the Hermitage.[6] The fact that the
pose in this drawing reverses that in the painting suggests
that Greuze may have known Rubens' composition from
one of the five engravings executed after it. In any case, the
heroic character of Greuze's figure suggests, as Thoré
commented,[7] a general familiarity with Rubens' style, one
which Greuze could have acquired while studying the
Medici Series in the Palais du Luxembourg in 1760 (see
No. 25).[8]

1   "*Parait être l'étude pour la
Charité romaine.*" ("Appears to be
the study for the Roman Charity.")
T. Thoré, catalogue of the Caroline
Greuze sale, lot 29
2   "*La Charité romaine. Femme nue
et couchée qui se presse le sein.
Sanguine, signée des initiales J. B. G.*"
("The Roman Charity. Nude
reclining woman pressing her
breast. Red chalk, signed with the
initials J. B. G.")
3   Monod-Hautecoeur, No. 134,
Pl. LV

4   See Martin-Masson, No. 226
5   Munhall, 1965, fig. 4, pp. 24, 27
6   R. Oldenbourg, *P. P. Rubens*,
Berlin-Leipzig, n. d., repr. p. 43
7   "*La souplesse du modelé et
l'abondance de l'exécution rappellent
la pratique de Rubens.*" ("The
litheness of the modelling and the
richness of the execution recall the
manner of Rubens.")
Thoré, *loc. cit.*
8   Wille, I, p. 139

60 Cimon and Pero (*La Charité romaine*)

Brush, black ink, gray ink wash, over pencil, on white
paper, 12¾ x 16⅜ in. (32.6 x 41.6 cm)
Paris, Musée du Louvre, Cabinet des Dessins

Collections: original collection of the Cabinet des Dessins,
Musée du Louvre[1]

Exhibitions: Paris, Louvre, Cabinet des Dessins, Dessins
français de 1750 à 1825: Le Néo-classicisme, 1972, No. 10,
Pl. VI

Bibliography: Brookner, p. 108, Pl. 36; Guiffrey-Marcel,
VI, No. 4542, p. 56; Martin-Masson, No. 226; J. Mathey,
"Greuze et Fragonard copistes de Rubens," *Bulletin de la
Société de l'Histoire de l'Art français*, 1933, No. 2, pp. 183–84;
Morel d'Arleux, "Inventaire des dessins du Louvre,"
[1797–1827], ms., Paris, Louvre, IX, No. 12645; Munhall,
1965, pp. 24, 27, fig. 5; A. Pigler, *Barockthemen*, Budapest,
1956, II, p. 284

For a discussion of the iconographical and historical
background of this drawing and related paintings and
drawings see No. 59.

The proximity of the present *Cimon and Pero* to Rubens'
painting of the same subject in the Hermitage is more
pronounced than is that of the *Seated Female Nude* included
in this exhibition (No. 59). The disposition of the two
figures is similar and not reversed, both heads are in profile,
Pero's arm encircles Cimon to draw him closer and a
barred window is indicated at left. It is conceivable that
Greuze had seen Rubens' painting, for it appeared as lot
97 in the de Jullienne sale, Paris, March 30–May 22, 1767.

In 1767, when Greuze most likely executed this powerful
drawing, both Bachelier and Lagrenée treated the same
subject in paintings which are now in the Ecole des
Beaux-Arts, Paris, and the Musée des Augustins, Toulouse,
respectively. Neither resembles the Greuze composition,
but they attest to the popularity of the theme and may
possibly have influenced Greuze in abandoning it as a
vehicle for his Académie reception piece.

The figure of Cimon is not unlike that of the Emperor in
Septimius Severus Reproaching Caracalla (No. 70), and may
have been drawn from the same model employed in Greuze's
pastel study for the latter.[2] The same bearded, thin old man
appears in two contemporary studies—one in the Musée
Bonnat at Bayonne (fig. 5),[3] the other formerly in the
Baderou collection, Paris—for the fallen figure in *The
Death of Cato of Utica*, another historical subject Greuze
experimented with in the late 1760s.

1 Since Martin-Masson (No. 226),
this drawing has occasionally been
erroneously identified with lot 111
in the Warneck sale, Paris,
November 26–27, 1841, which was
in fact a painting.

2 Munhall, 1965, fig. 10, p. 27
3 No. 1643; Martin-Masson,
No. 1337

61 Seated Woman Holding a Book
(Study for *Reflections*)
Brush, black and brown ink, over pencil, on white paper,
6 x 4⅜ in. (15.3 x 11.0 cm)
Tournus, Musée Greuze

Collections: marquis de Chennevières, Paris (Lugt 2072);
his sale, Paris, May 5–6, 1898, lot 223, acquired by the
museum
   Bibliography: Martin-Masson, No. 200; Munhall, 1964,
p. 7

This spirited little drawing is a study for a lost painting
entitled *Reflections* (*Le Retour sur soy-même*), which was
engraved by Louis Binet.[1] The subject of the print is an
elderly woman reflecting on the contents of a large book
she holds on her lap, clearly identified in the engraving as a
"*Vie des saints*" and open to the "*Chapitre de la Magdalein.*"
This is another of Greuze's representations of figures
absorbed in thought. Religious writers of the eighteenth
century, particularly Protestants, stressed the importance of
such reflective activity, in texts such as this by the Reverend
Ostervald: "*il y en a d'autres* [duties] *qui ne sont pas
moins essentiels, lesquels on néglige généralement: comme la
méditation, la lecture, l'examen de soi-même pour ne rien dire ici*

des devoirs de la sanctification."[2]
   In executing this drawing Greuze may have had in mind
a similar work by Gerrit Dou, his popular *Old Woman
Reading*, of which there were in the eighteenth century one
version in the Royal collection (Louvre) and another in
the de Jullienne collection (Hermitage). Wille (No. 39)
executed an engraving after the latter picture in 1761.[3]
   Greuze's painting of *Reflections*, according to the
inscription on Binet's engraving, belonged to the
miniaturist and engraver Johann Anton de Peters, who was
described by Wille as an "*habile peintre en miniature, qui a
un cabinet de tableaux.*"[4] It subsequently appeared in the
Robert de Saint-Victor sale, Paris, November 26, 1822, lot
530. De Peters' genre paintings were strongly influenced
by Greuze.
   Binet's print is undated, but marked formal similarities
between this drawing and Greuze's study for *Sophronie*
(No. 62) suggest a date around 1768.

1 Portalis-Béraldi, I, p. 189
2 "there are others [duties] no
less essential, which are generally
neglected: such as meditation,
reading, self-examination, to say
nothing here of the duties of
sanctification." J. F. Ostervald,

*Traité des sources de la corruption qui
règne aujourd'hui parmi les Chrétiens*,
Amsterdam, 1709, p. 239
3 Wille, I, pp. 171–72
4 "skillful painter of miniatures,
who has a collection of pictures."
Ibid., p. 251

1 "He throws himself at her feet.
You see her, cries he, darting a
touching glance at her. Ah!
Madame, let yourself be moved;
deign to grant me her hand, you
will fulfill all my wishes.
Sophronie appears confused; shame
lowers her brow, while a charming
modesty shines on her daughter's
face." Madame Benoist [F.-A. Puzin
de la Martinière], *Sophronie*, London,
1769, p. 40
2 "that he is rather annoyed
that his friend Greuze wastes
his time working like a Gravelot
or a Charles Eisen instead of
working like a Greuze; that he
will doubtless turn out these
sorry things better than the other
book illustrators; but that the
habit of making such trifles . . .
and the rage to put illustrations
into books will ruin the arts in
France, precisely because they
enable artists to earn a lot of money
in a short time; finally that he
wishes his friend Greuze would
concern himself only with glory
and scorn money, which, moreover,
he does not lack. . . ." Baron F.
Melchior von Grimm,
*Correspondance littéraire, philosophique
et critique*, ed. M. Tourneux, Paris,
VIII, 1879, pp. 356–57

62 Compositional Study for *Sophronie*

Brush, brown ink, on white paper, 9⁷⁄₁₆ x 9⁷⁄₁₆ in. (24.0 x
24.0 cm)

Karlsruhe, Staatliche Kunsthalle, Kupferstichkabinett

Collections: Groult, Paris (?); Baderou, Paris; anonymous
sale, Paris, December 9, 1961, lot 6; Matthieson, Ltd.,
London; Z. Bruck, Buenos Aires, 1964; acquired by the
museum from Stefanie Maison, London

  Bibliography: H. Cohen, *Guide de l'amateur de livres à
vignettes du XVIIIè siècle*, Paris, 1873, pp. 17–18; Martin-
Masson, No. 408; Munhall, 1961, pp. 237–42; Portalis-
Béraldi, III, p. 169

  Engraving: J.-M. Moreau *le jeune*, 1769

According to the inscription below Moreau *le jeune*'s
engraving of this subject, Greuze executed it in 1768 for the
frontispiece of Madame Benoist's novel *Sophronie, ou la
leçon prétendue d'une mère à sa fille*, published in London in
1769. The composition illustrates the book's climactic
incident, in which Sophronie, who had staged for her
daughter Adelle's edification a mock seduction with
Valzan, is embarrassed by Adelle's entrance into her boudoir
and by Valzan's impassioned request for the daughter's
hand. The text clarifies the subject: "*Il se jette à ses pieds.
Vous la voyez, s'écrie-t-il, en jettant sur elle un regard touchant.
Ah! Madame, laissez-vous fléchir; daignez m'accorder sa main,
vous comblerés tous mes voeux. Sophronie paroit confondue; la

honte abbaisse son front, tandis qu'une pudeur charmante brille
sur le visage de sa fille.*"1

  After being barred from the Salon of 1767 for not having
presented his reception piece, Greuze attempted to keep
himself before the public by entering the field of literary
illustration, then very profitable. So far as is known,
however, he executed only two other illustrations, one for
Billardon de Sauvigny's *La Rose, ou la fête de Salency* (study
with Colnaghi, London, in 1965) and one for the
Baskerville edition of *Orlando furioso*, published in
Birmingham about 1775 (fig. 13). In 1769 Baron Grimm
was sufficiently aware of this development in Greuze's
career to note "*qu'il est assez fâché que son ami Greuze
perde son temps à faire le Gravelot ou le Charles Eisen au lieu de
faire le Greuze; qu'il fera sans doute ces pauvretés mieux que
les autres faiseurs de dessins pour livres; mais que l'habitude de
faire de pareilles minuties . . . et la fureur de mettre des images
dans les livres perdront les arts en France, précisément parce
qu'elles font gagner aux artistes beaucoup d'argent en peu de
temps; enfin qu'il voudrait que son ami Greuze ne fît cas que de la
gloire et méprisât l'argent qui, d'ailleurs ne lui manque pas. . . .*"2

  The tempestuous character of this drawing—which is
probably too rough to have served as the direct model for
Moreau's engraving—and that of similar drawings reflects
once again Greuze's enthusiasm for Rembrandt. A drawing
for the figure of Valzan is included in this exhibition
(No. 63). Another, for Adelle, is in the Victoria and
Albert Museum, London.

63 Kneeling Youth with Arms Outstretched
(Study for *Sophronie*)
Red chalk, on white paper, 14¼ x 11¾ in. (36.2 x 29.9 cm)
Cambridge, Massachusetts, Fogg Museum of Art, Harvard
University, Meta and Paul J. Sachs Collection

Collections: Georges Bourgarel, Paris; his sale, Paris, June
15–16, 1922, lot 96; Baderou, Paris; acquired from Richard
Owen by Paul J. Sachs in 1927; entered the Fogg Museum
of Art in 1965

Exhibitions: Santa Barbara Museum of Art, 1943; New
York, Century Association, 1947; Detroit Institute of Arts
and Richmond, Virginia Museum of Fine Arts, French
Drawings of Five Centuries from the Collection of The
Fogg Museum of Art, 1951–52; Baltimore Museum of Art,
Age of Elegance: The Rococo and Its Effect, 1959, No. 56;
Cambridge, Fogg Museum of Art and New York, Museum
of Modern Art, Memorial Exhibition: Works of Art from
the Collection of Paul J. Sachs (1878–1965), 1965–66,
No. 31

Bibliography: A. Mongan and P. J. Sachs, *Drawings in The
Fogg Museum of Art*, Cambridge, 1940, I, No. 624, p. 332,
III, fig. 313; Munhall, 1961, pp. 237–38, 242, fig. 2, p. 239

This is a study for the figure of Valzan in Greuze's
frontispiece for Madame Benoist's novel *Sophronie*, a general
compositional sketch for which is also included in this
exhibition (No. 62). Valzan is here seen striking an
imploring stance as he requests the hand of Sophronie's
daughter in marriage.

Valzan's expression is more impassioned in this drawing
than in Moreau's *le jeune*'s engraving of the frontispiece.
The sword at his side is omitted in the print.

The medium is the same fabricated red chalk Greuze used
for the *Seated Female Nude* of about the same period (No. 59).

64 Female Nude with Arms Raised
Red chalk, on white paper, 13⁷⁄₁₆ x 18³⁄₁₆ in. (34.5 x 46.2 cm)
Paris, private collection

Collections: Caroline Greuze, Paris; her sale, Paris, January
25–26, 1843, lot 30; acquired in Paris in 1976

This vigorous study seems related to *Aegina Visited by
Jupiter* (No. 65). The association is strengthened by the
existence of a similar drawing (fig. 18) which resembles the
painting more strongly and which was coupled with this
one in the sale held in 1843 after the death of Greuze's
daughter Caroline (lots 30, 31). In comparison with the
figure in the painting, that in the present drawing appears to
be in a state closer to ecstasy than to apprehension.

Particularly in the late 1760s, Greuze's female nudes have
a muscular solidity totally unlike the luscious softness of
his contemporary Boucher's female figures. While this
disparity may be attributable in part to differences in
personal style and preferences in models, it more likely
reflects Greuze's familiarity with and emulation of antique
sculpture, after which he was making drawings during the
same period (see fig. 3, Nos. 67, 68).

Another drawing of the same model, shown with her
arms at her sides, is in the Musée Bonnat, Bayonne
(No. 1647).

65 Aegina Visited by Jupiter

Oil, on canvas, 57⅞ x 77⅛ in. (146.7 x 195.9 cm)
New York, The Metropolitan Museum of Art, Gift of
Harry N. Abrams and Joseph Pultizer Bequest, Pfeiffer,
Fletcher and Rogers Funds, 1970

Collections: Caroline Greuze, Paris (?); Lapeyrière, Paris;
his sale, Paris, April 19, 1825, lot 185, sold for 801 francs to
Dubois; E. Rhoné (or Rosné), Paris, 1846; Bonnet, Paris,
1860; his sale, Paris, June 2, 1885, lot 1, sold for 40,000
francs; Brame, Paris; Levesque, Paris, 1900; G. Trotti et
Cie., Paris, 1923;[1] baron Maurice de Rothschild, Paris,
1926; Wildenstein et Cie., Paris; William Randolph Hearst,
New York, 1939; his sale, New York, 1941, lot 301-4;
Wildenstein and Co., New York, 1941; H. N. Abrams,
New York, 1968 (in part); acquired by the museum in 1970
   Exhibitions: Paris, 26 boulevard des Italiens, Tableaux
. . . exposes au profit de la caisse de secours des artistes
peintres, 1860; Paris, Exposition Universelle, Exposition
centennale de l'art français, 1900, No. 334; Amsterdam,
Rijksmuseum, Exposition rétrospective d'art français, 1926,
No. 59; San Francisco, Golden Gate International
Exposition, Masterworks of Five Centuries, 1939, No. 116;
New York, Wildenstein and Co., The Nude in Painting,
1956, No. 15, Benefit Exhibition for The Arthritis

Fig. 18 Reclining Female Nude,
study for *Aegina Visited by Jupiter*,
red chalk, Camden, Maine,
Eric H. L. Sexton collection

Foundation, 1968, and Gods and Heroes: Baroque Images of Antiquity, 1968–69, No. 17

Bibliography: G. Brière, *Catalogue des peintures, Musée National du Louvre*, 1924, I, p. 120; L. Gillet, *La Peinture au Musée du Louvre*, I, 1929, p. 67; Goncourt, I, p. 347; T. Lejeune, *Guide . . . de l'amateur de tableaux*, Paris, 1864, p. 278; Martin-Masson, No. 1277; C. Sterling, *The Metropolitan Museum of Art: A Catalogue of French Paintings, XV-XVIII Centuries*, Cambridge, 1955, p. 177

Engravings: L. Flameng, 1860; M.-G. Desboutin

Despite its familiarity and imposing size, this picture remains relatively unstudied and presents problems both historical and iconographical.

There are no references to it dating from the eighteenth century, though Greuze may have had this subject in mind when he said to Diderot in 1767, *"je voudrais bien peindre une femme toute nue, sans blesser la pudeur."*[2] In 1860 Thoré thought he recalled having seen the painting in the studio of Caroline Greuze before her death in 1842.[3]

The subject has been identified both as Danaë, who was confined with her maid by her father Acrisius and was visited by Jupiter in the form of a shower of gold, and as Aegina, daughter of the river Asopus, who was visited by Jupiter in the guise of fire and was later carried off by him in the form of an eagle. The latter identification has the inclusion of the eagle in its favor, the former the presence of the maid and the suggestion of some indefinite form descending in the middle background. The existence of a small variant of the subject in the Louvre, with compositional differences but with a shower of gold clearly indicated, would support the

association with Danaë, but neither identification is entirely satisfactory. In the Lapeyrière sale of 1825, the present picture was listed as *Jupiter et Danaë*, but the catalogue noted that *"une lumière remplace ici la pluie d'or."*[4] Such is the case in another celebrated *Danaë* which Greuze might have known—Rembrandt's picture of 1636 (Hermitage), one of the major paintings in the Crozat collection at the time Greuze executed the present work.

Greuze was barred by the Académie from the Salon of 1767 for having failed to present his *morceau de réception*. Having decided to present himself as a history rather than a genre painter, he experimented in the late 1760s with a number of historical and mythological subjects before settling on the confrontation of Septimius Severus and Caracalla (No. 70). *Aegina Visited by Jupiter* may have been an attempt at the *morceau de réception*, left unfinished. Indeed, it shares a number of features with *Septimius Severus Reproaching Caracalla*: its size, the representation of a central nude figure of heroic proportions on a bed with ample draperies, the presence of a tripod table copied from the antique and hanging draperies employed as a backdrop.

A small copy of the present picture appeared in the Ricketts sale, Paris, December 8–12, 1846, lot 423, sold for 200 francs. In the museum at Metz is a version of the above-mentioned compositional variant in the Louvre. There is also a study for the head of Aegina in the Louvre. A preparatory drawing for the full figure of Aegina (fig. 18) appeared in the Caroline Greuze sale, Paris, January 25–26, 1843, lot 31, and is now in the Sexton collection, Camden, Maine. Another related drawing is included in this exhibition (No. 64).

1 See "Trotti et Cie., place Vendôme," *La Renaissance de l'art*, June, 1923, p. 362
2 "I should very much like to paint a woman totally nude, without offending modesty." Diderot, *Salons*, III, p. 109
3 W. Burger [T. Thoré], "Exposition de tableaux de l'école française ancienne, tirés de collections d'amateurs," *Gazette des Beaux-Arts*, November, 1860, p. 237, described as *"une des oeuvres les plus curieuses et les plus importantes de Greuze"* ("one of the most curious and most important works by Greuze").
4 "a light replaces here the shower of gold"

66 The Funeral of Patroclus

Red chalk, on white paper, 17¾ x 22⁷⁄₁₆ in. (45.0 x 57.0 cm)
Signed: *Greuze*
Paris, private collection

Collections: Madame de Conantré, Paris; her daughter,
baronne de Ruble, Paris; her daughter, Madame de Witte,
Paris; marquise de Bryas, née de Witte, Paris; Galerie
Cailleux, Paris

   Exhibitions: Paris, Galerie Cailleux, Le Dessin français de
Watteau à Prud'hon, 1951, No. 186, and Autour du
Néoclassicisme, 1973, No. 12

Apart from his early academic work, Greuze left few
studies of the male nude. This fine drawing must date from
the prolific period around 1767–68 when the artist resolved
to abandon genre scenes for the grander arena of history
painting. The anatomical precision of his early work
remains (compare No. 4), but this drawing has a fresh
emotional intensity and grandeur of composition which may
reflect Greuze's study of Rubens. Indeed, the recumbent
figure seen here recalls the sculpture representing the dead
Christ shown above the altar in Rubens' *Marriage by Proxy*
(Louvre), a painting from which Greuze copied two heads
in 1760 (No. 25). The reversal of the pose could have
resulted from another of Greuze's frequent uses of
counterproofs.

   The subject of this sheet has long resisted identification.
Considering Greuze's interest in antique themes at the
probable time of its execution, it seems plausible to suggest
that the artist may have intended it as a study for a
painting of the funeral of Patroclus, in which he planned to
show Achilles covering his fallen comrade's body with a
drapery. The funeral of Patroculus was in 1769 the
Académie's subject for the Prix de Rome competition, and
David's painting on this theme (Dublin, National Gallery
of Ireland), dated 1779, has as its focus a pair of figures
not unlike those shown here.[1]

1 See: Detroit Institute of Arts
and New York, Metropolitan
Museum of Art, French Painting
1774–1830: The Age of Revolution,
exhib. cat., 1975, No. 27, repr. p. 54

67 Studies of Male Heads after the Antique

Red chalk, on white paper, 6⅜ x 12⁹⁄₁₆ in. (16.3 x 31.9 cm)
Lyon, Musée Lyonnais des Arts Décoratifs

Collections: Musée d'Art et d'Industrie, Lyon, until 1890
(Lugt S 1699 a); Musée historique des Tissus, Lyon, until
1925

While this drawing bears no specific relationship to
Septimius Severus Reproaching Caracalla (No. 70), the fact
that it is drawn after antique models suggests that it was
executed around 1767–68 during the period when Greuze
was studying sources for a number of subjects taken from
Roman history, including his reception painting.

The drawing appears at first glance to support the theory
of Beaucousin, who wrote of *Septimius Severus* that *"les
têtes copiées d'après des médailles, ont la dureté et le ton de cuivre."*[1]
However, at least two of the heads in the painting were
based on Roman busts, and the sources for this drawing
apparently were not medals but relief sculptures and a seal.

The profile of a bearded man wearing a cap at lower
right and again at upper left would seem to derive from a
similar profile on the Column of Trajan, a cast of which,
made under Girardon's supervision, was in the Louvre in
the eighteenth century.[2] The head of the older bearded
man at bottom to the left of center, whose features are
strongly reminiscent of Socrates', resembles that carved on
an antique seal representing the Greek philosopher which
Diderot employed in sealing all his letters to Falconet,
some letters to Sophie Volland and perhaps also some to
Greuze.[3] As Seznec has pointed out, Diderot wrote in 1761
that in order to appreciate Challe's *Socrates About to Drink
the Hemlock, "il faut avoir vu beaucoup de bas-reliefs,
beaucoup de médailles, beaucoup de pierres gravées."*[4] Diderot
may have expressed similar ideas directly to Greuze during
the latter's search for antique models.

1 "the heads, copied after medals,
have the harshness and tone of
copper." M.-B. Beaucousin, *Lettres
sur le Salon de peinture de 1769*, Paris,
1769, p. 24
2 K. Lehmann-Hartleben, *Die
Trajanssaeule*, Berlin, 1926, I, fig.
28. This relationship and
information on the cast kindly
communicated by Dean Walker
3 J. Seznec, *Essais sur Diderot et
l'antiquité*, Oxford, 1967, pp. 21–22,
fig. 4
4 "it is necessary to have seen
many bas-reliefs, many medals,
many engraved stones." Diderot,
Salons, I, p. 124

1 "is drawn after the antique."
"The expression the artist has given to Severus seems to us less fortunate. If Poussin had had a comparable subject to treat he would have shed on the countenance of this Prince a calmer and more tranquil air, one suitable to an Emperor. . . . He would have made this Prince's indignation perceptible merely by a slight movement of the eyebrows, but one which would have caused him to lose nothing of that august character of grandeur which should always distinguish the Prince and the hero." "Arts: Exposition des peintures, sculptures, gravures de M.M. de l'Académie Royale," *L'Avant-Coureur*, September 11, 1769, p. 394
2 "I sought above all the art of putting expression into the faces." "I do not give in so easily on the character that you claim he [Poussin] would have given the Emperor. Everyone knows that Severus was the most fiery, the most violent of all men; and you would prefer that when he says to his son, *if you desire my death, order Papinian to give it to me with that sword*, he would have in his picture, like Solomon under comparable circumstances, a calm and tranquil air; I ask every sensible man to judge, was that the expression that should have been painted on the countenance of this redoutable Emperor?" J.-B. Greuze, "Lettre à l'auteur," *L'Avant-Coureur*, September 25, 1769, pp. 407–08

68   Head of Septimius Severus

(Study for *Septimius Severus Reproaching Caracalla*)
Red chalk, on white paper, 15⅞ x 11⅝ in. (40.4 x 29.6 cm)
Signed on mount: *Jean-Baptiste Greuze*
France, private collection

Collections: Caroline Greuze, Paris; her sale, Paris, January 25–26, 1843, lot 147; Madame de Conantré, Paris; her daughter, baronne de Ruble, Paris; her daughter, Madame de Witte, Paris; marquise de Bryas, née de Witte, Paris, until 1958; Galerie Cailleux, Paris; acquired in 1973

 Exhibitions: Paris, Galerie Cailleux, Autour du Néoclassicisme, 1973, No. 14

 Bibliography: Martin-Masson, No. 16; Munhall, 1965, pp. 27–28, fig. 8

Like the comparable study for the head of Caracalla (fig. 19), this preparatory study for the Emperor in the artist's *Septimius Severus Reproaching Caracalla* (No. 70) was drawn after a Roman portrait bust or cast in the Louvre. As the owner of the drawing has pointed out, in the painting Greuze changed the young and relatively placid features seen in the drawing to suit the Emperor's advanced age and the stormy drama in which he is engaged.

The critic of the *Avant-Coureur*, who noted that the head of Caracalla "*est dessiné d'après l'antique*," said of the head of Septimius Severus: "*L'expression que l'artiste a donné à Sévère nous paraît moins heureuse. Si le Poussin avait eu un pareil sujet à traiter il aurait répendu sur la phisionomie de ce Prince un air plus calme, plus tranquille et tel que devait l'avoir un Empereur. . . . Il aurait seulement fait appercevoir l'indignation de ce Prince par un leger mouvement des sourcils, mais qui ne lui aurait rien fait perdre de ce caractère auguste de grandeur qui doit toujours distinguer le Prince et le héros.*"[1]
In his reply to this critic Greuze, noting "*j'y ai surtout cherché l'art de mettre l'expression dans les figures*," insisted that his depiction of Septimius Severus was historically correct: "*je ne me rends pas si aisément sur le caractère que vous prétendez qu'il [Poussin] aurait donné à l'Empereur. Tout le monde sçait que Sévère était le plus emporté, le plus violent de tous le hommes; et vous voudriez que lorsqu'il dit à son fils*, si tu désires ma mort, ordonne à Papinien de me la donner avec cette épée, *il eût dans son tableau, comme Salomon en pareille circonstance, un air calme et tranquille; j'en fais juge tout homme sensé, était-ce là l'expression qu'il fallait peindre sur la physionomie de ce redoutable Empereur?*"[2]

69 Head of an Old Man

(Study for *Septimius Severus Reproaching Caracalla*)
Red chalk, on tan paper, 14⁹⁄₁₆ x 11¹⁵⁄₁₆ in. (36.8 x 30.4 cm)
Paris, Musée du Louvre, Cabinet des Dessins

Collections: acquired by the museum from M. Defer in 1842
for 25 francs
Exhibitions: Paris, Musée Royal au Louvre, 1841, No.
1 016, and 1845, No. 1 016[1]
Bibliography: Brookner, pp. 109, 110, Pl. 40; Guiffrey-
Marcel, VI, p. 60, No. 4576 (repr. as No. 4976); Martin-
Masson, No. 1684; Munhall, 1965, pp. 27-28, fig. 7;
Reiset, II, p. 770; J. Seznec, "Diderot et l'affaire Greuze,"
Gazette des Beaux-Arts, May–June, 1966, pp. 342, 345, 346,
347, 348, 350, fig. 4

This drawing of a deeply troubled old man is a study for
the head of Papinian in *Septimius Severus Reproaching
Caracalla* (No. 70). Unlike the comparable study for the
head of the Emperor (No. 68), it appears to have been
drawn from life. In this preparation for a history painting
Greuze utilized his familiar talent for capturing in
naturalistic fashion the subtleties of emotions.

The identification of the figure as the celebrated jurist
Papinian depends from Greuze's literary source, Pierre Le
Pesant's translation of the *Roman History* of Cassius Dio,
in which Papinian's presence at the confrontation of
Septimius and Caracalla is indicated twice (see No. 70).[2]
When Diderot saw a preparatory version of *Septimius
Severus* in 1767 he misidentified Papinian but admired
Greuze's painting of him, writing in a letter to Falconet:
"*Le centurion est au chevet, la tête baissée, et confondu d'étonne-
ment et d'indignation. C'est une belle, une très belle figure que ce
vieux soldat à longue barbe et à la tête demi-chauve.*"[3] In his
Salon commentary of 1769 Diderot, this time identifying

Papinian correctly, continued to admire the head: "*La
tête de Papinien est très belle mais elle n'est pas du reste du
corps, sa tête est faite pour être grande et le corps pour rester petit.*"[4]
Diderot suggested that Greuze should have cut up his
painting and gone home "*pour y encadrer les têtes merveilleuses
de Papinien et du sénateur qu'il aurait épargnées au milieu de
la destruction du reste.*"[5]

Cochin's official criticism of *Septimius Severus* spoke of
"*les expressions . . . malheureusement attachées à des caractères de
testes bas et triviaux.*"[6] Many critics repeated this opinion,
and many shared Diderot's initial difficulty in identifying
the obscure characters. Beaucousin found the heads failing
in expression: "*Vous avez voulu donner à vos personnages des
regards sombres, et ils n'ont que des yeux enfoncés. Le Père
malheureux, le Fils parricide, les Officiers fidèles, n'ont pas la
phisionomie plus heureuse les uns que les autres, ou plutôt ils n'en
ont personne.*"[7] The author of the *Sentimens sur les tableaux
exposés au Salon*, whom Mariette identified as Daudet de
Jossac, felt that, "*Les têtes en sont fort belles, modelées et
dessinées sçavamment, et peintes de ce style que vous lui
connoissiez.*"[8] The critic of the *Avant-Coureur* was impressed
specifically by the expressive character of the head of
Papinian: "*Papinien . . . a la tête penchée. Il est comme
accablé du poids des sentiments que doivent élever dans le coeur
d'un homme vertueux les reproches que L'Empereur fait à son fils.*"[9]

In his letter defending the painting published in the
Avant-Coureur, Greuze referred to Papinian only in passing:
"*Une autre injustice bien plus grande encore, c'est . . . d'avoir
voulu imaginer que j'eusse eu l'idée de peindre Geta, frère de
Caracalla, dans le personnage que j'ai placée derrière Papinien.*"[10]

A counterproof of the present drawing is in the Cabinet
des Dessins at the Louvre (No. 26970). Similar studies for
the heads of Caracalla and Castor (figs. 19, 20) are in the
Musée Bonnat, Bayonne (Nos. 1841, 1642).

1 *Notice des Dessins placés dans les galeries du Musée Royal au Louvre*, Paris, 1841 and 1845
2 Cassius Dio Cocceianus, *Histoire romaine*, trans. P. Le Pesant, Sieur de Boisguillebert, Paris, 1674, II, p. 224
3 "The centurion is at the head of the bed, his head lowered, and overwhelmed with astonishment and indignation. It is a beautiful, a very beautiful face, this old soldier with long beard and balding head." Diderot, *Correspondance*, VII, pp. 102–03
4 "The head of Papinian is very beautiful but it does not go with

the rest of the body, the head is made to be large and the body to remain small." Diderot, *Salons*, IV, p. 106
5 "to frame there the marvelous heads of Papinian and the senator, which he would have spared in the midst of destroying the rest." *Ibid.*, p. 104
6 "the expressions . . . unhappily attached to base and trivial sorts of heads." Quoted in J. Seznec, "Diderot et l'affaire Greuze," *Gazette des Beaux-Arts*, May–June, 1966, p. 345
7 "You wanted to give your characters somber looks, and all

they have are sunken eyes. The unfortunate Father, the parricidal Son, the faithful Officers, do not have a happier aspect some more than the others, or rather none of them does." M.-B. Beaucousin, *Lettres sur le Salon de peinture en 1769*, Paris, 1769, p. 24
8 "The heads in it are quite beautiful, skillfully modelled and drawn, and painted in the style that you used to associate with him." [Daudet de Jossac], *Sentimens sur les tableaux exposés au Salon*, Paris, 1769, p. 20
9 "Papinian . . . has his head lowered. He appears overwhelmed

by the weight of the feelings that the Emperor's reproaches to his son must raise in the heart of a virtuous man." "Arts: Exposition des peintures, sculptures, gravures de M.M. de l'Académie Royale," *L'Avant-Coureur*, September 11, 1769, p. 394
10 "Another injustice much greater still is . . . having wished to imagine that I should have had the idea of painting Geta, Caracalla's brother, in the person that I placed behind Papinian." J.-B. Greuze, "Lettre à l'auteur," *L'Avant-Coureur*, September 25, 1769, p. 408

70 **Septimius Severus Reproaching Caracalla**
(*L'Empereur Sévère reproche à Caracalla son fils,
d'avoir voulu l'assassiner dans les défilés d'Ecosse, et
lui dit: Si tu désires ma mort, ordonne à Papinien de
me la donner avec cette épée*)
Oil, on canvas, 48¹³⁄₁₆ x 63¹⁄₁₆ in. (124.0 x 160.0 cm)
Paris, Musée du Louvre

Collections: Paris, Académie Royale de Peinture et de
Sculpture

Exhibitions: Salon of 1769, No. 151; Cleveland Museum of
Art, Neoclassicism: Style and Motif, 1964, No. 33; R. A.,
1968, No. 307; R. A., 1972, No. 119; Antwerp, Le Néo-
classicisme, 1972, No. 15; Paris, Louvre, La "Mort de
Germanicus" de Poussin du Musée de Minneapolis, 1973,
No. 92

Bibliography: Bachaumont, *Mémoires secrets*, XIII, pp.
54–57; H. Bardon, "Les Peintures à sujets antiques au
XVIIIè siècle d'après les livrets de Salons," *Gazette des
Beaux-Arts*, April, 1963, p. 224, fig. 1, p. 219; Brookner,
pp. 67–70, 109–10, Pl. 41; [Daudet de Jossac], *Sentimens sur
les tableaux exposés au Salon*, Paris, 1769, pp. 19–20; D.
Diderot, *Lettres à Sophie Volland*, Paris, 1930, III, p. 215, and
Salons, IV, pp. 41–44, 103–07; A. Fontaine, *Les Collections
de l'Académie Royale de Peinture et de Sculpture*, Paris, 1910,
p. 200; T. W. Gaehtgens, "Diderot und Vien," *Zeitschrift
für Kunstgeschichte*, 1973, p. 65, fig. 9; Goncourt, I, pp.
306–10; Hautecoeur, pp. 20, 65–68; R. Ingrams,
"Bauchaumont: A Parisian Connoisseur of The Eighteenth
Century," *Gazette des Beaux-Arts*, January, 1970, p.
23; C.-L. F. Lecarpentier, *Notice sur Greuze lu dans la
séance de la Société libre d'Emulation de Rouen*, [Rouen], 1805,
p. 4; J. Locquin, *La Peinture d'Histoire en France de 1747 à
1785*, Paris, 1912, pp. 36, 168, 249, 250, 253, Pl. XIX;
Martin-Masson, No. 16; Munhall, 1965, pp. 22–29, 59;
Rosenberg, Reynaud and Compin, I, No. 319; R. Rosenblum,
Transformations in Late Eighteenth Century Art, Princeton,
1967, pp. 54–55; J. Seznec, "Diderot et l'affaire Greuze,"
Gazette des Beaux-Arts, May–June, 1966, pp. 339–56, fig. 1,
p. 340; J. Thuillier and A. Châtelet, *French Painting from
Le Nain to Fragonard*, Geneva, 1964, pp. 228–29; Valori,
p. 369; Wille, I, p. 415

Subjected to nearly universal abuse since its creation,
Septimius Severus Reproaching Caracalla was the long-awaited
morceau de réception with which Greuze was elected in 1769
to full membership in the Académie, but only in the
capacity of a genre painter and not that of a history
painter as the subject of the work indicated and as the
artist fully expected. The stylistic innovations of *Septimius
Severus Reproaching Caracalla*, and indeed its real quality,
have been obscured by the scandal that accompanied its

presentation and that all but obviated any influence the
picture might have had on the evolution of neoclassical
painting.

Seznec has most satisfactorily recounted and analyzed
the complex events surrounding its presentation, which was
for Greuze, in Diderot's words, "*une scène mortifiante.*"[1]

Barred from exhibiting in the Salon of 1767 because of his
fourteen-year delay in presenting a reception painting,
which normally was expected within six months of an
artist's being awarded associate membership, Greuze
aspired not merely to full membership but, like many
artists in 1767, to the post in the Académie that was about
to be left vacant by Michel van Loo and was reserved for
a history painter.[2] In addition to seeking the practical
advantages of that appointment, Greuze had an evaluation
of his own talents that made intolerable any classification
of them below the highest.

In the years between the Salon of 1765 and that of 1769
Greuze had experimented with a number of subjects drawn
from history and mythology, including *Aegina Visited by
Jupiter* (No. 65), *Cimon and Pero* (No. 60), *The Death of Cato
of Utica* (fig. 5) and *Vespasian and Sabinus* (Chaumont,
Musée d'Art et d'Histoire). He was also learning how to
compose a history painting with textual and archaeological
references, choosing to follow the example and style
of Poussin.

By 1767 Greuze had already selected as the subject for his
reception painting an event that followed the attempted
murder of Septimius Severus in Scotland by his son
Caracalla in A.D. 210. Greuze[3] and Saint-Aubin[4] both
indicated that the literary source for *Septimius Severus
Reproaching Caracalla* was Moréri's *Grand dictionnaire
historique*.[5] However, since Moréri's text omits the event
Greuze depicted, the artist probably consulted Moréri's
source, Cassius Dio's *Roman History*, whose text, as translated
in 1674 by Pierre Le Pesant, could serve as a caption to
Greuze's picture: "*il retourna au camp où appellant son fils avec
Papinien et Castor, il mit une épée au milieu, et après l'avoir
fort tancé d'avoir voulu commettre une action si exécrable . . . il
conclut ainsi son discours: si vous voulez m'oster la vie, tuez moy
présentement, car outre que je suis déjà dans l'âge, ie n'ay plus
de santé. Que si vous avez quelque peine à faire ce coup de vostre
main, voicy Papinien qui est Colonel des Gardes, donnez luy
cette commission, quoy que vous commandiez il vous obeyra,
puisque vous estes Empereur.*"[6]

In addition to its obscurity, the event described by Cassius
Dio presents peculiar problems for a painter in that it is
both episodic and verbal. Beaucousin lamented Greuze's
avoidance of a subject that was "*net et connu*" for "*un fait
énigmatique et compliqué que l'art ne peut rendre.*"[7] Bachaumont
also criticized Greuze's choice: "*Le premier défaut de M.
Greuze est donc d'avoir choisi un mot et non une action à peindre.*"[8]

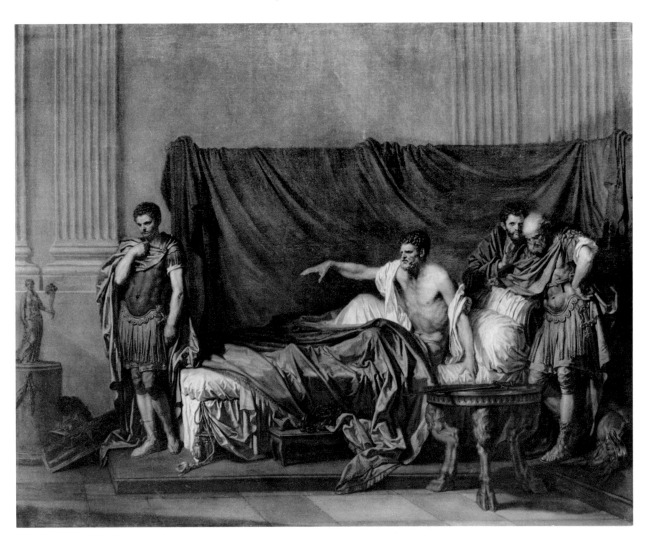

Apparently after he had already established the appearance of his principal figures through preparatory drawings after antique sculptures or casts (see fig. 19, Nos. 67, 68), Greuze painted at least two sketches of *Septimius Severus Reproaching Caracalla*, one which included the essentials of the final composition but with less space indicated around the figures and with a tent as the setting,[9] and the other a larger sketch, now lost,[10] in which the composition, according to Diderot, "*est restée le même.*"[11] Diderot saw and admired the latter version in August of 1767. He described to Falconet Greuze's daring change of genre—"*Le Greuze vient de faire un tour de force. Il s'est élancé tout d'un coup de la bambochade dans la grande peinture, et avec succès, autant que je m'y connais*"—and gave a sensitive interpretation of the picture with specific reference to its verbal quality: "*Et puis, beaucoup de simplicité dans les accessoires; un fond large et nu, avec un si grand silence qu'il semble que la voix de Septime Sévère retintisse dans le vague de l'appartement.*"[12] For Diderot in 1767, "*cette ébauche promettait un beau tableau.*"[13] But two years later, in describing to Falconet the scandal of Greuze's reception, Diderot wrote: "*Le fâcheux de tout cela c'est qu'en effêt le tableau ne vaut rien.*"[14]

Diderot's change of opinion reflects the nearly unanimous rejection of *Septimius Severus Reproaching Caracalla* when Greuze presented it to the Académie on July 23, 1769. After examining the painting with its unexpected historical subject, and no doubt recalling Greuze's acerbic attitude towards his colleagues, the members of the Académie first voted to elect him, by a majority of twenty-four to six, but then voted again on the matter of his classification and, in a vote of twenty-one to nine, received him "*aux mêmes droits que son agrément, c'est-à-dire comme peintre de genre.*"[15] Greuze was informed of this detail only after taking the oath of membership. Diderot reported that the artist, "*déchu de son espérance, perdit la tête, s'amusa comme un enfant à soutenir l'excellence de son tableau,*"[16] and Cochin's official record of the event written for Marigny noted, "*Il s'est cabré contre cette décision, a laissé échapper quelques traits de son estime qu'il a pour soy-même, et même du mépris qu'il a fait de tous les autres.*"[17] The final humiliation awaited Greuze at home, where his wife received the disappointing news with "*les reproches emportées de la femme la plus violente . . . qui se rongeait les poings de fureur,*"[18] in a scene probably similar to that represented in *The Angry Woman* (No. 96). Wille was touched by his friend's plight but piously accepted the verdict of the Académie: "*M. Greuze présenta, pour sa réception, un tableau historique à l'Académie royale pour être reçu comme peintre d'histoire. Cela lui causa bien de la peine; mais personne ne pourroit lutter contre le scrutin du corps en général.*"[19] Following all this Greuze decided not to participate in the Académie's future exhibitions and even attempted, without success, to resign his membership.

On August 25 the Salon opened, and the public and critics, alerted to the scandal, considered the case of *Septimius Severus Reproaching Caracalla*. They followed, nearly without exception, the judgment of the Académie: "*Le

Fig. 19 Head of Caracalla, study
for *Septimius Severus Reproaching
Caracalla*, red chalk, Bayonne,
Musée Bonnat

Fig. 20 Head of Castor, study for
*Septimius Severus Reproaching
Caracalla*, red chalk, Bayonne,
Musée Bonnat

Fig. 21 *Septimius Severus Reproaching
Caracalla* (detail)

*public confirme hautement la décision de l'Académie . . . le
genre historique vous est étranger*";[20] "*Ce genre est au-dessus de
ses forces*";[21] "*Ni composition, ni dessin, ni expression, ni
pinceau*";[22] "*C'est par accident qu'il l'a donné dans le pot au
noir*";[23] "*une exécution vague et distraite*";[24] "*c'est une jambe,
une cuisse droite qui ne finit pas*";[25] "*des draperies trop tourmentées*";[26] "*M. Greuze a mis l'agraphe du manteau de Caracalla du
côté gauche; mais . . . les romains attachaient leur toge sur
l'épaule droite.*"[27]

Perhaps inspired by Daudet de Jossac's sympathetic
invitation to speak out,[28] Greuze decided to defend himself
against this avalanche of criticism by responding to the
critic of the *Avant-Coureur*, who had offended him most by
comparing *Septimius Severus Reproaching Caracalla* unfavorably
to Poussin, the very artist he had tried to follow. It was,
however, not the deliberate recollections of Poussin that
Greuze had worked into his picture which struck that
critic, but the absence of picturesque detail and a supposed
deficiency in expression. The artist's response appeared in
the *Avant-Coureur* on September 25: "*J'ai étudié aussi bien
que vous l'avez pu faire, les ouvrages de ce grand homme*,"
replied Greuze, who went on to point out errors of
historical interpretation on the critic's part and to question
the very motive of his criticism, which struck the artist as
"*un dessein marqué de me désobliger.*" With justification he
asked, "*Pourquoi m'opposer seul entre tous me confrères au plus
savant peintre de notre école?*"[29]

Of all the aspects of *Septimius Severus Reproaching Caracalla*
that eluded Greuze's contemporaries, it is the nature of its
relationship with Poussin that now seems most obvious.
Although Gabriel de Saint-Aubin cited Poussin's *Death of
Germanicus* (Minneapolis Institute of Arts) in reference to
Greuze's work in the Salon of 1769, he did so in reference to
Greuze's drawing *The Death of a Father Lamented by his
Children* (No. 51) and not to *Septimius Severus*, despite the
fact that he made two sketches of the latter in his Salon
catalogue.[30] Greuze's reworking of Poussin's picture, which
he could have seen at the Palazzo Barberini when he was
in Rome,[31] has indeed passed largely unnoticed until recent
years,[32] though Diderot had said that Greuze was extolling
his picture "*comme un morceau à lutter contre ce que Poussin
avait fait de mieux.*"[33] Greuze's picture shares with *The Death
of Germanicus* several of its cardinal features: a subject with
strong moral overtones drawn from Roman history; the
general disposition of the figures in a frieze-like group—a
quality ridiculed by Diderot[34] and Boucher[35] alike—against
a curtain parallel to the picture plane; an image of
antiquity correct in archaeological detail, and the presentation of a dramatic subject through the means of
gesture and expression. In his attempt to revive Poussin's
sober manner Greuze had passed beyond the level of the
very history painters who judged his first history painting

and found it merely awkward and peculiar. It is David's
paintings of the 1780s that make obvious the originality of
Greuze's accomplishment with *Septimius Severus*.

In addition to the painted sketches and preparatory
drawings for the painting mentioned above or included in
this exhibition (Nos. 68, 69), there exist a pastel study for
the torso of Septimius Severus in the Ecole des Beaux-Arts,
Paris,[36] a red chalk study for the head of Caracalla formerly
with the Schab Gallery, New York, studies for the heads
of Caracalla and Castor in the Musée Bonnat, Bayonne
(figs. 19, 20),[37] and a nude study for the figure of Caracalla,
based on the Belvedere *Antinoüs* (Vatican), in the Musée
Greuze at Tournus.[38] The attempt to achieve historical
verisimilitude evident in these figures drawn after the
antique extended also to details such as the statue of
Fortuna at extreme left, which Greuze copied from an
engraving in Michel Ange de la Chaussée's *Grand Cabinet
romain*, where her relevance to the scene is made explicit:
"*on la représente amaiant un gouvernail et tenant une corne
d'abondance pour marquer qu'elle dispose des richesses et qu'elle
est la gouvernante générale du monde.*"[39] Various elements
of the setting and of Roman military dress were derived
from the illustrations in Dom Bernard de Montfaucon's
Antiquité expliquée.[40]

The severe architectural background of *Septimius Severus
Reproaching Caracalla*, which aids in flattening the composition,
recalls that of Vien's *Marchande d'amours* of 1763, with its
bare walls and thick Ionic pilasters, and also the work of
Greuze's classicizing contemporaries Chalgrin, Gondouin
and Ledoux.

1 "a mortifying scene." Diderot, *Salons*, IV, p. 105

2 "*Mais savez-vous, mon ami, la raison de cette rage de Greuze, de ce déchirement de Pierre, contre ce pauvre Doyen? c'est que Michel* [Van Loo] *qui tient l'Ecole* [des Elèves protégés] *laissera bientôt vacante une place à laquelle ils prétendent tous.*" ("But do you know, my friend, the reason for this rage of Greuze's, this outburst of Pierre's, against that poor Doyen? it is because Michel [Van Loo], who directs l'Ecole [des Elèves protégés], will soon leave vacant a post to which they all aspire.") *Ibid.*, III, p. 189

3 "*Premièrement, Geta n'était point présent à cette scène: c'était Castor . . . suivant Moréri.*" ("First of all, Geta was not even present at that scene: it was Castor. . . according to Moréri.") J.-B. Greuze, "Lettre à l'auteur," *L'Avant-Coureur*, September 25, 1769, p. 408

4 Alongside his sketch of Greuze's picture in his Salon catalogue Saint-Aubin noted, "*Castor Chambellan de Sévère et son plus fidèle domestique. Voy. Moreri.*" ("Castor Chamberlain of Severus and his most faithful servant. See Moréri.") Dacier, *Saint-Aubin*, II, p. 81

5 L. Moréri, *Le Grand Dictionnaire historique*, Paris, 1759, IX, p. 385

6 "he returned to camp, where, summoning his son with Papinian and Castor, he placed a sword before them, and after having strongly berated him for having wished to commit so detestable an act . . . he concluded his discourse thus: if you wish to take my life, kill me now, for I am already old and no longer have my health. But if you have some reluctance in striking this blow with your own hand, here is Papinian, who is Colonel of the Guards; give him this task, whatever you command he will obey, for you are Emperor."

Cassius Dio Cocceianus, *Histoire romaine*, trans. P. Le Pesant, Sieur de Boisguillebert, Paris, 1674, II, p. 224

7 "clear-cut and familiar" "an enigmatic and complicated event that art cannot treat." M.-B. Beaucousin, *Lettres sur le Salon de peinture en 1769*, Paris, 1769, p. 23

8 "M. Greuze's initial fault is, then, having chosen to paint a word and not an action." Bachaumont, *Mémoires secrets*, XIII, p. 55, letter of September 28, 1769

9 Rothan sale, Paris, May 29-31, 1890, lot 155, sold to Durand-Ruel for 4,150 francs; Bessoneau sale, Paris, June 15, 1954, lot 65; J. Seznec, "Diderot et l'affaire Greuze," *Gazette des Beaux-Arts*, May-June, 1966, pp. 339-56, fig. 2

10 Tonnelier sale, Paris, November 28, 1783, lot 27, sold for 89 livres; Parizeau sale, Paris, March 26, 1789, lot 99, sold for 100 livres to Delaroux

11 "remained the same." Diderot, *op. cit.*, p. 104

12 "That Greuze has just accomplished a tour de force. He has jumped in a single step from genre painting to history painting, and with success, so far as I can see." "And then, a great deal of simplicity in the accessories; a broad, naked background, with so great a silence that it seems the voice of Septimius Severus reverberates in the emptiness of the apartment." Diderot, *Correspondance*, VII, pp. 102-03

13 "this sketch gave promise of a beautiful picture." Diderot, *Salons*, IV, p. 104

14 "What is annoying in all this is that in effect the picture is worth nothing." Diderot, *Correspondance*, IX, p. 132

15 "with the same rights as his associateship, that is to say as a genre painter." A. de Montaiglon,

ed., *Procès-verbaux de l'Académie Royale de Peinture et de Sculpture*, Paris, 1888, VIII, pp. 18-19

16 "his hopes dashed, lost his head, indulged himself like a child in maintaining the excellence of his picture." Diderot, *Salons*, IV, p. 104

17 "He flew into a passion over this decision, let loose some remarks about the esteem he has for himself and even some about the scorn he felt for all the others." "Mémoire de Cochin à M. de Marigny ajouté en note au procès-verbal de l'Assemblée de l'Académie Royale du mercredi 23 juillet 1769," *Correspondance de M. de Marigny avec Coypel, Lépicié et Cochin*, Paris, 1904, XX, p. 183, No. 653

18 "the fiery reproaches of the most violent woman . . . who gnaw her fists in rage." D. Diderot, *Lettres à Sophie Volland*, Paris, 1930, III, p. 215, letter of October 1, 1769

19 "For his reception, M. Greuze presented to the Académie Royale a history painting in order to be received as a history painter. That caused him a great deal of trouble, but no one could oppose the vote of the general membership." Wille, I, p. 415

20 "The public loudly confirms the decision of the Académie. . . the historical genre is foreign to you." Beaucousin, *loc. cit.*

21 "This genre is beyond his capacities." "Lettre adressée aux auteurs du *Journal encyclopédique* au sujet des ouvrages exposés au Salon du Louvre en 1769," ms., Paris, Bibliothèque Nationale, Cabinet des Estampes, Fonds Deloynes, IX, No. 133, p. 364

22 "Neither composition, nor drawing, nor expression, nor brushwork." Beaucousin, *op. cit.*, pp. 23-24

23 "By accident he dropped it into a pot of black paint." [N. Cochin], *Réponse de M. Jérome,*

rapeur de tabac à M. Raphael, peintre de l'Académie de S. Luc, entrepreneur général des enseignes de la ville, fauxbourgs et banlieue de Paris, Paris, 1769, p. 23

24 "a vague and distracted execution." *Le Chinois au Salon*, Paris, 1769, p. 11

25 "it is a leg, a right thigh that never ends." [Daudet de Jossac], *Lettre sur les peintures, gravures et sculptures qui ont été exposées cette année au Louvre: par M. Raphaël, peintre, de l'académie de S. Luc, entrepreneur général des enseignes de la ville, fauxbourgs et banlieu de Paris: à M. Jérosme, son ami, rapeur de tabac et riboteur*, Paris, 1769, p. 27

26 "draperies too highly elaborated." *Lettre sur l'exposition des ouvrages de peinture et de sculpture au Sallon du Louvre*, Paris, 1769, pp. 37-38

27 "M. Greuze has placed the clasp of Caracalla's cloak on the left side; but . . . the Romans attached their toga on the right shoulder." "Arts: Exposition des peintures, sculptures, gravures de M.M. de l'Académie Royale," *L'Avant-Coureur*, September 11, 1769, p. 395

28 "*Si l'auteur lui-même prenoit la peine de vous rendre raison de tous ces doutes, vous seriez plus que jamais épris et convaincu de son mérite.*" ("If the artist himself took the trouble to account for all these misgivings, you would more than ever be taken by him and convinced of his merit." [Daudet de Jossac], *Sentimens sur les tableaux exposés au Salon*, Paris, 1769, p. 20

29 "I have studied as well as you could have the works of that great man." "an unmistakable intent to offend me." "Why set me alone of all my colleagues up against the most learned painter of our school?" Greuze, *op. cit.*, pp. 407-08

30 Dacier, *op. cit.*, II, pp. 81, 89

31 A. Blunt, *Nicolas Poussin,*

New York, 1967, I, pp. 77 ff.,
II, Pl. 22
32 See: Paris, Louvre, La "Mort
de Germanicus" de Poussin du
Musée de Minneapolis, exhib.
cat., 1973, No. 92
33 "as a piece to vie with what
Poussin had done best." Diderot,
Salons, IV, p. 104
34 Diderot, *Oeuvres*, XI, p. 461
35 "*le tableau . . . a été plaisamment
appellé par Monsieur* Boucher, un
bas-relief." ("the picture . . . has
been amusingly called by Monsieur
Boucher, a bas-relief.") Bachaumont,
op. cit., p. 57
36 Munhall, 1965, fig. 10
37 Nos. 1642, 1841
38 Munhall, *op. cit.*, fig. 11.
Diderot recognized the source:
"*c'est* l'Antinoüs *déguisé sous
l'habit romain*" ("it is the *Antinoüs*
disguised in Roman dress"),
Salons, IV, p. 106
39 "she is represented steering a
rudder and holding a horn of
plenty to indicate that she disposes
of riches and is the general
governess of the world." M. A. de
la Chaussée, *Le Grand Cabinet romain*,
Amsterdam, 1706, Pl. XX, p. 51;
Munhall, *op. cit.*, figs. 12, 13
40 Dom Bernard de Montfaucon,
L'Antiquité expliquée, Paris, 1719,
III, Pls. XXXIII, LVI

71 Madame Greuze Embracing Her Son after Twenty Years Absence (*Madame Greuze embrassant son fils, après vingt ans d'absence*)

Brush, gray and brown ink wash, over pencil, on white
paper, 12³⁄₁₆ x 8⅞ in. (31.0 x 22.5 cm)
Inscribed on mat: "*Madame Greuze embrassant son fils / après
vingt ans d'absence*"; inscribed on verso: "*J'ai donné ce dessin à
Mr Chambry, comme un léger témoignage de ma reconnaissance et
de mon amitié. A. G. Greuze.*" "*Ce dessin m'a été donné par la
fille du célèbre Greuze, en mai 1841; elle avait alors 80 ans.
J'avais demandé et obtenu qu'on réunit dans une même sépulture
les restes de son Père et de sa Mère, en 185[?], et ceux de sa
soeur ainée, morte 12 après.*"[1]
Paris, private collection

Collections: Anne-Gabrielle Greuze, Paris, until 1841;
Chambry, Paris; Léonce Coblentz, Paris; his sale, Paris,
December 15–16, 1904, lot 53; David David-Weill, Neuilly,
before 1928; anonymous sale, Paris, June 10, 1971, lot 217,
sold for 7,000 francs
   Bibliography: Brookner, p. 72; G. Henriot, *Collection David
Weill*, Paris, 1928, III, Pt. I, pp. 205, 207

If the inscription on its mat is to be believed, this
drawing is an important document in the artist's biography.
Brookner dates the drawing to about 1769, when Greuze
is thought to have left Paris and visited Angers and his
native Tournus. His first departure from Tournus for Paris
would thus have taken place around 1749. However, Louis
Gougenot wrote in his manuscript "Album de voyage en
Italie" that Greuze visited his family on his way to Italy
in 1755. This statement would suggest a date of 1775 for
the drawing, though there is no direct evidence that Greuze
was in Tournus that year.
   The drawing records Greuze's own appearance, with his
familiar coiffure and voluminous travel clothes, as well
as the distinctive features of his mother. The two are
linked not only in a physical embrace but also by an
intense visual exchange.
   Probably contemporaneously, Greuze executed another
drawing the same size as this one, slightly less finished
and more pathetic in subject, depicting the artist assisting
his invalid mother back to her chair (Paris, private
collection). There exists as well a portrait drawing of the
artist's mother probably also from the same period.[2]

1 "I have given this drawing to
Mr Chambry, as a slight token of
my gratitude and friendship. A. G.
Greuze." "This drawing was
given to me by the daughter of the
celebrated Greuze, in May 1841;
she was then eighty years old. I
had requested and obtained
permission to have the remains of
her Father and Mother reunited
in the same tomb, in 185[?], and
those of her elder sister, who died
twelve years later."
2 D. S. sale, Paris, December 17,
1924, lot 145, repr.

72 Woman with a Spaniel, Presumed Portrait of Madame de Porcin
Oil, on oval canvas, 27$\frac{15}{16}$ x 22$\frac{7}{16}$ in. (71.0 x 57.0 cm)
Angers, Musée d'Angers

Collections: Pierre-Louis Eveillard, marquis de Livois, Angers (d. 1790); acquired by the museum by the law of sequestration in 1792

Exhibitions: R. A., 1932, No. 271; Paris, Musée Carnavalet, Chefs-d'oeuvre des musées de province, 1933, No. 40; Copenhagen, Palais de Charlottenborg, L'art français du XVIIIè siècle, 1935, No. 82; Paris, Palais National des Arts, Chefs-d'oeuvre de l'art français, 1937, No. 169; San Francisco, Palace of the Legion of Honor, Rococo: Masterpieces of XVIII Century French Art from the Museums of France, 1949, No. 19; Milan, Palazzo Reale, Il Ritratto francese da Clouet a Degas, 1962, No. 101

Bibliography: J. Bouchot-Saupique, "La Part des musées de province à l'exposition des Chefs-d'oeuvre de l'art français," *Bulletin des Musées de France*, August–September, 1937, p. 119, repr. p. 120; Brookner, pp. 72, 117–18, Pl. 53; J. Denais, *Les Portraits conservés par les collections publiques d'Angers*, Angers, 1896, p. 12; B. Dorival, *La Peinture française*, Paris, 1942, II, p. 31; M. Florisoone, *La Peinture française: Le Dix-huitième siècle*, Paris, 1948, pp. 70, 129; L. Gonse, *Les Chefs-d'oeuvre des musées de France: La Peinture*, Paris, 1900, I, pp. 34–35, repr. facing p. 34; H. Jouin, *Musée d'Angers: Notice des Peintures*, Angers, 1870, No. 44; Martin-Masson, Nos. 501, 818, 1233; H. de Morant, *La Peinture au Musée d'Angers*, Angers, 1968, p. 10, No. 53; E. Munhall, "Greuze's Portrait of Comtesse Mollien, Study of a Motif," *Baltimore Museum of Art News*, Fall, 1962, p. 20, fig. 8; R. Planchenault, "La Collection du marquis de Livois: L'Art français," *Gazette des Beaux-Arts*, October, 1933, pp. 226–27; L. Réau, *Histoire de la peinture française au XVIIIè siècle*, Paris, 1925, II, p. 22, Pl. VII; C. de Ris, *Les Musées de province*, Paris, 1872, pp. 32–33

Engraving: C. Guérin[1]

The traditional identification of the subject of this portrait, one of Greuze's best known and most highly admired, as Madame de Porcin goes back to Pierre Sentout's catalogue of the collection of the marquis de Livois, compiled after the latter's death in 1790. However, no record of a Porcin family can be found. It has also been supposed that Greuze executed this portrait during a trip to Angers which Florisoone dates to 1769 and de Morant to 1774, neither citing any evidence. Planchenault hesitantly suggested the possibility that the subject might have been Livois' servant, Agathe Bouteiller, who bore him a daughter. In any case, Livois was a provincial collector of eighteenth-century paintings and was on close terms with many of the artists represented in his distinguished collection. He owned no other works by Greuze.

Martin and others have stated that a copy of this painting was in the Palais des Beaux-Arts at Lille, but no such copy appears in any inventory of that museum.[2] A copy of the portrait by Emile-Auguste Hublin, an Angevin painter, is in the Musée Municipal at Château-Gontier (Mayenne).[3] Another copy was on the art market in 1965.[4]

Greuze also utilized the motif of a woman encircling a dog's head with a crown of flowers in his portrait of Princess Varvara Nikolaewna Gagarine (1762–1802) in the Metropolitan Museum of Art, New York.

1 Portalis-Béraldi, II, p. 357
2 Information kindly communicated by M. Albert Châtelet in a letter dated November 27, 1963
3 Musée de Château-Gontier, *Notice des peintures, sculptures et des antiquités*, Château-Gontier, 1876, No. 10

4 Mak van Waay, Amsterdam, catalogue No. 163, 1965, No. 187, 71.5 x 58.0 cm. This might be the version cited by Martin as having been in the Armengaud and Turby collections.

73 The Dreamer

Oil, on canvas, 15¾ x 12¾ in. (40.0 x 32.4 cm)
New York, Wildenstein and Co.

Collections: comtesse du Barry, Louveciennes; her sales,
Paris, December 22, 1775, lot 22 (bought in ?), and Paris,
February 17, 1777, lot 54; comte de Merle, Paris; his sale,
Paris, March 1–4, 1784, lot 24, sold for 1,880 livres to Le
Rouge; comte de Vaudreuil, Paris; his sale, Paris, November
26, 1787, lot 97, sold for 1,880 livres to Quesnay; Countess
Mensdorff; Prince Dietrichstein, Vienna

   Exhibitions: Cincinnati Art Museum, An Exhibition of
French Paintings of the Eighteenth and Early Nineteenth
Centuries, 1937, No. 10; New York, Wildenstein and Co.,
French Painting of the Eighteenth Century, 1948, No. 18

   Bibliography: M. Breuning, "Luxurious France," *Art
Digest*, February 1, 1948, p. 19; Martin-Masson, No. 756

Freely inspired by Rubens' *The Birth of Louis XIII*, part of
the Medici Series (Louvre) which Greuze and Wille were
studying in 1760 (see No. 25), this picture is a prototype of
the unique mixture of voluptuousness and reflection with
which Greuze excited both his contemporaries and late-
nineteenth-century collectors. Diderot's enthusiastic
remarks over Greuze's lost portrait of his wife exhibited in
the Salon of 1763 could apply equally well to the present
picture: "*La délicatesse avec laquelle le bas de ce visage est
touché et l'ombre du menton portée sur le col est inconcevable.
On serait tenté de passer sa main sur ce menton, si l'austerité de
la personne n'arrêtait et l'éloge et la main. L'ajustement est
simple: c'est celui d'une femme le matin dans sa chambre
à coucher.*"[1]

---

1 "The delicacy with which the lower part of this face is handled and the shadow of the chin cast on the neck is inconceivable. You would be tempted to pass your hand over this chin, if the austerity of the subject did not stop both your praise and your hand. The arrangement is simple: it is that of a woman in the morning in her bedroom." Diderot, *Salons*, I, p. 237

74 Portrait of Marie-Jeanne Bécu, comtesse du Barry

Oil, on canvas, 23½ x 18⅝ in. (59.7 x 47.3 cm)
New York, Wildenstein and Co.

Collections: Mainnemare, Paris; his sale, Paris, February 21, 1843, lot 15, sold for 1,500 francs (?); Baron Llangattock, The Hendre, Monmouth; his sale, London, November 28, 1958, lot 27, sold for 1,200 guineas to Nicholls
   Bibliography: Martin-Masson, No. 1104; L. Willoughby, "Lord Llangattock's Monmouth Seat: The Hendre and its Art Treasures," *Connoisseur*, March, 1907, p. 158, repr. p. 152

This pensive and intimate portrait was painted at the height of Madame du Barry's success around 1771, the year she inaugurated her celebrated pavilion at Louveciennes designed by Claude-Nicolas Ledoux. The mistress of Louis XV is represented casually garbed in a dressing gown, without jewels and with her hair not yet done up. Her pose suggests that she has just turned from her mirror to pause reflectively. In a well-known color print Edouard Gauthier-Dagoty also represented Madame du Barry at her dressing table, being served coffee by her black servant Zamor.[1] A similar upholstered chair appears in both portraits.

Born in Vaucouleurs in 1746, Marie-Jeanne Bécu began working in a milliner's shop in Paris in 1762. She became involved with Jean, chevalier du Barry, who arranged a private introduction to Louis XV and who subsequently married her to his brother Guillaume, comte du Barry, so that she might have a title and be formally presented at court. Her presentation occurred on April 22, 1769. From then until the death of Louis XV in 1774 Madame du Barry wielded great power as the Royal mistress. Exiled after the King's death, she was eventually permitted to return to Louveciennes. She was arrested on September 22, 1793, for conspiring against the Republic, and was guillotined at nightfall on December 7.

Madame du Barry took a greater interest in Greuze than did her predecessor, Madame de Pompadour. Her sale on December 22, 1775, following the death of the King and her disgrace, included Greuze's *Child Playing with a Dog* (No. 55), which she had purchased at the sale of her enemy the duc de Choiseul, a *Boy with a Dog*, probably identical with the *Matelot napolitain* exhibited as No. 118 in the Salon of 1757 (London, Wallace Collection), two female busts (see No. 73) and a reduced version of *The Votive Offering to Cupid* (Wallace Collection).[2] Two female busts by Greuze appeared in the sale of Madame du Barry's nephew, the comte du Barry, on November 21, 1774.

It is impossible to identify the marble-topped piece of furniture at right in this painting among the quantities of such pieces listed in the inventory of Madame du Barry's possessions made on March 6, 1793.[3] Its severe lines are characteristic of her advanced taste.

Greuze executed another portrait of Madame du Barry, similar to the present one but in an oval format. It belonged to Alfred de Rothschild when it appeared in the Fair Women exhibition held in 1894 at the Grafton Galleries, London. Its present whereabouts are unknown.

1 J. Levron, *Le Destin de Madame du Barry*, Paris, 1961, repr. facing p. 60; Portalis-Béraldi, I, pp. 615–16
2 In addition to these pictures Martin-Masson list as other works by Greuze having belonged to Madame du Barry their Nos. 442, 609, 1105.
3 Paris, Archives Nationales, F7 4682. The inventory mentions only one portrait of Madame du Barry, in the vestibule of the pavilion: "*Un Tableau représentant la citoyenne du Barri en grand avec bordure dorée.*" ("A Picture representing citizen du Barri full-length with a gilded frame.") This presumably is the portrait of the comtesse by Drouais now in the Chambre de Commerce at Versailles.

75   Presumed Portrait of Mademoiselle Raucourt
Red and black chalk, stumped, on cream paper, 16$\frac{9}{16}$ x 12$\frac{5}{8}$
in. (42.0 x 32.0 cm)
Dijon, Musée Magnin

Collections: Magnin, Paris, until 1938
  Bibliography: Musée Magnin, *Peintures et dessins de l'Ecole
rançaise*, Dijon, 1938, p. 107, No. 467

The subject of this portrait drawing has traditionally been
identified as the actress Françoise-Marie-Antoinette-Joseph
Saucerotte, called Mademoiselle Raucourt (1756–1815).
If this identification is correct, Greuze executed it probably
between 1772, when the actress made her debut at the
Comédie Française in Paris, and 1776, when she abruptly
disappeared. Her life was scandalous, her expenditures so
extravagant that she was imprisoned for debt, and even her
funeral provoked a riot between her admirers and the
clergy who refused to accept her body.
  Greuze here softened the severe style that typifies most of
his profile portrait drawings (compare Nos. 36, 50) by
employing a combination of chalks and an extreme
delicacy in the stumping, so effective in the rendering of the
various textures of flesh, hair, pearls, fur and silk.

76 Woman with Hands Clasped
(Study for *The Charitable Woman*)
Red chalk, on white paper, 12⅝ x 9⅞ in. (32.1 x 25.2 cm)
Dijon, Musée des Beaux-Arts

Collections: given to the museum by Mademoiselle Pourpry in 1931

   Exhibitions: Dijon, Musée des Beaux-Arts, Dessins français, XVIIè et XVIIIè siècles, 1960, No. 35

Though this drawing and versions of it have been related to the central pleading figure in *The Father's Curse: The Ungrateful Son* (No. 84), they actually resemble more closely the figure of the invalid wife in the painting *The Charitable Woman* (Lyon, Musée des Beaux-Arts). The fact that the wife's pose in the painting is reversed may have resulted from Greuze's regular habit of utilizing counterproofs of preparatory drawings.

   Although Massard engraved a sketch for *The Charitable Woman* in 1772, the final painting does not seem to have been completed until 1775. After describing the ill and indigent recipient of the charitable woman's generosity, François de Laharpe referred to the subject of this drawing as "*sa femme malade comme lui*," commenting of her gesture: "*La reconnaissance de la femme qui est dans le lit semble plus vive, et celle du gentilhomme semble plus noble.*"[1] Bachaumont also singled out this figure in his description of the painting: "*Sa femme auprès de lui, recueillie en elle-même, les mains jointes, exprime le même sentiment* [of thanks] *d'une manière plus conforme à son sexe dévot, qui commence par rapporter à la providence une visite aussi généreuse et par la remercier intérieurement.*"[2]

   In addition to the lost counterproof of this or a related drawing which Greuze presumably utilized for the painting, there are versions of this sheet in the Pierpont Morgan Library, New York (No. I. 285), and the Musée Greuze at Tournus (No. 21; Martin-Masson, No. 1648). A smaller version appeared in the Jules Boilly sale, Paris, March 19-20, 1869, lot 136.

1 "his wife ill like himself." "The gratitude of the woman in the bed seems more intense, and that of the gentleman seems more noble." F. de Laharpe, *Correspondance littéraire*, Paris, 1804, I, p. 268
2 "His wife beside him, absorbed in herself, her hands clasped, expresses the same feeling [of thanks] in a manner more consistent with her devout sex, which begins by ascribing to providence so generous a visit and by inwardly giving thanks." P. de Bachaumont, "Observation de Bachaumont sur la Dame de charité, tableau de Mr Greuze," ms., [1775], Paris, Bibliothèque Nationale, Cabinet des Estampes, Fonds Deloynes, p. 2

77 Seated Girl (Study for *Wavering Virtue*)
Red and black chalk, stumped, gray ink wash, on white
paper, 17½ x 12¹⁵⁄₁₆ in. (44.5 x 31.3 cm)
Signed: *Greuze*
Paris, Musée du Louvre, Cabinet des Dessins

Collections: original collection of the Cabinet des Dessins,
Musée du Louvre
   Exhibitions: Paris, Palais National des Arts, Chefs-d'oeuvre
de l'art français, 1937, No. 551
   Bibliography: Guiffrey-Marcel, VI, No. 4543; Martin-
Masson, Nos. 216, 1407

A study for Greuze's *Wavering Virtue* in the Alte
Pinakothek, Munich,[1] a picture engraved by Massard in
1776, this drawing is close in size and detail to one in the
Museum Boymans-van Beuningen, Rotterdam.[2] The latter,
which is reversed, may be a counterproof of the present
drawing, reworked by the artist using brush and ink over
the red chalk transfer. In neither is the girl depicted holding
the crucial watch that appears in the painting. A third
study of the same subject, facing right, appeared in the
Bourgarel sale, Paris, June 15–16, 1922, lot 97, repr.; her
head is only summarily indicated, but there is a spot on
her hand that corresponds to the watch.

The garret interior with its casement window and the
chair placed alongside the bed recall the setting of *The
Death of a Cruel Father Abandonned by His Children* (No. 52),
exhibited in 1769. The model appears to be the same as the
one seen in the *Girl Weeping over Her Dead Bird* of 1765
(No. 44).

In the painting of *Wavering Virtue*, the girl has less
elongated proportions than in this drawing, her sleeves
are raised above her elbows and her bodice is more open,
details that help convey the dilemma of a hitherto
innocent girl now abandoned in her dishevelled room and
contemplating the ominous gift of a gold watch.

1 H. Bauer, *Meisterwerke des 18.
Jahrhunderts . . . in der Alten
Pinakothek*, Munich, 1966, pp.
30–31, repr.

2 See: Paris, Institut Néerlandais,
Le Dessin français dans les
collections hollandaises, exhib. cat.,
1964, No. 93, Pl. 75

78 The Love Letter
Brush, black ink wash, heightened with white gouache,
on white paper, 16 x 12 in. (40.7 x 30.5 cm)
New York, Mr. Emile E. Wolf

Collections: vicomte de Pluvinel, Paris; his sale, April 19–20,
1830, lot 79, sold for 20 francs; anonymous sale, Paris,
March 21, 1840, lot 56; Wildenstein and Co., New York;
acquired in 1966
　Bibliography: A. Brookner, "Aspects of Neo-classicism in
French Painting," *Apollo*, September, 1958, p. 70, fig. VIII;
Martin-Masson, Nos. 92, 98

In size and composition this drawing resembles Greuze's
painting *The Inconsolable Widow* of 1763 (London, Wallace
Collection),[1] in which the subject attempts, as here, to
communicate with an absent husband or lover through the
medium of a portrait bust mounted on a circular pedestal.
However, the sumptuous neoclassical architectural background and furnishings in the present work suggest a date
later than that of the Wallace Collection picture, perhaps
in the mid-1770s. Greuze had been familiar with advanced
neoclassical furniture design since he painted the portrait
of Lalive de Jully in 1759 (No. 22). The incense burner
in the foreground of this drawing recalls the vase designs
of Saly, which were engraved in 1746 and later republished
by Basan, as well as the architectural compositions of
de Neufforge.[2]

1 Wallace Collection Catalogues,
Pictures and Drawings, London,
1968, No. P454, pp. 137–38

2 S. Ericksen, *Early Neo-classicism
in France*, London, 1974, Nos.
291, 310, pp. 375, 379

79   The Return of the Young Hunter
Brush, black ink, over black chalk, heightened with white
gouache, on cream paper, 20¾ x 26¼ in. (52.0 x 66.5 cm)
Minneapolis Institute of Arts

Collections: Réjane (Madame Porel), Paris; comte Jacques de
Bryas, Paris; his sale, Paris, April 4–6, 1898, lot 72, sold for
2,000 francs; Lucien Goldschmidt, New York; purchased
by the museum in 1970, John R. Van Derlip Fund
   Exhibitions: Toronto, Ottawa, San Francisco and New
York, French Master Drawings of the Seventeenth and
Eighteenth Centuries in North American Collections,
1972–73, No. 57
   Bibliography: Martin-Masson, No. 365; Minneapolis
Institute of Arts *Bulletin,* 1970, pp. 81, 90; "Recent
Accessions of American and Canadian Museums," *Art
Quarterly,* Autumn, 1970, p. 324, fig. 2, p. 330

The existence of a preparatory drawing for this sheet,
about half its size, in the British Museum, London (No.

1925.5.11.9), and the fact that no painting of the subject
is known suggest that this is a characteristic example of
the highly finished drawings Greuze produced as complete
works in themselves, not merely as studies for paintings.
Such drawings were avidly sought after by important
collectors in the eighteenth century. Mariette stated that
they were "*payés prodigeusement par quelques curieux.*"[1]
   In the British Museum drawing the essentials of the
composition are roughly indicated in reverse, but with the
dog lying down and without the figure standing at
far right.
   The elaborate neoclassical setting is characteristic of the
late 1770s, though the painting in the oval frame at center
appears to represent an amorous chase with a flying Cupid,
a subject more characteristic of previous decades. The
swagged table and the bowl or incense burner with
figures on it reappear in *The Love Letter* (No. 78), suggesting
that they may have been among Greuze's household
possessions.

1   "sold for prodigious prices to
some collectors." P.-J. Mariette,
Abécédario, ed. P. de Chennevières
and A. de Montaiglon, Paris,
1853–54, II, p. 331

80 The Return of the Outlaw

Brush, gray ink wash, over pencil, on white paper,
8¹⁵⁄₁₆ x 14½ in. (21.1 x 36.7 cm)
Hartford, Wadsworth Atheneum, Henry and Walter
Keney Fund

Collections: baron d'Holbach, Paris; his sale, Paris, May
6–7, 1861, lot 183, sold for 70 francs to Thuillier;
Antoine-François Marmontel, Paris; his sales, Paris,
January 25–26, 1883, lot 132, sold for 190 francs, and Paris,
March 28–29, 1898, lot 31, sold for 250 francs; acquired by
the museum from J. N. Streep, Fine Arts, New York,
in 1963
   Exhibitions: Toronto, Ottawa, San Francisco and New
York, French Master Drawings of the Sevententh and
Eighteenth Centuries in North American Collections,
1972–73, No. 59
   Bibliography: Martin-Masson, No. 364; "Accessions of
American and Canadian Museums," *Art Quarterly*, Winter,
1963, p. 486; "Chronique des arts," *Gazette des Beaux-Arts*,
February, 1965, Supplement, p. 53, fig. 215

In composition and manner of execution this drawing
resembles the *Return of the Hunter* in the British Museum,
London (No. 1925.5.11.9), discussed in relation with the
Return of The Young Hunter included in this exhibition (No.
79). However, the present drawing is made more intensely
dramatic by the apprehensive female figures crowding
about the newly arrived young man, provocatively
identified in nineteenth-century sales as a "*proscrit*"
(outlaw). With its reminiscences of the subject of the
Prodigal Son, this drawing also relates to studies for *The
Father's Curse* of the mid-1770s (see Nos. 84, 88).
   The pose of the male figure at right is recalled in a
drawing of a slightly older man in the Cabinet des Dessins
at the Louvre (No. 29756; Guiffrey-Marcel, No. 4547).

81   Compositional Sketch
Pen and brush, gray and brown ink wash, over pencil, on
white paper, 12½ x 19¾ in. (31.8 x 50.2 cm)
Inscribed: *Greuze fec*
New York, Mrs. Herbert N. Straus

Collections: acquired from Richard Ederheimer in New York
about 1909
   Exhibitions: New York, Jacques Seligmann and Co.,
Exhibition of Original Drawings by the Old Masters,
1925, No. 105; Montreal, Museum of Fine Arts, Five
Centuries of Drawings, 1953, No. 171; Rotterdam, Museum
Boymans-van Beuningen, Paris, Musée de l'Orangerie and
New York, Metropolitan Museum of Art, French Drawings
from American Collections, Clouet to Matisse, 1958–59,
No. 59
   Bibliography: R. Shoolman and C. E. Slatkin, *Six Centuries
of Master Drawings in America*, New York, 1950, p. 80,
Pl. 44; H. Tietze, *European Master Drawings in the United
States*, New York, 1947, No. 106, p. 212

The subject of this violent drawing remains an enigma. The
sheet has traditionally been related to *The Father's
Curse: The Punished Son* (No. 88) because of general
composition similarities. However, there is only the bare
suggestion of a figure entering at right, and few specific
details correspond.
   In manner of execution the drawing resembles an equally
enigmatic *Scene of a Murder* in the Cabinet des Dessins at
the Louvre,[1] as well as the crowded *Domestic Scene* in the
Metropolitan Museum of Art, New York.[2] The supine
figure at left recalls similar figures in three other
drawings: *The Death of a Cruel Father Abandoned by His
Children* (No. 52), *The Death of Cato of Utica* in the Musée
Bonnat, Bayonne (No. 1643) (fig. 5), and *The Death of
Cato of Utica* in the Musée des Beaux-Arts, Rouen. It also
seems related to the head of the father in the Smith College
Museum of Art counterproof study for *The Punished Son*.
   Despite the iconographical mysteries of this sheet—one
of Greuze's best-known drawings in the United States—its
dramatic power and bold calligraphy have changed many
connoisseurs' ideas about the nature of Greuze's art.

1 No. 26988; Guiffrey-Marcel,
VI, No. 4544
2 No. 1972.224.3. See: New York,
Metropolitan Museum of Art,
Drawings Recently Acquired,
1972–75, exhib. cat., 1975–76,
No. 47, repr.

82 Portrait of Benjamin Franklin

Pastel, on oval paper, 31½ x 25⅛ in. (80.0 x 64.1 cm)
Washington, United States Department of State,
Diplomatic Reception Rooms

Collections: Prince Nicolas Nikitich Demidoff (d. 1828); his
son Prince Anatole Demidoff, San Donato Palace near
Florence; his sale, Paris, February 21–22, 1870, lot 397, sold
for 660 francs to Thomas Lawrence; Thomas Lawrence,
Boston; his widow, who became Mrs. Thomas Liddall
Winthrop; her son James Lawrence; his son James Lawrence;
acquired by The Franklin Mint in 1973; given to the
Department of State in 1976

Bibliography: Martin-Masson, No. 1126; C. C. Sellers,
Benjamin Franklin in Portraiture, New Haven, 1962, pp.
112–14, 297–98, No. 1, Pl. 22, and " 'La Noblesse d'une
Ame Libre': The Franklin of Greuze and de Véri," *Art
Quarterly*, Spring, 1963, pp. 2–6

As this simple but imposing image demonstrates, few
portrait subjects and their artists were as attuned to each
other as Benjamin Franklin and Greuze. Even the timing of
their encounter was propitious. Franklin's fame flattered
Greuze's vanity, his principles appealed to the artist's
mind and heart and his understated appearance recalled the
simple, virtuous people Greuze had depicted throughout
his career. This is rightfully considered Franklin's
finest portrait.

Benjamin Franklin (1706–1790), already well known in
Paris from his previous visits in 1767 and 1769, arrived in
France on December 4, 1776, in hope of arranging a treaty
with the French government. The impression he made on
this occasion was amusingly described by his companion
John Adams: "His reputation was more universal than that
of Leibnitz or Newton, Frederick or Voltaire, and his
character more beloved and esteemed than any or all of
them. . . . His name was familiar to government and
people . . . to such a degree that there was scarcely a
peasant or a citizen, a *valet de chambre*, coachman or footman,
a lady's chambermaid or a scullion in a kitchen who was
not familiar with it, and who did not consider him as a
friend to human kind. When they spoke of him, they
seemed to think he was to restore the Golden Age."[1]

This pastel was done by Greuze as a preliminary study
for a painted portrait of Franklin, the commission of which
Jean-Baptiste Jacques Elie de Beaumont had requested
from Franklin on March 8, 1777. Writing to the American
statesman, the eminent French lawyer at first requested
that Franklin pose for the sculptor Dufourny de Villiers
for a bust that would serve as a model for a painted
portrait, in order *"m'assurer d'après ce buste votre portrait
pour le placer dans ma bibliothèque au rang des amis de leur*

patrie et de l'humanité."[2] The sculpted bust apparently was
either not approved or not required, for Bachaumont
reported on June 10 that Greuze was progressing with the
present portrait as a sketch for de Beaumont's commission:
*"M. Greuze, ce peintre excellent pour les têtes de caractère, s'est
emparé de celle de Franklin, dont on voit l'esquisse. Il y a
beaucoup de ressemblance et d'expression."*[3] By July 25
Bachaumont reported that the painted portrait based on
this pastel was ready for de Beaumont's library, just as de
Beaumont had originally planned to install it: *"On a dit
que le Sr Greuze faisoit le portrait de M. Franklin qui ne
manquera pas d'être gravé. M. Elie de Beaumont Avocat célèbre
par son éloquence, par ses intrigues et par un génie romanesque, a
disposé d'avance dans son cabinet une niche pour ce personnage
illustre, entre d'autres grands hommes anciens et modernes qu'il
y a placés, et a fait d'avance cette inscription pour mettre au bas:
Alterius orbis Vindex, utriusque Lumen."*[4] The de Beaumont
painted portrait is now in a private collection in Delaware.

Contrary to Bachaumont's prediction the portrait was not
engraved, but Greuze did paint another version of it for his
admirer the abbé Joseph Alphonse de Véri, whose journal
records his pride over it: *"Si je vieillis autant que ce bienfaiteur
de l'humanité, je me vanterai, auprès de mes petits-neveux, d'avoir
connu ce grand homme, de l'avoir souvent reçu chez moi et d'avoir
obtenu de lui qu'il se laissât peindre par Greuze pour que j'eusse
son portrait de la main de ce grand maître. Ce portrait me suivra
partout jusqu'au tombeau. Je le chéris d'autant plus, qu'étant
ressemblant, Greuze y a peint toute la noblesse d'une âme libre,
toute la sagesse d'une tête bien organisée et toute la sagacité
d'un homme d'état."*[5] De Véri's version is now in a French
private collection. Sellers admirably catalogues the
numerous and often confused contemporary and subsequent
copies of Greuze's portrait.

Bachaumont reported on September 6, 1777, that Greuze
was displaying one of these portraits of Franklin in his
studio, once again at the time of the biennial Salon: *"M.
Greuze, qui n'expose plus depuis longtemps au Sallon, en a aussi
ouvert un chez lui, et il admet le public qui vient s'y présenter.
On y voit surtout le portrait de M. Franklin. On juge aisément que
ce personnage a échauffé sa verve; il est difficile de trouver une
tête mieux caractérisée. On y remarque la bonté heureusement alliée
à la fierté, et l'amour de l'humanité y respire avec la haine de
la tyrannie."*[6]

Among Franklin's papers at the Sterling Memorial
Library, New Haven, is an undated letter from Madame
Greuze to Franklin introducing a friend, as well as a copy
of some verses she had had inscribed on a porcelain urn in
which she preserved the petals of a bouquet of roses
Franklin gave her. These verses, composed by Aimé Ambroise
Joseph Feutry, were afterward printed with a date of
reference for the encounter between the artist's wife and
Franklin, which presumably took place when Greuze went

to Passy to execute the present pastel: "*Inscription que Madame Greuze a mise sur une urne de porcelaine, où elle garde les restes d'un bouquet de roses, que M. Franklin lui a donné, en juin, 1777.*"[7] This date corresponds with Bachaumont's first reference to the portrait.

Greuze was later associated with Franklin in the influential Paris Masonic Lodge known as Les Neufs Soeurs, which through Franklin's participation became a vehicle for American propaganda. Bachaumont noted that the lodge had elected Greuze on November 28, 1778, after failing to attract d'Alembert: "*La loge désolée de ne pouvoir faire cette acquisition, en a été un peu endommagée par le peintre Greuze, très-utile aux travaux dans sa partie.*"[8] Greuze's initiation took place in Franklin's presence during an elaborate "*Apothéose de Voltaire,*" who had died the previous May. The artist, who was eulogized as "*ne cessant jamais d'être naïf lors même qu'il est sublime; devenu enfin le peintre de toutes les conditions, de tous les âges, comme La Fontaine en est le poète,*"[9] placed a wreath on the head of Franklin, who in turn laid it before a representation of Voltaire, setting off spectacular effects of light and sound. Following this much discussed "*Apothéose*" Louis XVI ordered the lodge to disband, later permitting its reorganization only on condition that Franklin become its Worshipful Master, which he did.[10]

83 Head of a Boy

(Study for *The Father's Curse: The Ungrateful Son*)
Red chalk, on cream paper, 19⅛ x 12⁷⁄₁₆ in. (48.5 x 31.5 cm)
Paris, Madame Frédéric Megret

Collections: baron Gourgaud
   Exhibitions: Paris, Galerie Charpentier, L'Enfance, 1949, No. 111; Paris, Galerie Cailleux, Le Dessin français de Watteau à Prud'hon, 1951, No. 66
   Bibliography: F. Boucher and P. Jacottet, *Le Dessin français au XVIIIè siècle*, Lausanne, [1952], No. 78; *Dessins français du XVIIIè siècle: La Figure humaine*, Paris, 1959, Pl. 35

The troubled countenance seen in this drawing is that of the boy in the center background of *The Father's Curse: The Ungrateful Son* (No. 84), a figure who seems to observe the violent action before him with fearful incomprehension. In reference to Greuze's 1765 drawing of *The Ungrateful Son* (No. 48), in which a younger boy corresponding to this one is represented at far right, Diderot wrote, "*Derrière le fauteuil du vieillard, le plus jeune de tous a l'air intimidé et stupéfait.*"[1]

Greuze's uncanny ability to create images of such emotional subtlety was highly appreciated by his contemporaries. In summarizing Greuze's art shortly after his death, Gault de Saint-Germain described this aspect of it as crucial: "*Greuze, que l'on doit regarder comme le peintre des passions de l'âme, est unique dans l'école française.*"[2]

The scale and sculpturesque character of this drawing suggest that it was executed around the time of the painting—that is, about 1777. The same boy appears with a similarly dumbstruck expression in the background of *The Father's Curse: The Punished Son* (No. 88).

1   J. Adams, *Works*, 1856, I, p. 660
2   "to assure myself of having your portrait after this bust to place it in my library among the friends of their homeland and of mankind." Quoted in C. C. Sellers, *Benjamin Franklin in Portraiture*, New Haven, 1962, pp. 112–13
3   "M. Greuze, the excellent painter of character heads, has taken on that of Franklin, the sketch of which can now be seen. There is much resemblance and expression in it." Bachaumont, *Mémoires secrets*, X, p. 179
4   "We have said that Sʳ Greuze was doing the portrait of M. Franklin, which will not fail to be engraved. M. Elie de Beaumont, the Attorney celebrated for his eloquence, his intrigues and a romantic spirit, has already arranged in his study a niche for this illustrious personnage among other great men, ancient and modern, whom he has placed there, and has composed in advance this inscription to put below it: *Champion of the one world, and light of both.*" *Ibid.*, p. 196
5   "If I should grow as old as this benefactor of humanity, I shall boast to my grandnephews of having known this great man, of having received him often in my home and of having obtained his consent to let himself be painted by Greuze so that I might have his portrait from the hand of that great master. This portrait will follow me everywhere until my grave. I cherish it all the more because, being a good likeness, Greuze has

painted in it all the nobility of a free spirit, all the wisdom of a well-ordered mind and all the sagacity of a statesman." Quoted in Sellers, 1962, p. 300
6   "M. Greuze, who for some time now no longer exhibits in the Salon, has opened one of his own in his studio, and he admits the public who drop by. To be seen there especially is the portrait of M. Franklin. One easily judges that this prominent figure has stimulated his spirit; it is difficult to find a head better characterized. One observes in it goodness happily allied with pride, and the love of humanity breathes in it with the hatred of tyranny." Bachaumont, *op. cit.*, pp. 234–35
7   "Inscription Madame Greuze has placed on a porcelain urn in which she keeps the remains of a bouquet of roses M. Franklin gave her in June, 1777." Quoted in Sellers, 1962, p. 114
8   "The lodge, grieved at being unable to make this acquisition, has been somewhat compensated by the painter Greuze, most useful for tasks in his field." Bachaumont, *op. cit.*, XI, p. 174
9   "never ceasing to remain unaffected even though he is sublime; become finally the painter of all ranks, of all ages, as La Fontaine is their poet." L. Amiable, *Une loge maçonnique d'avant 1789, la R*** L*** Les Neuf Soeurs*, Paris, 1897, p. 329
10   B. Faÿ, *Revolution and Freemasonry, 1680–1800*, Boston, 1935, pp. 267–68

1   "Behind the old man's armchair, the youngest of all appears frightened and stupefied." Diderot, *Salons*, II, p. 156
2   "Greuze, who should be regarded as the painter of the passions of the soul, is unique in the French school." P. M. Gault de Saint-Germain, *Les Trois Siècles de la peinture en France*, Paris, 1808, p. 251

84   The Father's Curse: The Ungrateful Son
(*La Malédiction paternelle: Le Fils ingrat*)
Oil, on canvas, 57$\frac{3}{16}$ x 63$\frac{11}{16}$ in. (130.0 x 162.0 cm)
Paris, Musée du Louvre

Collections: marquis de Véri, Paris, with pendant; his sale, Paris, December 12, 1785, lot 20, sold with pendant for 21,000 francs; Laneuville, Paris; his sale, Paris, November 15–16, 1813, lot 94, sold with pendant for 15,000 francs; Ville-Serre, Paris; purchased from him with pendant in 1820 for 10,000 francs for Louis XVIII

Exhibitions: Paris, Musée Carnavalet, Paris au XVIIIè siècle: Rétif de la Bretonne, Le Paris populaire; Carmontelle, Le Paris mondain, 1934–35, No. 58

Bibliography: Bachaumont, *Mémoires secrets*, X, p. 153; Bouchot-Saupique, No. 8; Brookner, pp. 73–75, 121–23, Pl. 61; Diderot, *Oeuvres*, X, p. 354; Duchesne, *Museum of Painting and Sculpture*, London, 1831, p. 395; Goncourt, I, pp. 322, 324; L. Hautecoeur, *Greuze*, Paris, 1913, pp. 54, 74–77, 113–14, 147; C.-L. F. Lecarpentier, *Notice sur Greuze lu dans la séance de la Société libre d'Emulation de Rouen*, [Rouen], 1805, p. 4; Martin-Masson, No. 167; Munhall, 1964, pp. 15–19; Rosenberg, Reynaud and Compin, I, No. 322; Smith, No. 40; J. Thuillier and A. Châtelet, *French Painting from Le Nain to Fragonard*, Geneva, 1964, p. 226; Valori, pp. 364–65

Engravings: J.-M. Moreau *le jeune*, 1777, with pendant; R. Gaillard, with pendant; J.-J. Avril [1]

The two majestic paintings Greuze executed in 1777–78 on the theme of *The Father's Curse* (see also No. 88) are the masterpieces of the artist's mature years. Following a habit he had established by 1757, they were conceived as dramatic pendants in which the events depicted in one picture are inextricably linked to those in the other. They present in contemporary dress an age-old theme of family dissension that goes back to the parable of the Prodigal Son. By means of pose and expression Greuze draws the viewer into sympathetic participation in these scenes of searing emotion. Highly regarded in the eighteenth century, their quality has been appreciated afresh only in recent years.

Returning to the subject of *The Ungrateful Son* which he had treated in 1765 (No. 48), Greuze represents here the eldest son of a large family who, having quarrelled with his father, is stunned and angered by the curse the latter hurls at him as he is about to leave their country home, his right hand raised in horror, his left fist clenched in rage. Other members of the family react to the violent discord according to their individual characters—some restraining, pleading or remonstrating, others simply registering fright. A recruiting officer, who has given, or is about to give, the young man money for enlisting, awaits

his subject with a supercilious air.

Though the theme recalls in a general way the departure of the Prodigal Son, it more specifically relates to a scene in Diderot's prose drama *Le Père de famille* of 1758, in which a father curses his son in words appropriate to Greuze's picture and to its title: "*Eloignez-vous de moi, fils ingrat et dénaturé. Je vous donne ma malédiction; allez loin de moi.*"[2] Diderot had also included an article on "*Malédiction*" in the *Encyclopédie*, defining it as an "*imprécation qu'on prononce contre quelque objet. mal faisant. Un père maudit son enfant . . . on croit que la malédiction assise sur un être est une espèce de caractère.*"[3] In 1780, inspired by Greuze's picture, Rétif de la Bretonne published his *Malédiction paternelle*, the story of a man driven to depravity and tragedy through the curse his father had placed upon him.

Compared to the drawing of 1765, the composition of *The Father's Curse: The Ungrateful Son* is reversed, more frieze-like in composition and less picturesque in detail. Greuze's experience with history painting in the intervening years had led him to a nobler style, with a clearer delineation of expression and with more generalized clothing—particularly in the case of the mother, whose flowing draperies are reminiscent of Hellenistic sculpture. Sauerländer has even seen in the haunting pose of the son an echo of that of Laocoön in the Vatican group.[4] In reference to antique models it is worth noting that the recruiting officer is depicted with his hand on his hip in an affected pose Greuze adapted from the Belvedere *Antinoüs* and used frequently (see for example No. 70).

Writing in June of 1777, Bachaumont claimed Greuze was currently hurrying to complete *The Father's Curse: The Ungrateful Son* not only in time to compete with the biennial exhibition of the Académie, but also in anticipation of a visit from the Queen's brother, the Emperor Joseph II, who was visiting France that summer under the assumed title of comte de Falkenstein: "*Monsieur Greuze, toujours piqué de son exclusion de l'académie, continue à préparer pour le temps de l'exposition des tableaux, quelque chef-d'oeuvre qui attire la foule chez lui. Cette année il a pris pour sujet la* malédiction paternelle. *Instruit de l'arrivée de l'Empereur, il a pressé son ouvrage, afin de pouvoir le montrer à ce prince dans un état de perfection; ce qui fait qu'on peut déjà l'aller admirer chez cet artiste. On en dit beaucoup de bien.*"[5] The Emperor's visit took place and apparently was a success, for that August, Joseph II offered Greuze the title of baron and purchased a painting from him for 4,000 ducats.[6]

Greuze's strategy of exhibiting his latest productions in his studio at the same time as the Académie's exhibitions gave rise to numerous comments concerning *The Ungrateful Son* in 1777. They are almost unanimously enthusiastic, but few merit quoting at length. While Greuze's skill was admired, it still was regarded as that of a genre painter:

"*Greuze est le Molière de la peinture, mais il n'en est ni le Corneille ni le Racine.*"[7] More favorably than was the case with *Septimius Severus Reproaching Caracalla* (No. 70), his achievement was compared with those of Poussin and other masters of expression: "*Enfin, ce tableau est un chef-d'oeuvre en tout point, et tel, à mon avis, que les plus grands maîtres en fait d'expression, qu'un* Poussin, *un* Le Sueur *et* Raphaël *peut-être, ne l'auroient pas désavoué.*"[8] Even the fact that Greuze had painted an essentially verbal or literary subject, as he had in *Septimius Severus*, was this time appreciated: "*On croit entendre sortir de sa bouche les paroles terribles. Cependant, à travers son indignation, on sent le déchirement du coeur paternel, qui gémit de la nécessité de maudire, et ce mélange de sentimens opposés étoit sans doute bien difficile à exprimer.*"[9] *La Prêtresse* found "*la couleur fraîche, vigoureuse et quelquefois transparente.*"[10] However, the artist's tendency to arrange

his figures as in a frieze was not appreciated, as one critic of Gaillard's engraving noted: "*On seroit même tenté de croire en voyant la disposition du sujet composé de huit figures placées à peu près sur la même ligne et collées en quelque sorte sur le fond, que l'estampe a été gravée d'après un bas-relief.*"[11]

Nevertheless, Greuze was hailed as the inventor of a new kind of moralizing art capable of affecting people's behavior. Following him, artists would depict "*sous tant de traits odieux les désordres des familles qu'il ne tient qu'aux spectateurs, pères, mères, filles, époux d'en faire leur profit.*"[12] Most significantly, Greuze's ability to involve his viewers in the emotions of his subjects was fully appreciated: "*Il y a dans toute cette scène une âme, une chaleur, un caractère, une énergie de sentiment qu'il m'est impossible de vous rendre. J'ai surtout été frappé du mouvement général qui l'anime. Elle est comme d'un seul jet. . . . C'est le sublime de l'expression touchante.*"[13]

Fig. 22 Standing Male Nude,
study for *The Father's Curse: The
Ungrateful Son*, red chalk,
whereabouts unknown

A copy of *The Father's Curse: The Ungrateful Son* described
as "*faite par Greuze lui-même, ou du moins par un élève très-
habile, et retouchée par lui*," appeared without pendant in
the Brossard de Beaulieu sale, Paris, August 2, 1832, lot 1.[14]
A full-scale copy of *The Ungrateful Son*, said to be
contemporary and to have come from the Juigné and
Talleyrand-Périgord collections, appeared, with pendant,
in the Boittelle sale, Paris, March 13, 1891, lot 10, sold for
950 francs. This may be the copy that appeared, with
pendant, in a sale in Paris, June 30—July 1, 1941, and
again at a sale in Paris, December 2, 1970.

Numerous drawings for *The Father's Curse: The Ungrateful
Son* are known. In addition to the Lille preliminary drawing
of 1765 (No. 48), there exists a highly finished preparatory
study for the painting, or possibly a record of it, executed
by Greuze; formerly in the collection of the baronne
Salomon de Rothschild, it appeared in the René Fribourg
sale, London, October 16, 1963, lot 548, and was
subsequently in the Avnet collection, New York. A third
drawing of the full composition, in the Albertina, Vienna
(No. 15374), shows the young man in the cavalier stance
of the Lille drawing. A fourth drawing of the full
composition, now lost, done in ink heightened with white
on blue paper, appeared in the Saint-Maurice sale, Paris,
February 1 and 6, 1786, lot 382, with pendant.

A study of three figures for *The Ungrateful Son* appeared
in the van den Zande sale, Paris, April 30, 1855, lot 2986,
sold for 180 francs to Cormante. A counterproof of a study
for the daughter at left is in the Lepeltier collection, Paris.
A study for the boy behind her is included in this
exhibition (No. 83). In the Cabinet des Dessins at the
Louvre is a drawing of the imploring sister with her hands
clasped together beneath her chin (Inv. 26997), as well as a
counterproof of the same sheet (Inv. 27001).[15] A study for
the child clutching at his brother—described in 1777 as
"*un petit frère, encore enfant*" who "*s'accroche à la veste du
ainé et s'efforce aussi de l'arrêter*"[16]—appeared in the Jacques
Doucet sale, Paris, June 5, 1912, lot 25, sold for 5,600
francs to Lasquin. A superb nude study for the departing
son (fig. 22) was in 1951 with the Galerie Cailleux, Paris,[17]
and a counterproof of it is in the Lepeltier collection, Paris.
An important study for the mother, in red, black and
white chalks heightened with watercolor, appeared in the
Walferdin sale, Paris, April 12–16, 1880, lot 307. A study for
the father is in the Hermitage.[18]

Fig. 23 *The Father's Curse: The Ungrateful Son* (detail)

1 Portalis-Béraldi, III, p. 123, II, p. 224, I, p. 62. The Moreau print is inscribed "*de mémoire*" (from memory).

2 "Get away from me, ungrateful and unnatural son. I give you my curse; go far from me." Diderot, *Oeuvres complètes*, VIII, p. 227

3 "imprecation uttered against some evil-doer. A father *curses* his child . . . it is believed that a curse placed on someone is a kind of mark." Diderot, *Encyclopédie*, IX, p. 944

4 Sauerländer, p. 150, figs. 9, 10

5 "Monsieur Greuze, still piqued over his exclusion from the Académie, continues to prepare for the time of the exhibition of paintings some masterpiece that will attract the crowd to his studio. This year he has taken for his subject the *father's curse*. Informed of the Emperor's arrival, he has hurried on with his work in order to be able to show it to that prince in a state of perfection; which means that one can already go to admire it in the artist's studio. People are saying a lot of good things about it." Bachaumont, *Mémoires secrets*, X, pp. 167–68

6 "*M. le comte de Falkenstein, loin d'envier à la France les grands hommes qui honorent leur Patrie, vient d'envoyer à M. Greuze un diplôme de Baron et quatre mille ducats, en lui demandant seulement un de ses tableaux. Tout le monde doit applaudir à cette générosité qui justifie le haut degré de perfection auquel ce peintre a porté son talent.*" ("M. the comte de Falkenstein, far from envying France the great men who honor their Country, has just sent M. Greuze a certificate of Baron and four thousand ducats, asking from him only one of his pictures. Everyone should applaud this generosity which justifies the high degree of perfection to which that artist has brought his talent.") J.-J. Métra, *Correspondance secrète, politique et littéraire*, Paris, 1787, V, p. 113

7 "Greuze is the Molière of painting, but he is neither its Corneille nor its Racine." *Seconde lettre de M. le comte D*** en réponse à celle qui est avant celle sur la partialité*, Paris, 1777, p. 3

8 "Finally, this picture is a masterpiece in every respect, and so much so, in my opinion, that the greatest masters in matter of

expression, such as a *Poussin*, a *Le Sueur* and perhaps *Raphael*, would not have disavowed it." *Lettres pittoresques, à l'occasion des tableaux exposés au Sallon, en 1777*, Paris, 1777, *Septième lettre*, p. 45

9 "You feel you can hear the terrible words issuing from his mouth. And yet, through his indignation, you sense the rending of the paternal heart, which bemoans the necessity of cursing, and this mixture of opposed sentiments was no doubt very difficult to convey." *Ibid.*, p. 43

10 "the coloring fresh, vigorous and sometimes transparent." *La Prêtresse, ou nouvelle manière de prédire ce qui est arrivé*, Rome—Paris, 1777, p. 22

11 "One would even be tempted to believe, in seeing the arrangement of the subject composed of eight figures placed nearly on the same line and somehow glued onto the background, that the print was engraved after a bas-relief." *Lettres d'un voyageur à Paris à son ami Charles Lovers . . . sur les nouvelles estampes de Mr Greuze*, Paris, 1779, p. 34

12 "family disorders in so many odious images that it would simply be up to the viewers, fathers, mothers, daughters, husbands, to profit from them." *Lettres pittoresques, Cinquième lettre*, p. 20

13 "There is throughout this entire scene a soul, a warmth, a character, an energy of feeling impossible for me to convey to you. I was especially struck by the overall movement that animates it. It is as if it were all done at one go. . . . It is the sublime of affective expression." *Ibid.*, *Septième lettre*, p. 44

14 "done by Greuze himself, or at least by a very skilled pupil, and touched up by him." Information kindly communicated by M. Jean Adhémar

15 Guiffrey-Marcel, VI, p. 56, Nos. 4553, 4554; Martin-Masson, Nos. 1503, 1504

16 "a little brother, still a child." "hangs on to his elder brother's waistcoat and also tries to detain him." *Lettres pittoresques, Septième lettre*, p. 44

17 See: Paris, Galerie Cailleux, *Le Dessin français de Watteau à Prud'hon*, exhib. cat., 1951, No. 61

18 Monod-Hautecoeur, No. 57

85 Head of a Man

Red chalk, on white paper, 12¾ x 16½ in. (32.4 x 41.9 cm)
Baltimore, private collection

Collections: Fairfax-Murray, London; Prince W. Argoutinsky-Dolgoronkoff, Paris (Lugt 2602 d); his sale, London, July 4, 1923, lot 41, sold for 15,000 guineas to Borenius; T. Borenius; Mrs. W. H. Hill, Boston; acquired from a Mrs. Smith, New York, about 1943

Exhibitions: Los Angeles, University of California Art Council, French Masters: Rococo to Romanticism, 1961, No. 42

This important drawing is clearly related to *The Father's Curse: The Ungrateful Son*, but it cannot be considered a preparatory study for the head of the departing son as he appears in either the drawing of 1765 (No. 48) or the painting of 1777 (No. 84). Instead this sheet belongs to the genre of the *tête d'expression*, a drawn or painted representation of a specific emotional state—in this case, pain.

This *Head of a Man*, and another related one formerly in the Hermitage (fig. 8),[1] depend from Charles Lebrun's representation of *douleur corporelle* (physical pain) in his *Conférence sur l'expression générale et particulière* (fig. 7), which in turn was based on the *Laocoön* group. Just as Greuze transposed traditional subjects of history painting into scenes of contemporary life, so in this drawing he brings the representations of the passions up to date, yet still conforming in a general way to Lebrun's description of the physical manifestations of pain: *"Tous les mouvemens du visage paroîtront aigus, car les sourcils qui s'élèvent en haut, le seront encore plus que dans la précédente passion* [sadness], *et s'approcheront plus près l'un de l'autre; la prunelle sera cachée sous le sourcil, les narines s'éleveront aussi de ce côté là, et marqueront un pli aux joües, la bouche sera plus ouverte . . . et plus retirée en arriere, et fera une espece de figure carrée en cet endroit là. Toutes les parties du visage paroîtront plus ou moins marquées, et plus agitées selon que la douleur sera violente."*[2]

At about the time Greuze must have executed this work, his skill in depicting expressions was praised in these terms: *"Je le connais, et il a réelement la plus grande vérité de caractère et d'expression. . . ."*[3] In 1779 another critic linked this skill with the artist's experience in naturalistic drawing: *"Ayant souvent copié la nature il sait indiquer par de justes masses, les principaux traits de caractère des passions propres à son sujet."*[4]

The power of this drawing no doubt accounts for the existence of four copies of it, the highest in quality being that in the Pierpont Morgan Library, New York (I. 826). Others, not by Greuze, are in the Louvre (No. 27000; Guiffrey-Marcel, No. 4580), in the Musée des Beaux-Arts, Lyon (No. 322), and in a private collection, Paris.[5] A counterproof roughly the size of the present sheet is in the Musée Greuze, Tournus (No. 51).

1   Monod-Hautecoeur, No. 78, Pl. XXI
2   "All the movements of the face will appear intense, for the eyebrows, which are raised up, will be so even more than in the preceding passion [sadness], and will be drawn closer to one another; the pupil will be concealed beneath the eyebrow, the nostrils will also be raised in the same way and will form a crease in the cheeks, the mouth will be more open . . . and drawn back further, and will form a sort of square shape in that area. All parts of the face will appear more or less affected, and more or less agitated according to the violence of the pain." Quoted in H. Jouin, *Charles Le Brun et les arts sous Louis XIV*, Paris, 1889, II, p. 386
3   "I know him, and he really has the greatest truth in character and expression." *Dialogues sur la peinture*, Paris, 1773, p. 42
4   "Having often drawn from nature, he knows how to indicate by appropriate masses the principal characteristics of the passions peculiar to his subject." *Lettres d'un voyageur à Paris à son ami Charles Lovers . . . sur les nouvelles estampes de Mr Greuze*, Paris, 1779, p. 5
5   Red chalk drawing, 44.5 x 32.5 cm, formerly in the Rouzé-Huet collection (Lugt 1742), sold in Paris, June 22, 1965, lot 23

175

86 Woman Embracing a Recumbent Old Man
(Study for *The Father's Curse: The Punished Son*)
Pen and brush, brown ink, on white paper, 4¾ x 7¹⁵⁄₁₆ in.
(12.0 x 20.2 cm)
Signed: *Greuze*
Paris, Fondation Custodia (Coll. F. Lugt), Institut
Néerlandais

Collections: Grosjean et Maupin, Paris; acquired by the
institute in 1959

This intense little drawing is a study for *The Father's Curse:
The Punished Son* (No. 88). It represents a daughter embracing
her expiring father and suggests—more than either the
early drawing of that subject (No. 49) or the later painting,
in both of which she is depicted hovering over the bed—
the feeling that, as Diderot put it, she "*ne sauroit pas se
persuader qu'elle n'a plus de père.*"[1]

1 "cannot bring herself to believe
she no longer has a father." Diderot,
Salons, II, p. 157

87 Head of a Man
(Study for *The Father's Curse: The Punished Son*)
Oil, on white paper (counterproof), reworked with brush
and brown ink, 8½ x 7⅜ in. (21.6 x 18.7 cm)
Paris, Musée du Louvre, Cabinet des Dessins

Collections: original collection of the Cabinet des Dessins,
Musée du Louvre (Lugt 1886)
   Exhibitions: Paris, Louvre, Cabinet des Dessins, Le
Théâtre et la Danse en France au XVIIIè Siècle, 1959, No. 66
   Bibliography: Guiffrey-Marcel, VI, No. 4549; Martin-
Masson, No. 1686;[1] Reiset, II, p. 39, No. 775

This apparently simple drawing of the returning son in
The Father's Curse: The Punished Son (No. 88) is in effect a
monotype made from a sketch in oil, counterproved and
then reworked in brown ink—a unique example of such a
procedure in Greuze's oeuvre. The combination of media
would suggest that Greuze executed the drawing late in
1778 while working on the canvas for which it is a study.
Other studies for the same head are less complex spatially,
being in pure profile, and less intense emotionally, as they
do not show the head so painfully bowed in grief. The
fact that the hand is here depicted delicately supporting
the brow is the only essential difference from the same
head in the drawing of 1765 (No. 49), which Diderot
described thus: *"Le fils ingrat paroît consterné; la tête lui tombe
en devant, et il se frappe le front avec le poing."*[2]

   Greuze's abundant use of counterproofs in evolving his
compositions remains to be studied. In the inventory of
his possessions made in 1793 no less than forty-seven
counterproofs were listed in one portfolio, *"la plupart
maculées et dans le plus mauvais ordre"*[3]—an observation
justified by the spotted edges of the present sheet.

1   Guiffrey and Marcel, No. 4549,
list the present drawing as
corresponding to Martin-Masson
No. 1689, which is in fact Louvre
drawing No. 26977 (Guiffrey-Marcel
No. 4579)
2   "The ungrateful son appears
overwhelmed; his head falls
forward, and he strikes his forehead
with his fist." Diderot, *Salons,*
II, p. 158
3   "most of them stained and in
the worst order." M. Barroux,
ed., "Procès-verbal d'apposition
de scellés chez Greuze après son
divorce," *Bulletin de la Société de
l'Histoire de Paris et de l'Ile-de-France,*
XXIII, 1896, p. 89

88 The Father's Curse: The Punished Son
(*La Malédiction paternelle: Le Fils puni*)

Oil, on canvas, 57⅜₆ x 64¼ in. (130.0 x 163.0 cm)
Paris, Musée du Louvre

Collections: Same as No. 84

Exhibitions: Paris, Musée Carnavalet, Paris au XVIIIè
siècle: Rétif de la Bretonne, Le Paris populaire; Carmontelle,
Le Paris mondain, 1934–35, No. 58; Paris, Louvre, Chefs-
d'oeuvre de la peinture, 1945, No. 98; Paris, Louvre, La
"Mort de Germanicus" de Poussin du Musée de
Minneapolis, 1973, No. 93

Bibliography: Brookner, pp. 73–75, 121–25, Pl. 62; Diderot,
Oeuvres, X, p. 356; *L'Espion anglais ou correspondance secrète
entre Milord All'Eye et Milord All'Ear*, London, 1784, X,
Lettre XI; Goncourt, I, pp. 322, 324, 349–50; Hautecoeur,
pp. 74–77, 113–14, 147; C.-L. F. Lecarpentier, *Notice sur
Greuze lu dans la séance de la Société libre d'Emulation de Rouen*,
[Rouen], 1805, p. 4; Martha, *La Délicatesse dans l'art*, Paris,
n.d., p. 133; Martin-Masson, No. 167; Munhall, 1964,
pp. 15–19; E. Prechin, *Le XVIIIè siècle*, Paris, 1952, p. 730;
Rosenberg, Reynaud and Compin, I, No. 323; R. Rosenblum,
Transformations in Late Eighteenth Century Art, Princeton,
1967, pp. 37–38, 53–55, fig. 33; Smith, No. 41; J. Thuillier
and A. Châtelet, *French Painting from Le Nain to Fragonard*,
Geneva, 1964, p. 226; Valori, pp. 364–65; *Lettre en vers d'un
amateur à M. Greuze*, Paris, 1780, pp. 4–5

Engravings: J.-M. Moreau le jeune, 1778, with pendant; R.
Gaillard, with pendant; Bligny; Civil[1]

As with its pendant, *The Father's Curse: The Ungrateful Son*
(No. 84), it is Bachaumont who supplies a date for the
execution of the present work. In summarizing its content
on November 28, 1778, he wrote: "*On commence à aller voir
chez M. Greuze un tableau faisant partie de celui de la
malédiction paternelle. Le père infortuné a succombé à sa
douleur; le fils arrive dans ce moment; la mère lui montre le
cadavre, et il paroît en proie à ses remords et à sa douleur; les
autres enfants remplissent et secondent chacun dans leur genre
cette scène touchante. Tel est le fond de l'action, dont on parlera
plus au long quand de jugement des connoisseurs sera fixé.*"[2]

The Father's Curse: The Punished Son repeats the general
scheme of the sketch Diderot admired so highly in 1765
(No. 49), but with a number of crucial changes that move
it away from the anecdotal and picturesque toward the
noble and timeless. Various details have been eliminated in
favor of a concentration on expression and gesture. For
example, in the 1765 sketch and in other preparatory
studies (see below) the son is represented supporting his
wounded lower left leg on a wooden stump;[3] in the painting
he is depicted merely with a crutch, which he has let

fall to the floor. Greuze has omitted also the delimiting
elements of the crucifix held by the woman at left and the
holy-water vessel and candle at the foot of the bed. The
total effect has become that of a classical history painting.
Indeed, the composition even recalls complex Hellenistic
sculpture such as *The Farnese Bull* or the *Niobe* group, in
which each figure plays a unique emotional role. That
Greuze's public was beginning to appreciate this fusion of
the grand style of history painting with subject matter of
both universal and contemporary significance was indicated
by the anonymous author of the *Lettres pittoresques*, who
had written of *The Father's Curse: The Ungrateful Son*: "*Qu'on
leur donnât d'autres habillemens, quoique les leurs soient
très-bien entendus; qu'on les revêtît de costume héroïque, et nous
aurions un des plus beaux tableaux d'histoire.*"[4]

Poussin's *Death of Germanicus* is echoed in this work even
more strongly than in *Septimius Severus Reproaching Caracalla*
(No. 70) or *The Death of a Beloved Father Mourned by His
Children* (No. 51). Indeed, Pierre Rosenberg has called *The
Punished Son* "*sans doute la plus intelligente retranscription dans
le monde du quotidien de la 'Mort de Germanicus.'* " Going on
to call the painting, quite justly, "*un des chefs-d'oeuvre de
l'art du XVIIIè siècle*," he summarized its significance with
an understanding no one has brought to the painting
before: "*dans ce drame de tous les jours, de la mort, de la
souffrance, de l'incompréhension, de l'émotion retenue et du
repentir, passe le souffle du grand art. Evitant la mièvrerie et le
sentimentalisme dont l'on accuse encore si souvent bien à tort,
Greuze avait su être le peintre d'histoire de la réalité quotidienne.*"[5]

In addition to Poussin, Greuze may have drawn as well
from Rembrandt, an earlier favorite of his. *The Punished Son*
recalls Rembrandt's etching *The Raising of Lazarus* of
1631–32 in the two figures on the far side of the bed
extending their arms in astonishment over the corpse, in
the majestic draperies defining the void in which the figures
move and in the dominant, statuesque figure of the mother.

Perhaps because it was acquired by the marquis de Véri
soon after its completion in 1778, *The Punished Son* did not
receive the critical publicity accorded its pendant. Scattered
allusions to it were made in the 1780s, and Rétif de la
Bretonne wove the picture into his novel *Les Contemporaines*
(1780–85), suggesting, in terms that widen the significance
of Greuze's painting, the tragedy awaiting all who are
involved in a curse: "*Ce n'est pas dans les Campagnes
seulement que les Pères maudissent leurs Enfans; ils usent dans
les grandes villes de ce droit funeste, si contraire à la nature;
puisqu'il dépouille Celui qui maudit du titre sacré de Père, pour
ne lui laisser que l'odieuse qualité de persécuteur et d'ennemi de
son sang. C'est se maudire soi-même, que de maudire son Fils;
c'est une sorte de suicide, puisque le Fils n'est que le
prolongement de l'existence du Père.*"[6]

A copy of *The Father's Curse: The Punished Son*, along with one of its pendant, appeared in a sale in Paris, June 30—July 1, 1941. This copy may be the one, described as contemporary and as having come from the Juigné and Talleyrand-Périgord collections, that appeared in the Boittelle sale, Paris, March 13, 1891, lot 11, sold for 950 francs, with pendant, and in a sale in Paris, December 2, 1970, with pendant. The latter was in 1975 with the Banque de l'Union Orientale, Paris.

Writing of Lagrenée's prolific entries in the Salon of 1767, Diderot noted: "*dix-sept tableaux; en deux ans, sans compter ceux qui ne sont pas exposés; tandis que Greuze couve pendant des mois entiers la composition d'un seul, et met quelquefois un an à l'exécuter.*"[7] The quantity of drawings for *The Punished Son* that have survived attests to the accuracy of Diderot's description of Greuze's working methods. In their subtle variations these drawings help explain the impact of the final painting, which incorporates the resolutions Greuze laboriously made for each element in his preparatory studies.

No less than six compositional studies for *The Punished Son* survive, in addition to a lost drawing with nine figures, done in wash heightened in white on blue paper, that appeared in the Saint-Maurice sale, Paris, February 1 and 6, 1786, lot 382, with pendant. In probable chronological order they are: a) a signed chalk and wash study in the Albertina, Vienna (No. 12–759), very similar to b) the drawing from the Musée des Beaux-Arts, Lille, included in this exhibition (No. 49); c) a rough wash drawing in the Ecole des Beaux-Arts, Paris (No. 1042),[8] which shows three figures on the far side of the bed, the mother wearing draperies after the antique and the dog moving parallel to the picture plane, as in d) a signed wash drawing in the Albertina (No. 12–760) and e) a rather stiff drawing, perhaps not by Greuze, also in the Albertina (No. 15–375) which includes the weeping boy in the foreground; and f) a study representing the corpse, three lamenting figures on the far side of the bed and the weeping boy in the foreground, in the Schmitz-Hille collection, Thun,

Switzerland.[9] All but the last include a candle and holy-water vessel at the foot of the bed.

Numerous studies for the figures also survive. Proceeding from left to right across the final painting, they include the following. A red chalk study for the boy shown reaching up to the woman sitting by the bed—as he had been represented reaching up to the departing son in *The Ungrateful Son*—appeared in the Léon Michel-Lévy sale, Paris, June 17–18, 1925, lot 69, sold for 15,000 francs. A counterproof of a study for the woman sitting by the bed, depicted in the drawings as holding a crucifix which according to Diderot *"elle a fait baiser à son père,"*[10] is in the Smith College Museum of Art, Northampton, Massachusetts. A study for her head appeared in a sale in Paris, April 3, 1837, lot 43; this may be the original of a counterproof in the Cabinet des Dessins at the Louvre (No. 26965).[11] In the Musée Bonnat at Bayonne is a superb study in red and black chalks for the head of the father (No. 1640). A drawing for the same figure appeared in the Joinville sale, London, 1848, lot 41. A pen and brush drawing in brown ink representing the young woman on the far side of the bed passionately embracing the old man, an early study for this dramatic figure, is included in this exhibition (No. 86). A study for her full figure is in the Louvre (No. 26980).[12] A study for her head appeared in the Mirecourt sale, July 9, 1943, lot 56, and in a sale in Paris, March 20, 1956, lot 13; a counterproof of this sheet appeared in the Galipe sale, Paris, March 27, 1923, and in a sale in Paris, November 30, 1927, lot 76. Two red chalk studies for the boy weeping in the foreground are in the Louvre (Nos. 26972, 26976).[13] For the boy beyond the bed, *"les bras en l'air, et les doigts écartés,"* who *"semble concevoir les premières idées de la mort,"* there exists a red chalk study which appeared in a sale in London, October 21, 1963, lot 124; its counterproof appeared in sales in Paris on July 9, 1943, lot 57, and March 20, 1956, lot 14. A full-length study in red chalk for the mother appeared in the Walferdin sale, Paris, May 18, 1860, lot 85.[14] A fine study of her head in red chalk, formerly in Baron Schwiter's collection, now belongs to Kurt Meissner, Zurich (fig. 25) and another was sold in Leipzig, June 27, 1899, lot 241, having previously appeared in the Storck sale, Berlin, June 25, 1894, lot 239. A full-length study for the returning son was also in the Walferdin sale of 1860, lot 86.[15] A counterproof, perhaps of the latter drawing, representing the full figure of the son is in the Musée Greuze, Tournus (No. 24),[16] and a study for his torso is in the Louvre (No. 26956).[17] In addition to the study for the son's head included in this exhibition (No. 87), other drawings for his head include one in pen and ink at the Louvre (No. 26975),[18] one in brush and ink also at the Louvre (No. 26977)[19] and three formerly in the Hermitage.[20]

A representation of *The Father's Curse: The Punished Son* appears in A.-C. G. Lemonnier's painting *Une Lecture chez Madame Geoffrin* in the Musée des Beaux-Arts, Rouen. Greuze's picture is evoked with dramatic significance in the scene of the grand ball at the end of Giuseppe di Lampedusa's *Il Gattopardo*.[21]

1 Portalis-Béraldi, III, p. 123, II, p. 224, III, p. 721. The Moreau print is inscribed *"de mémoire"* (from memory).
2 "People are starting to go to M. Greuze's studio to see a picture that forms part of the *father's curse*. The unfortunate father has succumbed to his suffering; the son arrives at just that moment; the mother shows him the corpse, and he seems to fall prey to his remorse and his grief; the other children fill out and implement, each in their own way, this touching scene. Such are the essentials of the action, about which we shall speak at further length once the judgment of the connoisseurs has been determined." Bachaumont, *Mémoires secrets*, XI, p. 173
3 Though occasionally described as partially amputated, the leg is clearly depicted intact.
4 "Let them be given other garments, though the ones they wear are very well arranged; let them be dressed in heroic costumes, and we would have one of the most beautiful of history paintings." *Lettres pittoresques, à l'occasion des tableaux exposés au Sallon, en 1777*, Paris, 1777, *Septième lettre*, pp. 44–45
5 "without doubt the most intelligent retranscription of the *Death of Germanicus* into the everyday world." "one of the masterpieces of the art of the eighteenth century." "into this everyday drama of death, of suffering, of incomprehension, of emotion held back and of regret, passes the inspiration of great art. Avoiding the finicky affectation and sentimentality of which he is still accused so often quite wrongly, Greuze knew how to be the history painter of daily life." See: Paris, Louvre, La "Mort de Germanicus" de Poussin du Musée de Minneapolis, exhib. cat., 1973, No. 93, p. 58
6 "It is not in the Countryside alone that Fathers curse their Children; in the great cities they make use of this deadly power, so contrary to nature; for it strips the One who curses of the sacred title of Father, leaving him only the odious quality of persecutor and the enemy of his own blood. To curse one's Son is to curse oneself; it is a kind of suicide, for the Son is only the continuation of the existence of the Father." See: Paris, Musée Carnavalet, Paris au XVIIIè siècle: Rétif de la Bretonne, Le Paris populaire; Carmontelle, Le Paris mondain, exhib. cat., 1934–35, No. 59, p. 13
7 "seventeen pictures; in two years, without counting those that are not exhibited; while Greuze broods over the composition of a single one for months at a time, and sometimes takes a year to execute it." Diderot, *Salons*, III, p. 113
8 P. Lavallée, "La Collection de dessins de l'Ecole des Beaux-Arts," *Gazette des Beaux-Arts*, October–December, 1917, p. 428
9 The drawing bears a partially illegible inscription on the verso: *"Donné à . . . par son ami Greuze le 6 7bre / 1793 . . . de la République."*
10 "she has had her father kiss." This and the following descriptive quotation ("his arms in the air, and his fingers spread apart" "seems to grasp his first ideas of death") from Diderot, *op. cit.*, II, pp. 157–58
11 Guiffrey-Marcel, No. 4585
12 *Ibid.*, No. 4573; Martin-Masson, No. 1553
13 Guiffrey-Marcel, Nos. 4545, 4546; Martin-Masson, Nos. 1514, 1515
14 Martin-Masson, No. 1431, described as *"étude du pied de la mère dans le tableau du Fils puni"* ("study for the foot of the mother in the picture of *The Punished Son*"); the catalogue of the Walferdin sale lists it as *"étude en pied de la mère"* ("full-length study of the mother").
15 Martin-Masson, No. 1432, same confusion as described in preceding note
16 *Ibid.*, No. 1522
17 Guiffrey-Marcel, No. 4578
18 *Ibid.*, No. 4548
19 *Ibid.*, No. 4579
20 Monod-Hautecoeur, Nos. 87, 89, 90
21 See J. Meyers, "Greuze and Lampedusa's 'Il Gattopardo,'" *Modern Language Review*, April, 1974, pp. 308–15

Fig. 24 *The Father's Curse: The Punished Son* (detail)

Fig. 25 Head of a Woman, study for *The Father's Curse: The Punished Son*, red chalk, Zurich, Kurt Meissner collection

89 The Boat of Happiness

Brush, black ink, on white paper, 5⅛ x 14⅛ in. (21.9 x
35.8 cm)
Signed: *Greuze*
Rotterdam, Museum Boymans-van Beuningen

Collections: Franz Koenigs, Haarlem (Lugt 1023 a); D. G.
van Beuningen, Rotterdam; given by him to the Museum
Boymans Foundation in 1940

In *The Boat of Happiness* and a drawing related to it,
The Boat of Misfortune (No. 90), Greuze treats an autobiographical subject with characteristic frankness, for the
drawings refer to the early aspirations and late disappoint-
ments he experienced in his marriage with Anne-Gabrielle
Babuti.

Madame de Valori, in her account of Greuze first published
in 1813, describes a composition similar to this one, but
with certain important differences: "*Dans la première barque,
qui glisse légèrement sur une onde pure et tranquille, on voit deux
époux occupés à ramer pour atteindre l'autre bord, où l'on aperçoit
le temple du Bonheur qui s'élève au milieu d'une île semée de roses
et de myrtes. Au milieu de la barque, sont deux enfants qui
jouent en regardant leurs parents qui jouissent de leurs jeux, et
semblent redoubler d'efforts pour atteindre l'île fortunée. Pour s'en
approcher, il faut éviter un précipice, qui semble en rendre péril-
leuse l'approche; mais l'accord qui règne entre ces heureux époux, les
fait braver et vaincre le danger, et l'Amour, qui vole au-dessus
de la proue, les anime et sourit à leur bonheur.*"[1] The boat
imagery, the flying Cupid and the island with roses and
myrtle recall Watteau's *Pilgrimage to Cythera* (Louvre).

Stylistic comparisons suggest that these two drawings
were done in the late 1770s. Madame de Valori stated that
Greuze intended to execute paintings after them,[2] but none
are known. Prud'hon took up the subject in a drawing,[3]
which his pupil Constance Mayer-Lamartinière developed
in a painting entitled *The Dream of Happiness*, exhibited in
the Salon of 1819 and acquired by the Louvre. In her
picture, similar in shape to the present drawing, a woman
aided by a winged Cupid rows a boat at left as a man and
a sleeping woman and child recline at right. There is no
precipice nor temple.

1 "In the first boat, which glides
lightly on a pure and tranquil
wave, we see a husband and wife
busily rowing to reach the
opposite bank, where we perceive
the temple of Happiness rising in
the middle of an island strewn with
roses and myrtle. In the center of
the boat are two children playing
as they watch their parents, who
rejoice in their games and seem to
double their efforts to reach the
fortunate island. In order to
approach it, they must avoid a
precipice, which seems to make the
approach perilous; but the harmony
that reigns between these happy
spouses enables them to face and to
overcome the danger, and Love,
flying over the prow, encourages
them and smiles on their
happiness." Valori, p. 373
2 *Ibid.*
3 See: Paris, Institut Néerlandais,
Le Dessin français dans les
collections hollandaises, exhib. cat.,
1964, No. 135, Pl. 110

90 The Boat of Misfortune

Brush, gray ink wash, and pencil, on white paper, 14⁹⁄₁₆ x 9¹⁄₁₆ in. (37.0 x 23.0 cm)
Tournus, Musée Greuze

Collections: marquis Philippe de Chennevières, Paris
(Lugt 2072); his sale, Paris, April 4, 1900, lot 222
   Bibliography: Martin-Masson, No. 80

Different in shape and separate in provenance from *The Boat of Happiness* (No. 89), this drawing nonetheless relates closely to that one, which alludes to the optimistic earlier phase of Greuze's marriage. As in *The Angry Woman* (No. 96) and *The Reconciliation* (No. 97), Greuze stresses in these two drawings the autobiographical note of the subjects, in this case by including two children who recall his own two daughters.

Madame de Valori, a pupil of Greuze, may echo the artist's own words in describing the present drawing and its symbolism: "*Dans la seconde barque, que la scène qui s'y passe est différente de la première! Elle n'offre plus l'image du bonheur qu'on admirait dans l'autre. Les flots contre lesqueles elle lutte sont soulevés, les nuages amoncelés; l'éclair qui les fend et la foudre qui est tombée sur le temple du Bonheur, dont on n'aperçoit plus que les débris, annoncent le courroux du ciel, qui ne protége jamais les époux désunis. Les vents et les vagues déchaînés poussent cette malheureuse barque vers le précipice qu'elle avait su éviter. L'époux seul fait en vain des efforts pour l'empêcher de tomber dans l'abîme; ses mains affaiblies peuvent à peine soutenir les rames; le gouvernail est brisé. L'épouse assise sur le banc opposé à celui de son malheureux époux, la tête appuyée non-chalamment sur une de ses mains, semble insensible au danger qui l'environne, et tandis que ses enfants se battent en se disputant un morceau de pain, elle les fixe sans intérêt, et ne paraît pas même songer à les séparer, tant l'insouciance et la légerté de son caractère ont glacé son coeur. L'Amour, dont le flambeau est éteint, vole loin de cette barque où règne la discorde, et qui bientôt va disparaître sous les flots.*"[1]

Madame de Valori further recalled Greuze's advice to her on the subject of marriage as treated in these two drawings: "*Voilà . . . l'aspect d'un ménage dont un seul soutient tout le poids: souviens-toi, mon enfant, si jamais tu deviens épouse et mère, qu'il te faut partager les peines de ton mari, les adoucir, et avoir pour ses erreurs un grand fonds d'indulgence; car enfin la dernière personne qui reste à une femme, c'est son mari; elle doit donc tout employer pour conserver son amitié et son estime. Etre excellente mère; car une mauvaise mère est une erreur de la nature, et celle qui l'offre, excite le mépris. Sois donc bonne mère, épouse douce et indulgente, et la barque saura braver les orages pour arriver au port.*"[2]

1 "In the second boat, how different the scene that passes is from the first! It no longer offers the image of happiness that we admired in the other. The billows against which it struggles have risen, clouds have piled up; the lightning that tears through them and the thunderbolt that has struck the temple of Happiness, of which we now see only the wreckage, announce the wrath of the heavens, which never protect a disunited couple. The winds and the unleashed waves push this unfortunate boat toward the precipice it had succeeded in avoiding. The husband alone makes vain efforts to prevent it from falling into the abyss; his weakened hands can hardly support the oars; the rudder is broken. The wife, seated opposite her unhappy husband, her head nonchalantly resting on one hand, seems insensitive to the danger that surrounds her, and while her children fight with each other and quarrel over a piece of bread, she stares at them without interest, and does not even appear to dream of separating them, so much has her heart been frozen by the unconcern and frivolity of her character. Love, whose torch is extinguished, flies far away from this boat in which discord reigns, and which will soon disappear under the waves." Valori, pp. 373–74

2 "That is . . . the aspect of a household when only one member carries all the weight: remember, my child, if ever you become a wife and mother, that you must share your husband's troubles, assuage them, and have for his errors a great store of forgiveness; for after all, the last person left to a woman is her husband: she should therefore do everything to preserve his affection and esteem. Be an excellent mother; for a bad mother is an error of nature, and she who offers herself as such arouses contempt. So be a good mother, a gentle and indulgent wife, and the boat will succeed in braving the storms to arrive at port." *Ibid.,* p. 374

91 The White Hat

Oil, on oval canvas, 22$\frac{7}{16}$ x 18$\frac{1}{8}$ in. (57.0 x 46.0 cm)
Boston Museum of Fine Arts

Collections: Thomas Dowse, Cambridge; bequeathed by him
to the Boston Athenaeum in 1859; on loan from the
Athenaeum 1876–1975; acquired by the museum with
Jessie Wilkinson, Grant Walker, Seth K. Sweetser and
Abbot Lawrence Funds in 1975
   Exhibitions: Boston Athenaeum, Annual Exhibitions
from 1857 to 1873, Sanitary Fair Exhibition, 1863, No. 107,
and National Sailors Fair Exhibition, 1864, No. 99; Paris,
Palais National des Arts, Chefs-d'Oeuvre de l'art français,
1937, No. 172
   Bibliography: Boston Museum of Fine Arts, *Catalogue of
Paintings*, Boston, 1921, No. 267, p. 102

The White Hat is a fine and relatively early example of a
type of picture that Greuze, his followers and his
imitators proliferated in the late eighteenth and early
nineteenth centuries and that came to represent for the
general public a typical Greuze: the image of a young
woman in which innocence is fused with voluptuousness.
The present picture is remarkable for its suave composition
within the oval format Greuze frequently employed and
for its nuances of color within an extremely restricted
palette dominated by white.
   The unidentified subject's pleated organdy hat with
plume and her simple muslin dress, casually open, reflect
the vogue in France around 1780 for the "natural" clothing
favored by Marie-Antoinette, who wore plain white
dresses as early as 1775.[1]
   In his oval portrait of Countess Shuvalova (Hermitage),[2]
painted around 1780, Greuze adapted the informal schema
of *The White Hat* to the demands of an important
portrait commission.

1 See F. Boucher, *Histoire du
costume en occident de l'antiquité
à nos jours*, Paris, 1965, p. 303
2 Brookner, Pl. 55

92 Standing Male Figure with Right Arm Raised
(Study for *The Drunken Cobbler*)
Red chalk, on white paper, 20⅛ x 12¹¹⁄₁₆ in. (51.1 x 32.3 cm)
Signed: *J. B. Greuze*
London, British Museum, Lent by the Trustees

Collections: Sir Charles Greville, London (d. 1832) (Lugt
549); bequeathed to his nephew, George Guy, fourth Earl
of Warwick, Warwick Castle (Lugt 2600); his sale,
London, May 2–21, 1896, lot 158; J. P. Heseltine, London;
his sale, London, May 27–29, 1935, lot 246, purchased by
the museum with the aid of a donation from I. de Bruÿn
   Bibliography: E. Senior, "Two Drawings by Greuze,"
British Museum Quarterly, March, 1936, pp. 90–91

This image of an amiable, unstable drunkard is a study
for *The Drunken Cobbler* of about 1780 (No. 94). In contrast
to the figure in the painting, however, this one lacks the
significant apron identifying his trade as that of shoemaker.
   A counterproof of this sheet is in the Cabinet des Dessins
at the Louvre (No. 26989; Guiffrey-Marcel, No. 4562).
A study for the drunkard's hands is also in this exhibition
(No. 93).

93 Two Hands (Study for *The Drunken Cobbler*)
Red chalk, on white paper, 12 x 18¹¹⁄₁₆ in. (30.5 x 47.5 cm)
New Haven, Yale University Art Gallery, Everett V.
Meeks Fund

Collections: K. E. Maison, London; acquired by the museum
in 1963
  Bibliography: E. Haverkamp-Begemann and A.-M. S.
Logan, *European Drawings and Watercolors in The Yale
University Art Gallery*, New Haven—London, 1970, I, No. 54,
pp. 31-32, II, Pl. 38; "New Acquisitions," *Yale
University Art Gallery Bulletin*, August, 1964, p. 19

Peter O. Marlow has identified this drawing as a study for
the hands of the father in *The Drunken Cobbler* (No. 94).
In the final painting Greuze emphasized facial expressions
and gestures in order to convey with maximum clarity the
emotions of the subjects. To achieve such differentiations
he executed a quantity of preparatory drawings such as
this one, which even isolated succeeds in conveying the
weak protestations of the drunkard.

   In Greuze's drawing for the cobbler's full figure (No.
92) the hands are only roughly blocked in. Numerous
drawings of hands by Greuze exist, the closest comparable
ones in size and style being three studies for *Filial Piety* in
the Hermitage.[1] The 1793 inventory of Greuze's possessions
listed in his studio no less then eighty-one studies of
hands and feet.[2]

1 Monod-Hautecoeur, Nos. 3-5
2 M. Barroux, ed., "Procès-verbal
d'apposition de scellés chez Greuze
après son divorce," *Bulletin de la
Société de l'Histoire de Paris et de
l'Ile-de-France*, XXIII, 1896, p. 90

94 The Drunken Cobbler (*L'Ivrogne chez lui*)
Oil, on canvas, 29⅝ x 36⅜ in. (75.2 x 92.4 cm)
Portland Art Museum

Collections: marquis de Véri, Paris; his sale, Paris, December 12, 1785, lot 22, sold to Paillet; Grimod de la Reynière, Paris; his sale, Paris, April 3, 1793 (given in catalogue as November, 1792), lot 27, sold for 505 livres to Lebrun *l'aîné*; Huard, Paris; his widow's sale, Paris, April 6–11, 1835, lot 245; Duval, Geneva; his sale, London, May 12–13, 1846, lot 109, sold for 9,975 francs; comte d'Arzujon, Paris; his sale, Paris, March 2–4, 1852, lot 10, sold for 8,200 francs; Pillot, Paris; his sale, Paris, December 6–8, 1858, lot 48; baron James de Rothschild, Paris, 1860; Réne Gimpel and Wildenstein and Co., 1920; sold by the latter for $15,000 to Mrs. Bowles, Portland, in 1923; Mrs. Marion Bowles Hollis, Portland; given by her to the museum in 1959.

Exhibitions: Paris, 26 boulevard des Italiens, Tableaux et Dessins de l'Ecole française principalement du XVIIIè siècle, 1860, No. 173; San Francisco Museum of Art, Paintings by Old Masters, 1920, No. 93; Pittsburgh, Carnegie Institute, Pictures of Everyday Life: Genre Painting in Europe, 1500–1900, 1954, No. 59; Los Angeles, University of California Art Council, French Masters: Rococo to Romanticism, 1961, p. 27; San Francisco, M. H. de Young Memorial Museum, Man: Glory, Jest and Riddle, 1964–65, No. 189; London, R. A. and Victoria and Albert Museum, The Age of Neoclassicism, 1972, No. 120; Paris, Grand Palais, Detroit Institute of Arts and New York, Metropolitan Museum of Art, French Painting 1774–1830: The Age of Revolution, 1974–75, No. 85

Bibliography: Brookner, pp. 116, 120, 124, 127, Pl. 65; R. Gimpel, *Diary of an Art Dealer*, New York, 1966, p. 231; Goncourt, I, p. 353; E. Haverkamp-Begemann and A.-M. S. Logan, *European Drawings and Watercolors in The Yale University Art Gallery*, New Haven—London, 1970, I, pp. 31–32, fig. 4; H. Honour, *Neoclassicism*, Harmondsworth, 1968, pp. 143–44, 199, fig. 33; Martin-Masson, No. 158; *A Handbook of the Collections of The Portland Art Museum*, Portland, 1971, p. 80, repr. p. 105

The poverty to which the drunken subject of this picture has reduced his family is apparent in the barren setting, but it is most eloquently expressed in the superbly painted bare feet of the children. Ironically, though the catalogue of the Grimod de la Reynière sale, referring to the father's apron, noted that he was dressed in *"habit de travail"* (work clothes) and though the catalogue of the Mrs. Lyne Stephens sale listed a copy of this picture under the title *Le Savetier ivre* (The Drunken Cobbler), no one has yet remarked the obvious relation of this picture to the familiar proverb, "The shoemaker's children never have shoes" (*"Les cordonniers sont les plus mal chaussés"*). It was characteristic of Greuze to give his moralizing depiction of the evils of drunkenness a universal significance by recalling this common adage.

In terms of content, *The Drunken Cobbler* recalls Greuze's much earlier *Indolence* (No. 10), in which the vivid depiction of a specific vice was also intended to fill the viewer with revulsion. But here Greuze enlarges the context to embrace an entire family, shown on the brink of financial and spiritual destruction due to the irresponsible behavior of the father. Writing of drunkenness in the more rarefied context of bacchants, Michel Ange de la Chaussée gave an eighteenth-century view applicable to Greuze's picture: *"L'ivrognerie est la mère des meurtres et des querelles, c'est elle qui suggère et suscite ce qui se peut commettre de plus funeste. Celui qu'elle possède ne se possède pas lui-même. Celui qui en est entièrement adonné n'est plus homme; et ce ne serait pas assez de dire que cet homme pèche, il est le péché en original. L'ivrognerie est un Démon agréable, un doux poison, une rage volontaire, un ennemi recherché avec empressement et désiré avec passion, c'est l'acceuil de l'honnêteté et de la pudeur."*[1]

In the work of the Dutch painters Greuze emulated in his youth—Ostade, Brauwer, Quast—are frequent representations of drunkenness, but there the intent was generally a lighthearted one of mocking human frailty. Here, however, Greuze is in earnest. All that is known of the artist's own drinking habits is that a 1793 inventory listed in his cellar *"une pièce de vin entière et la valeur d'une demi-pièce en bouteilles."*[2]

It is possible that in evolving the deftly conceived figure of the father Greuze had in mind two celebrated sculptures he had probably seen in Florence: Michelangelo's *Bacchus* (Museo Nazionale), whose unsteady legs and sinking posture are similar to those of Greuze's figure, and the *Bacchus* of Sansovino (Museo Nazionale), who raises a bent arm bearing a cup.

The first recorded owner of *The Drunken Cobbler* was the marquis de Véri, who owned as well Greuze's *The Father's Curse: The Ungrateful Son* of 1777 (No. 84), which this work resembles in many ways—for example in the similarities between the drunkard's wife and the central, pleading woman in *The Ungrateful Son*, in the dramatic gesture of the right arm thrown into the air by both of the principal male figures and in the drapery hanging from a rafter. In the intervening years, which probably were not many, Greuze came to conceive an even sparer design, arranging his figures in profile as in a shallow frieze and, through scale and lighting, stressing even more the distinct nuances of expression.

A study for the father's hands and a preparatory drawing for his full figure are included in this exhibition (Nos.

1 "Drunkenness is the mother of murders and quarrels, it is she who suggests and gives birth to the deadliest deeds that can be committed. He whom she possesses does not possess himself. He who is totally given over to her is no longer a man; and it would not be enough to say that this man sins, he is sin itself. Drunkenness is an agreeable Demon, a sweet poison, a voluntary madness, an enemy eagerly sought out and passionately longed for, it heartily welcomes honesty and decency." M. A. de la Chaussée, *Le Grand Cabinet romain*, Amsterdam, 1706, p. 9

2 "a full cask of wine and the equivalent of a half-cask in bottles." M. Barroux, ed., "Procès-verbal d'apposition de scellés chez Greuze après son divorce." *Bulletin de la Société de l'Histoire de Paris et de l'Ile-de-France*, 1896, p. 88

3 No. 26989; Guiffrey-Marcel, No. 4562; Martin-Masson, No. 1517

4 No. 26960; Guiffrey-Marcel, No. 4567; Martin-Masson, No. 1404

5 No. 26971; Guiffrey-Marcel, No. 4572

6 No. 26968; Guiffrey-Marcel, No. 4592

7 "The girl [is] more wonderful in expression; a multitude of diverse and indefinable movements of the soul, brought together in her charming head and in her entire person, end up producing a feeling of profound sadness."

8 *Catalogue des tableaux du Musée de Lille*, Lille, 1893, No. 359

9 L. Berthomieu, *Catalogue descriptif et annoté de peintures et sculptures*, Toulouse, 1923, No. 129

93, 92). A counterproof of the latter is in the Louvre.[3] A superb full-length study for the wife, represented as leaning further forward, also is in the Louvre,[4] along with a counterproof of another study showing her with a different headdress[5] and a counterproof of a study for the head of the daughter.[6] The daughter's poignant expression was justly singled out for comment in 1846 by the compiler of the Duval sale catalogue: "*La jeune fille* [is] *plus étonnante d'expression, une multitude de mouvements divers et indéfinissables de l'âme, réunis sur sa charmante tête et sur toute sa personne, finissent par produire un sentiment de profonde tristesse.*"[7]

A number of copies of *The Drunken Cobbler* are known. One, attributed to Philiberte Ledoux (No. 103), was lost in a fire in 1916 at the Musée des Copies, Lille,[8] and another survives in the Musée d'Art et d'Histoire at Narbonne.[9] Although Martin and subsequent historians have listed Mrs. Lyne Stephens as a former owner of the present picture, the catalogue of her sale, London, May 9–17, 1895, specified that lot 354 was only "a replica of the celebrated engraved [*sic*] work in the Louvre [*sic*]." At least five additional copies are known.

95 Portrait of the Artist

Oil, on canvas, 28¾ x 23³⁄₁₆ in. (73.0 x 59.0 cm)
Paris, Musée du Louvre

Collections: Spontini, Paris; acquired from him for 2,000
francs in 1820 for Louis XVIII
   Exhibitions: Paris, Grand Palais, Detroit Institute of Arts
and New York, Metropolitan Museum of Art, French
Painting 1774–1830: The Age of Revolution, 1974–75, No. 86
   Bibliography: L. Goldscheider, *500 Self-Portraits*, London—
Vienna, 1937, No. 331; Goncourt, I, p. 345; Hautecoeur,
p. 39, Pl. I; Martin-Masson, No. 1133; Rosenberg, Reynaud
and Compin, I, No. 327; Smith, No. 2

While this austere self-portrait can hardly be called
seductive, its honesty is undeniable. The artist retains in
this image—painted, as Pierre Rosenberg has suggested,
probably around 1785—much of the arrogance of the early
self-portrait of about 1763 included in this exhibition
(No. 36) and gives only a hint of the poignant self-
revelations of the late one he exhibited in 1804 (No. 114).
Here pride mingles with disappointment in features depicted
with absolute but understated sureness. The smoky coloristic
atmosphere is characteristic of the artist's best work of
the 1780s, such as the *Widow and Her Priest* in the
Hermitage. The soft, blurred manner he utilized to such
effect during those years in depictions of female subjects
works in this picture to soften his aging features and,
within the restricting oval, to remove the subject from too
intimate a consideration by the viewer.
   A crude copy of this portrait is in the Musée Greuze,
Tournus.

96 The Angry Woman (*La Femme colère*)

Pen and brush, black ink, gray and black washes,
heightened with white gouache, over black chalk, on
white paper, 20½ x 25³⁄₁₆ in. (52.1 x 64.0 cm)
Inscribed on the back of the original mat: "*dessin original de
Greuze. Acheté dans son cabinet après sa mort par Monsieur
Joseph Joubert, auteur des Pensées et Maximes*"[1]
New York, The Metropolitan Museum of Art, Joseph
Pulitzer Bequest

Collections: Joseph Joubert, Paris (d. 1824); Hesme de
Villeneuve, Paris; his sale, Paris, March 3–4, 1856, lot 89;
anonymous sale, Paris, March 9, 1950, lot 16; Galerie
Cailleux, Paris; purchased by the museum in 1961

   Exhibitions: Paris, Galerie Cailleux, Le Dessin français
de Watteau à Prud'hon, 1951, No. 187; R. A., 1968, No.
326; New York, Metropolitan Museum of Art, French
Drawings and Prints of the Eighteenth Century, 1972–73,
No. 25

   Bibliography: J. Bean, *One Hundred European Drawings in The
Metropolitan Museum of Art*, New York, 1964, No. 59;
Martin-Masson, Nos. 143, 1692

   Engraving: R. Gaillard

With this drawing the viewer is introduced into the midst
of Greuze's own household, disrupted by the fiery spirit
of Madame Greuze. It is reasonable to assume that the
artist has depicted himself between his two surviving
daughters, facing the wrath of his wife. In the "Mémoire
de Greuze contre sa femme" the artist dictated with
the intention of obtaining a legal separation are
descriptions of several scenes reminiscent of the one
represented here. For example, when Greuze asked his wife
to wait a certain period before hiring a servant, he
recorded that "*Pour toute réponse, elle m'appliqua un
soufflet à tour de bras.*"[2] And again: "*Nous couchions toujours
dans la même chambre, lorsque je me réveille en sursaut; j'aperçu
Madame Greuze à la lumière d'une lampe de nuit qui alloit*

*m'écraser la tête avec son pot de chambre, et alors je lui fis, comme
vous devez bien penser de vives reproches, elle me dit: 'Si tu
raisonnes je crie à la garde par la croisée et je dirai que tu
m'assassines.'*"[3]

   The presumed personal quality of this drawing is further
heightened by the similarity between several of the
furnishings depicted here and corresponding items listed
in the 1793 inventory of Greuze's possessions. The clock
on the mantelpiece is probably the one described as "*une
pendule incrustée à cadran de cuivre.*"[4] According to Winthrop
Edey, it appears to be a *religieuse* of about 1680, with its
dome missing (leaving the bell exposed), with inlaid
gilt-copper or gilt-bronze Corinthian columns and with a
signature bronze below the dial. The overturned armchair
may have been one of the set of "*six fauteuils de velours
d'Utrecht,*"[5] and the mirror is possibly the one listed as
"*sur la cheminée une glace dans son parquet.*"[6]

   The severe neoclassical style of the interior and the fact
that Greuze was treating such an autobiographical subject,
which he was willing to publicize further through an
engraving, suggest that this drawing must date from 1785,
the year in which the artist and his wife took separate
apartments and in which the engraver of the drawing,
Robert Gaillard, died.

   In addition to its personal overtones, this drawing is of
interest as another instance of Greuze depicting a specific
vice—in this case, anger—with the aim of inciting the
viewer's revulsion (compare Nos. 10, 94). Nineteen years
after its execution, an anonymous critic of the *Journal des
débats* reviewed a play entitled "*La Jeune Femme colère*" in
terms that echo the artist's perennial moralizing attitude:
"*La pièce montre tout l'odieux et toute la difformité de la
colère. . . . Il en est de la colère comme de l'ivresse; dans ces
deux espèces de délire, l'âme se montre à découvert.*"[7]

   A pendant to this drawing, *The Reconciliation*, is included
in this exhibition (No. 97). A counterproof of a study for
the head of the male figure is in the Louvre.[8]

1   "original drawing by Greuze.
Bought in his studio after his
death by Monsieur Joseph Joubert,
author of the *Pensées et Maximes*"
2   "Her only response was to slap
me with all her might." J. Boilly,
ed., "Mémoire de Greuze contre
sa femme," *Archives de l'art
français*, II, 1852–53, p. 161
3   "We were still sleeping in the
same bedroom, when I awoke
with a start; in the glow of a
night light I saw Madame Greuze
about to smash my head with her
chamber pot, and when, as you
should well imagine, I reproached
her strongly, she said to me: 'If
you are going to argue, I am calling
out the window for the police
and I shall say that you are
murdering me.' " *Ibid.*, p. 170

4   "an inlaid clock with a copper
dial." M. Barroux, ed., "Procès-
verbal d'apposition de scellés
chez Greuze après son divorce,"
*Bulletin de la Société de l'Histoire
de Paris et de l'Ile-de-France*,
1896, p. 88
5   "six armchairs in Utrecht
velvet." *Ibid.*, p. 87
6   "over the mantelpiece a mirror
in its wooden molding." *Ibid.*
7   "The play demonstrates all the
odium and all the deformity of
anger. . . . It is with anger as
with drunkenness; in these two
forms of madness, the soul shows
itself naked." "Variétés," *Journal
des débats*, November 1, 1804, [p. 4]
8   No. 26985; Guiffrey-Marcel,
No. 4566; Martin-Masson, No. 1692

97 The Reconciliation
Brush, gray and black ink washes, over pencil, on white
paper, 19 x 24⅝ in. (48.2 x 62.5 cm)
Phoenix Art Museum

Collections: Hippolyte Walferdin, Paris; his sale, Paris, May
18, 1860, lot 76, sold for 400 francs; marquis Charles de
Valori, Paris; his sale, Paris, November 25-26, 1907, lot
118, sold for 280 francs (?); Wildenstein and Co., New
York; gift to the museum of Mr. and Mrs. Randall Barton
in memory of Mr. Bruce Barton, Jr., in 1964

   Exhibitions: New York, Wildenstein and Co., Drawings
through Four Centuries, 1949, No. 38, Timeless Master
Drawings, 1955, No. 74, and Treasures of French Art, 1964,
No. 39; El Paso, Museum of Art, French Painting and
Sculpture from the Phoenix Art Museum, 1965, No. 25;
Ann Arbor, University of Michigan Museum of Art,
French Watercolors: 1760–1860, 1965, No. 8; Notre Dame,
University of Notre Dame Art Gallery, Eighteenth Century
France, 1972, No. 41

   Bibliography: J. Harithas, *Painting, Drawings and
Sculpture in the Phoenix Art Museum Collection*, Phoenix,
1965, p. 50; Martin-Masson, No. 357; "Accessions of
American and Canadian Museums," *Art Quarterly*, Spring-
Summer, 1965, p. 109

Though slightly smaller and less finished than *The Angry
Woman* (No. 96), this drawing may be considered its
pendant. Greuze has substituted a boy for one of the girls
in the other work and has introduced a large cat—
reminiscent of that in *The Surprised Housekeeper* (No. 29)—to
join the dog, which is now represented as larger and of a
different breed. The positions of the husband and wife
are reversed.

   When J.-B.-P. Le Brun summed up Greuze's oeuvre in his
Almanach historique of 1776 he could almost have been
speaking of this drawing and its pendant, which were
executed probably a decade later: "*Peindre l'homme dans
sa vie privée, est le grand talent de M. Greuze.*"[1] Greuze
did indeed exploit his skill at expression and gesture to
lead the viewer into the midst of countless intimate scenes
of family quarrels and reconciliations, joys and tribulations,
in which each member of the household is depicted playing
a specific and recognizable role.

   A chalk study for the man in this drawing is in a
private collection, Paris. A crude copy of the drawing,
with variations, is in the Musée Grobet-Labadié, Marseille.

1   "To paint man in his private
life is the great talent of M.
Greuze." J.-B.-P. Le Brun,
Almanach historique, Paris, 1776.
(Minkoff reprint, 1972), p. 92

1   *Catalogue du Musée Vivenel,*
Compiègne, 1870, No. 138, p. 21
2   Portalis-Béraldi, II, p. 456.
These authors shed further light
on Benazech's character: "*Il faut
croire que les lauriers de Debucourt
empêchaient Benazech de dormir, car*

*il chercha très-visiblement à imiter la
manière de cet artiste.*" ("It must be
assumed that the laurels of
Debucourt kept Benazech from
sleeping, for he tried quite
obviously to imitate the style of
that artist." *Ibid.*, I, p. 158

98   The Recompense Refused

Brush, gray ink wash, over black chalk, heightened with
white, on blue paper, 14$\frac{3}{16}$ x 21 in. (36.0 x 53.3 cm)
London, British Museum, Lent by the Trustees

Collections: Sir Charles Greville, London (d. 1832) (Lugt
549); bequeathed to his nephew, George Guy, fourth Earl
of Warwick, Warwick Castle (Lugt 2600); his sale, London,
May 2–21, 1896, lot 159, acquired by the museum
    Bibliography: J. Vergnet-Ruiz, "Les Dessins français du
XVIIIè siècle au British Museum," *Bulletin de la Société de
l'Histoire de l'Art français,* 1932, pp. 19–20

In this image of natural virtue Greuze has represented a
shepherd and his companions refusing a reward for having
slain a boar. They and their dog are about to return to
their sheep, visible at right. One shepherd holds a birdcage.
    The classical profiles of the central figures and the
elaborate technique and pictorial style of the drawing
suggest that it was executed around 1785–90.
    This polished work is related to two drawings done in a
remarkably different manner. One, in the Musée Vivenel,
Compiègne, represents a man with a stick and a child

similar to the boy with his arm raised in the present
composition but seen from behind.[1] The other, in the
Städelsches Kunstinstitut, Frankfurt (No. 1074), shows
two men dragging a dead boar. Both have a spontaneous,
documentary quality lacking in the present sheet, suggesting
that Greuze might have actually observed and recorded an
event such as the one depicted here before elaborating it
in a literary manner.
    A curious transformation of this subject is to be found in
Charles Benazech's *The Poacher and the Landowner* in the
Ateneumin Taidemuseo, Helsinki, a picture bearing a
false signature of Greuze and a presumably false date of
1778. In that work the group at right in the present
drawing has been revised to represent a poacher and his
family being pardoned by a rich landowner, who stands at
left with his wife and child. Benazech's composition was
engraved by François-Robert Ingouf in 1789 and exhibited
in the Salon of 1793 as *La Liberté du braconnier*.[2] The print
identifies Benazech as the originator of the subject. Since
Benazech is known to have studied with Greuze only in
1789, he must have seen the present drawing in the artist's
studio and made quick use of it.

1 Portalis-Béraldi, III, p. 723
2 L. Armand-Calliat, *Musée Vivant-Denon: Catalogue de la Section des Beaux-Arts*, Chalon-sur-Saône, 1963, No. 257

99 The Fortune Teller (*La Diseuse de bonne aventure*)
Brush, gray ink wash, over pencil, on white paper,
12 x 16 in. (30.5 x 40.6 cm)
Signed: *Greuze*
Paris, M. Gaston Palewski

Collections: Carrier, Paris; his sale, Paris, March 9–10, 1846, lot 171; Hippolyte Walferdin, Paris; his sale, Paris, April 12–16, 1880, lot 318
  Bibliography: Goncourt, I, p. 351; Martin-Masson, No. 276
  Engraving: de Bréa[1]

Greuze's treatment of this traditional subject, with its powerful emotional overtones, was drawn probably in the mid-1780s. The eager, inquisitive child at right resembles a similar one in *The Angry Woman* of about 1785 (No. 96), and the frieze-like arrangement of the figures against a bare wall is typical of the artist's work during that period.

A version of this drawing, executed by Greuze probably slightly earlier, is in the Musée Vivant-Denon, Chalon-sur-Saône.[2] Three drawings in the Cabinet des Dessins at the Louvre (Nos. 26984, 26996, 26998) associated by Martin with *The Fortune Teller* are more likely studies for the seated mother in *The Twelfth-Night Cake* (Montpellier, Musée Fabre).

100 Innocence Carried off by Cupid

Oil, on canvas, 57½ x 77³⁄₁₆ in. (146.0 x 196.0 cm)
Paris, Musée du Louvre

Collections: commissioned by the comte d'Artois and sold to
Catherine II (?); Count Gregory Alexandrovitch Stroganoff,
Saint-Petersburg; acquired for 25,000 francs before 1900 by
baron Basile de Schlichting, Paris; bequeathed by him to
the museum in 1914

Exhibitions: Paris, Petit Palais, Exposition rétrospective
de l'art français, 1900, No. 4576; Paris, Louvre, Exposition
de 700 tableaux tirés des réserves, 1960, No. 619; Bregenz,
Landesmuseum and Vienna, Osterreichisches Museum für
angewandte Kunst, Angelika Kauffmann und ihre Zeitgenossen, 1968–69, No. 262

Bibliography: Brookner, p. 125, Pl. 68; G. Lafenestre,
"Les Arts à l'exposition universelle de 1900, la peinture
ancienne," *Gazette des Beaux-Arts*, December, 1900, p. 559;
J. Locquin, *La Peinture d'histoire en France de 1747 à 1785,*
Paris, 1912, p. 240; Martin-Masson, Nos. 71, 76; G.
Migeon, "L'Exposition rétrospective de l'art français,"
Revue de l'art ancien et moderne, May, 1900, pp. 373, 374;
Rosenberg, Reynaud and Compin, I, No. 324

Executed shortly before 1786, *Innocence Carried off by Cupid*
marks a conceptual change in Greuze's art and allots a
new importance to landscape and architecture. In this
triumphal allegory on the loss of innocence are distant
echoes of *A Marraige Contract* of 1761 (No. 34) and *The
Father's Curse: The Ungrateful Son* of 1777 (No. 84), in
each of which a young adult is shown leaving the confines
of the family propelled by some elemental force and
abetted by a figure from outside the household. Previously
Greuze had presented such general themes in images of
contemporary life, but here he sets his subject in a
timeless world where real and mythological beings
intermingle. Floating on clouds of smoke, Cupid holds
a flaming torch and gently leads away his conquest,
whose new freedom is symbolized by the dove being let
loose at right—a detail recalling the bird imagery in
A Marriage Contract. The tragic figure who seeks to
restrain the girl is reminiscent of Demeter trying to hold
back her child. A boy resembling an infant Bacchus
flourishes the crown of Hymen at left.

As with the *Girl Weeping over Her Dead Bird* (No. 44),
Greuze's inspiration for this picture seems to have been
Catullus. The Roman poet's lengthy *Collis o Heliconii/
Cultor, Uraniae genus*, a hymn to marriage, includes a
number of images similar to details of *Innocence Carried
off by Cupid:*

> "Sprung from Urania
> You inhabit Helicon
> Young girls you carry off
> To men, O Hymenaeus
> O Hymen Hymenaeus
>
> To the wild youth you hand over
> The girl who is just fluorescent
> Straight from the arms of mother. . . .
>
> Open the door, she is coming
> And in she comes, the torches

> Shake their hair. . . .
> But shyness holds her back
>
> Preferring to listen to this
> She cries because she must go
>
> In the varied garden
> Of the expensive householder
> The hyacinth stand so
> You waste time, day is going
> Bride, come out
>
> This is the house, a large
> and pleasant one. . . .
>
> The child who leads the girl
> Lets go her slender arm;
> Go to your husband's bed."[1]

Though none of Greuze's contemporaries mentions
specifically that he was familiar with Catullus, Madame
de Valori stated that *"il étoit instruit, possédait plusieurs
langues."*[2] In any case, the poetry of Catullus was available
to him in translations.

Unfortunately, only a few of what must have been a
considerable number of studies for this important painting
remain. A reduced version of the picture figured in the
comte d'Espagnac sales in Paris, March 1–3, 1866, lot
239, and May 8, 1868, lot 16, sold for 5,150 francs, and
appeared again in the H. Dugied sale, Paris, June 10–11,
1890, lot 13. A study for the head and shoulders of Cupid
is in the collection of baronne Alain de Gunzburg, Paris.[3]
Two similar studies less directly related to the painting
are in the Museum Boymans-van Beuningen, Rotterdam
(F I 242), and the Metropolitan Museum of Art, New
York (No. 50.145.20), where there is also a study for
the head of the figure at left (No. 49.131.3). A study for
the winged putto between Cupid and Innocence appeared
in the Biron sale, Paris, June 9–11, 1914, lot 24. The
curious drawing *A Family in a Park* in the Museum
Boymans-van Beuningen (F I 277) includes a circular
temple with columns like the one beyond Cupid in this
painting. Several drawings representing groups of putti
appeared in the Caroline Greuze sale, Paris, January
25–26, 1843, lots 11, 15–17, 56, 95.

A number of paintings Martin and others considered
preparatory studies for *Innocence Carried off by Cupid* were
more likely executed after it, with important changes. These
include the *Cupid* in the Hermitage, dated 1786,[4] and the
Cupid Flying with a Torch and two versions of *Psyche*,
one dated 1786, in the Wallace Collection, London.[5]

A related composition appeared as *L'Innocence séduite
par l'Amour et les plaisirs* in the chevalier Erard sale, Paris,
August 7, 1832, sold for 2,000 francs to Spontini.

1 *Catullus*, trans. C. H. Sisson,
London, 1966, pp. 39, 41, 42,
44, 45
2 "he was educated, knew
several languages." Valori, p. 252
3 Exhibited London, R. A.,
1954–55, No. 613

4 Smith, No. 7; Hermitage,
Catalogue of Paintings, Leningrad,
1958, p. 281, No. 4969
5 Wallace Collection Catalogues,
Pictures and Drawings, London,
1968, Nos. P434, P338, P440,
pp. 129–30, 135

101 Anacreon in His Old Age Crowned by Love

Brush, gray ink wash, heightened with white gouache,
on gray paper, 12⅜ x 16⅛ in. (31.4 x 41.0 cm)
New York, Mrs. Herbert N. Straus

Collections: Gil de Meestre; his sale, Paris, April 1, 1862 (?);
acquired from Jacques Seligmann and Co., New York, in 1959
  Bibliography: Martin-Masson, No. 77

The youthful figure of Love appears to have alighted
suddenly on the lap of the startled Greek poet Anacreon
to place a crown of laurel on his head. Like many of
Greuze's historical or literary subjects, the present
drawing has its autobiographical overtones, for Greuze's
gallantry toward women led him to be compared specifically
to this ancient author of amorous poetry. Writing shortly
after Greuze's death, Lecarpentier noted: *"Il se montra
toujours très-galant auprès du sexe qu'il idolâtra toute sa vie;
et il eut le talent bien rare aujourd'hui de savoir prodiguer des
louanges aux femmes, avec cette grâce, cet air affectueux qui
leur plaît sans leur causer d'inquiétude. Il eut la délicatesse
d'Anacréon, et comme cet agréable poëte de l'antiquité, il effleura
les roses du plaisir jusque dans l'âge le plus avancé."*[1]

The neoclassical setting of this drawing, which recalls
that of *The Love Letter* (No. 78), includes at right a
reduction of the Medici *Venus* (Uffizi), first sketched in
roughly with the arms in their proper positions and then
rendered more completely with the placement of the
arms reversed. A bronze-colored plaster replica of the
Medici *Venus* appears in the inventory of Greuze's
possessions made after his divorce.[2]

Greuze depicted a similar winged Cupid, asleep and
with a crown of leaves over his arm, in a drawing that
appeared in the de Musigny sale, Paris, March 7-8, 1845,
lot 79 bis.[3] Another similar Cupid is seen in the painting
Psyche Crowning Love (Lille, Musée des Beaux-Arts).

1 "He always behaved most
gallantly toward the sex that he
idolized all his life; and he had
the talent, very rare today, of
knowing how to lavish compliments
on women with that grace, that
affectionate air which pleases
them without causing them
uneasiness. He had the delicacy
of Anacreon, and like that agreeable
poet of antiquity, he lightly
stroked the roses of pleasure until
the most advanced age." C.-L. F.
Lecarpentier, *Notice sur Greuze lu
dans la séance de la Société libre
d'Emulation de Rouen*, [Rouen],
1805, pp. 6-7
2 M. Barroux, ed., "Procès-verbal
d'apposition de scellés chez Greuze
après son divorce," *Bulletin de la
Société de l'Histoire de Paris et de
l'Ile-de-France*, 1896, p. 90
3 Martin-Masson, Nos. 57, 63

102   Portrait of Charles-Athanase, baron Walckenaer
Oil, on canvas, 17¾ x 15⅛ in. (45.5 x 38.5 cm)
Paris, baron Walckenaer

Collections: Walckenaer family

This arresting portrait was executed about 1788. It conveys
the sympathy that the aging Greuze could still feel
toward an intelligent and handsome subject, in this case one
whom he probably knew well, for Charles-Athanase
Walckenaer was the natural son of Duclos-Dufresnoy,
Greuze's notary and one of the most avid collectors of the
artist's work.[1]

Born on Christmas Day in 1771, Walckenaer received
under Duclos-Dufresnoy's supervision a brilliant education.
He was a member of the first class to be graduated from
the Ecole Polytechnique in 1793, after which he continued
his studies at Oxford. Through changing political climates
he remained an important governmental functionary.
Elected a member of the Institut de France (Académie
des Inscriptions et Belles-Lettres) in 1813, he was named
chevalier of the Légion d'Honneur in 1814 and in 1823 was
created baron by Louis XVIII. Walckenaer was a prolific
writer in many areas; his publications range from an
Histoire de la vie et des ouvrages de La Fontaine and an *Histoire
de la vie et des poésies d'Horace* to his *Histoire naturelle des
insectes aptères*. He died at Villeneuve-Saint-Georges in 1852.

1   Duclos-Dufresnoy was guillotined
in 1794. The sale of his collection
held in Paris on August 28, 1795,
included twenty-two paintings
by Greuze, among them the *Child
Playing with a Dog* (No. 55), the
blond version of *Saint Mary of
Egypt* (see No. 113), *The Charitable
Woman* (Lyon, Musée des Beaux-
Arts) and *The Twelfth-Night Cake*
(Montpellier, Musée Fabre). Two
portraits of Duclos-Dufresnoy by
Greuze are in Paris collections.
On this interesting figure see the
excellent study by J. -P. Poisson,
"Le Notariat parisien à la fin du
18è siècle," *Dix-huitième Siècle,*
No. 7, 1975, pp. 105–27

103   Portrait of Jeanne-Philiberte Ledoux
Oil, on panel, 23½ x 19¼ in. (59.7 x 48.8 cm)
Durham, North Carolina, Dr. and Mrs. James H.
Semans

Collections: E. Secrétan, Paris; his sale, Paris, July 1, 1889,
lot 121, sold for 10,900 francs to Sedelmeyer; Galerie
Sedelmeyer, Paris; Mrs. Lyne Stephens, London (?); her
sale, London, May 9–17, 1895, lot 356 (?); James Simon,
Berlin; M. Knoedler and Co., New York; Wildenstein
and Co., New York, 1929; Henry E. Stehli, New York;
his sale, New York, November 30, 1950, lot 18, sold for
$9,000; Hirschl and Adler Galleries, New York; acquired
in 1960
  Exhibitions: Princeton University Art Museum, European
and American Art from Princeton Alumni Collections,
1972, No. 24
  Bibliography: Martin-Masson, No. 1178

As a portrait of one of Greuze's most gifted pupils,
Jeanne-Philiberte Ledoux (1767–1840), this picture,
painted around 1790, has a freshness and personal aura
lacking in Greuze's contemporary images of anonymous
young women. Daughter of the important architect
Claude-Nicolas Ledoux, Jeanne-Philiberte concentrated
her talents on the very sort of image her master produced
of her here. She exhibited in the Salons from 1793 until
1819. Greuze also executed portraits of her father (Martin-
Masson, No. 1203) and her brother (Martin-Masson,
No. 1179; lot 136 in the Walferdin sale, Paris, April
12–16, 1880, a picture frequently confused with the
present one). The motif of the wreath of flowers recalls
Greuze's earlier portrait of Madame de Porcin (No. 72).
  An unfinished oval sketch on canvas for a portrait of
Mademoiselle Ledoux appeared in the Henri Cousin sale,
Paris, March 19–20, 1841, lot 108.

104 Portrait of a Woman as Callisto
Oil, on panel, 20½ x 1(½ in. (52.1 x 44.5 cm)
New York, Mr. and Mrs. George T. Delacorte

Collections: marquis de la Tourette, Tournon; marquise
de la Rivière de la Tourette, château de Corsas; Schaeffer
Galleries, New York
   Bibliography: Martin-Masson, No. 591; "Masters in the
Art News," *Art News*, January, 1967, p. 20

Even without the leopard skin and arm bracelet this
would remain one of Greuze's most startling, even tragic,
portraits. Comparison with Robert Gaillard's engraving
of a much earlier picture in Wille's collection entitled
Callisto identifies the mythological guise in which Greuze
depicted this unknown woman, probably around 1790.
There is a tradition that the sitter was an ancestor of
the marquise de la Rivière de la Tourette, a former owner.
   The haunted look of the subject is appropriate to
Callisto, nymph and companion of Artemis, by whom
she was slain after she had born a child to Zeus and was
transformed into a bear. Callisto was eventually set among
the constellations as Ursa Major, the She-Bear.

105 Homer Saved by Time from the Ruins of the World (*Homère sauvé par le Temps des ruines du monde*)
Pen and brush, brown ink, on white paper, 12⁹⁄₁₆ x 20¹⁄₁₆ in. (32.0 x 51.0 cm)
Dijon, Musée Magnin

Collections: Anatole Fouquet, Clichy-la-Garenne (d. 1852); sale, Paris, February 27, 1858, lot 36; Magnin, Paris
Bibliography: Martin-Masson, No. 81; Musée Magnin, *Peintures et dessins de l'Ecole française*, Dijon, 1938, p. 107, No. 298; M. Sandoz, "The Drawings of Gabriel François Doyen," *Art Quarterly*, Summer, 1971, pp. 156, 174, fig. 23, and *Gabriel François Doyen*, Paris, 1975, p. 54

This important late drawing was justly reattributed to Greuze by Pierre Rosenberg.[1] It had previously been catalogued as the work of Gabriel-François Doyen on the recommendation of Mathey, who nevertheless noted that the sheet "*a de grands rapports avec certains dessins de Greuze.*"[2]

Madame de Valori knew the drawing in 1813 and described it fully: "*Parmi la foule immense des dessins de Greuze, on remarque celui d'Homère sauvé par le Temps des ruines du monde. Les anciens regardaient la mer comme la principale cause des révolutions du globe; Greuze a saisi cette idée. On voit, à droite du dessin, Neptune armé de son trident, poussant la mer sur la terre, et entraînant les empires, figurés par des débris de palais et par les pointes de quelques pyramides. C'est au-dessus de cette destruction universelle, que le Temps, poursuivant sa marche infatigable, soutient et emporte l'immortel Homère, et lui fait braver la nuit des temps. Cette composition hardie et pleine de verve, est un hommage que Greuze, qui, comme Homère, savait être poëte, a voulu rendre au chantre d'Ilion, qui doit à plus d'un titre être regardé comme le père de la peinture, de même qu'il est celui de la poésie.*"[3]

Anatole de Montaiglon, nephew of Anatole Fouquet, a former owner of the drawing, spoke of it slightingly: "*Quant au dessin de Greuze, il* [Fouquet] *le conservait pour sa curiosité plus que pour son mérite; car il était impossible de voir quelque chose de plus creux, de plus emphatique et de plus insignifiant.*"[4]

A lost drawing of the head of Homer by Greuze appeared in the Villenave sale, Paris, December 1–8, 1842, lot 648, sold for 12 francs, and in the Leperlier sale, Paris, February 17–18, 1879, lot 74, sold for 4 francs. That work cannot be identified with the considerably smaller *Head of Homer* in the Cabinet des Dessins at the Louvre (No. 27016), which Guiffrey and Marcel (No. 4602) rightfully hesitated to attribute to Greuze. But if the Louvre drawing reflects the style of the lost sketch, the latter must have been similar to the studies after the antique that Greuze executed for *Septimius Severus* (see fig. 19, Nos. 67, 68).

The cosmic scope of the present drawing is as appropriate to Homer as are the intimacy and grace of Greuze's evocation of Anacreon (No. 101) to that other Greek poet.

1 Oral communication, March, 1976
2 "relates closely to certain drawings by Greuze." J. Mathey, "G. -F. Doyen, An Allegorical Subject," *Old Master Drawings*, September, 1934, pp. 30–31, Pl. 32
3 "Among the host of drawings by Greuze, one notes that of Homer saved by Time from the ruins of the world. The ancients regarded the sea as the principal cause of the revolutions of the globe; Greuze seized upon that idea. One sees at right in the drawing Neptune armed with his trident, driving the sea over the earth and sweeping away the empires, represented by the ruins of palaces and the summits of some pyramids. It is over this universal destruction that Time, pursuing his tireless progress, sustains and carries off the immortal Homer, and has him brave the mists of time. This bold composition, full of verve, is an hommage that Greuze, who like Homer could be a poet, wanted to render to the bard of Ilium, who should on more grounds than one be considered the father of painting just as he is that of poetry." Valori, pp. 372–73
4 "As for the drawing by Greuze, he [Fouquet] kept it more for its curiosity than for its merit; for it was impossible to see anything more hollow, more bombastic and more insignificant." *Ibid.*, p. 373, n. 1

106   Portrait of Adèle Dutilleul, comtesse
Mollien, as a Child
Oil, on oval canvas, 24⅝ x 19½ in. (62.5 x 49.5 cm)
Inscribed on a label attached to the stretcher: *"ce petit
portrait est le mien à l'âge de six ans et demi, fait par Greuze
en 1791/ Adèle Dutilleul, comtesse Mollien"*[1]
Baltimore Museum of Art, Gift of the William Randolph
Hearst Foundation in memory of William Randolph
Hearst

Collections: Dutilleul family, Paris; acquired by William
Randolph Hearst in the 1920s; given to the museum in 1961
   Exhibitions: Paris, Galerie Georges Petit, Cent Chefs-
d'oeuvre, 1892, No. 14; Baltimore Museum of Art, From El
Greco to Pollack: Early and Late Works by European and
American Artists, 1968, No. 30; Baltimore, Walters Art
Gallery, Maryland Heritage: European Art at the Time of
the Revolution, 1976
   Bibliography: Martin-Masson, No. 1209; E. Munhall,
"Greuze's Portrait of Comtesse Mollien, Study of a Motif,"
Baltimore Museum of Art News, Fall, 1962, pp. 14–23; *Masters
in Art: Greuze,* Boston, 1904, p. 38, Pl. V

The inscription on the stretcher of this portrait identifies the
subject as Adèle Collart-Dutilleul (1784–1878), daughter of
a prominent financier during the reign of Louis XVI.[2] In
1802, at the age of seventeen, she married the recently
ennobled comte Nicolas-François Mollien (1758–1850),
who was well over twice her age. His memoirs record the
beginning of this marriage, which was to be regarded by
contemporaries as one of exemplary mutual devotion: *"Je
venois d'épouser mademoiselle Dutilleul, fille d'un ancien premier
commis qui, malgré la grande différence de nos âges, n'avait pas
craint de me confier son bonheur et se charger du mien."*[3] As
minister of the treasury, Mollien is best remembered for the
creation of a group of tollhouses encircling the city of Paris,
unusual masonry structures designed by Claude-Nicolas
Ledoux.
   This likeness demonstrates Greuze's lasting ability to
capture the seriousness and individual character of children.
The compositon may be a conscious reworking of the much
earlier *Girl with Dogs* in the Musée des Beaux-Arts at Rouen,
a drawing dated 1759.

1   "this little portrait is of me
at the age of six and a half, done
by Greuze in 1791/ Adèle Dutilleul,
comtesse Mollien"
2   Biographical information
kindly provided by M. Serge
Grandjean, in a letter dated
May 22, 1971

3   "I had just married mademoiselle
Dutilleul, daughter of a former
head clerk, who, despite the great
difference in our ages, was not
afraid to entrust her happiness to
me and to assume responsibility
for mine." N.-F. Mollien,
*Mémoires d'un ministre du trésor
public, 1780–1815,* Paris, 1845,
I, p. 315, n. 1

107 Portrait of Jean-Nicolas Billaud-Varenne

Oil, on panel, 23¼ x 19¼ in. (59.1 x 48.8 cm)
Dallas Museum of Fine Arts

Collections: Madame de Mandrot (?); Grenville L. Winthrop,
New York, 1936; Wildenstein and Co., New York; acquired
by the museum in 1962

  Exhibitions: New York, Wildenstein and Co., The French
Revolution, 1943, No. 1, p. 99; Houston, Museum of Fine
Arts, George Washington's World, 1954, No. 160

This portrait testifies to Greuze's ability in his late career
to produce a sober and convincing image of a brilliant
political figure of the times. The work dates from the early
years of the Revolution, a period particularly active for
Greuze in portrait commissions. The artist's own political
sympathies are unknown, but he seems to have maintained
a flexible attitude as the climate turned, profiting from
such innovations as the legalization of divorce in 1793.

  Jean-Nicolas Billaud-Varenne was born in 1756 at La
Rochelle. In 1785 he came to Paris, where he bought a
position as *avocat* in the Parlement. His attitude toward the
ancien régime was made clear in his *Despotisme des ministres en
France* published in 1789, to be followed by *L'Acéphrocratie*
issued after Louis XVI's flight to Varenne in 1791 and by his
Eléments du républicanisme in 1793. The book he is depicted
removing from his jacket is presumably one of these.
Billaud-Varenne was a virulent anti-Royalist, voting for
the death of Louis XVI *"dans vingt-quatre heures"* (within
twenty-four hours), and was accused of complicity in the
massacres that took place in the prison of the Abbaye of
Saint-Germain-des-Prés (see No. 108). His appearance at
the Abbaye was grimly recorded by a contemporary: *"Il
était cinq heures du soir, arrive Billaud de Varenne, substitut de
la Commune, il avait son écharpe et le petit habit puce et la
perruque noire qu'on lui connaît; il marche sur les cadavres, fait au
public une courte harangue et finit ainsi: 'Peuple, tu immoles tes
ennemis, tu fais ton devoir.'"*[1] As the Revolution cooled, the
Convention voted his deportation to Guiana on April 1,
1795. He remained there until 1816, when he moved to
Port-au-Prince, Haiti, where he died of dysentery three years
later.

  The schema of this painting is typical of Greuze's terse
male portraits of the 1790s, with most details obliterated so
that the viewer focuses on the stark presentation of the
subject. Greuze's natural skill in rendering likenesses is
united here with his ability to evoke an awesome personality
such as that of Billaud-Varenne, whose appearance in his
final days would be described thus: *"sa figure, plus pâle que
jamais était devenue d'une maigreur effrayante. . . . Ses regards
seuls avaient conservé leur premier feu et quelquefois leur fixité
terrible. On sentait bien en l'approchant, qu'il y avait encore en
lui quelque chose de grand caractère et un reste de fierté qu'il ne
pouvait cacher."*[2]

1 "It was five o'clock in the
evening, Billaud de Varenne
arrives, the deputy prosecutor of
the Commune, he had on his
scarf and the plain grayish-purple
suit and black wig that one
associates with him; he walks over
the corpses, makes a brief harangue
to the public and concludes thus:
'People, you are immolating your
enemies, you are doing your
duty.'" Quoted in J. Guilaine,
*Billaud-Varenne, l'ascète de la
Révolution*, Paris, 1969, p. 85
2 "his face, paler than ever,
had become frighteningly emaciated
. . . . His eyes alone had retained
their original fire and sometimes
their terrible steady gaze. One
certainly felt on approaching
him that there was still in him
something of great character and
a remnant of pride which he could
not conceal." Quoted in Guilaine,
op. cit., p. 374

108   Monsieur de Sombreuil Seized during the Revolution
Black and white chalk, over pencil, on blue-gray paper,
15⅜ x 7¹⁄₁₆ in. (39.0 x 18.0 cm)
Inscribed: *G sep 1792;* and on verso: *"Mʳ de Sombreuil/*
gouverneur des Invalides au/ massacres de septembre 1792"
France, private collection

Collections: descendant of the Sombreuil family

Thanks to the inscription on this rare and chilling drawing
from one of the darkest moments of the Revolution—the
September Massacres of 1792—the sheet can be identified
with a celebrated incident. Shortly after the Royal family
had been imprisoned in the Temple, hundreds of Royalist
prisoners were killed by "spontaneous" mobs. Among those
seized was Monsieur de Sombreuil, *gouverneur* of the Hôtel
des Invalides in Paris, whose arrest Greuze must have
personally witnessed. After Sombreuil was incarcerated in
the prison of the Abbaye of Saint-Germain-des-Prés, his
young daughter, Marie-Maurine Virot de Sombreuil,
voluntarily joined him there and saved his life by throwing
her body on his and pleading with his would-be assassins.
The tradition that she accomplished this only after con-
senting to drink a cup of human blood is persistent but
dubious. In a macabre fashion this story recalls the subject
of the Roman Charity which had interested Greuze many
years before (Nos. 59, 60).

A portrait of Sombreuil by Greuze appeared in the
Lucien Bonaparte sale, Paris, March 17-20, 1834, lot 13.

The only other Revolutionary subject known to have
been treated by Greuze is the so-called *Scène de la Révolution*
française in the Musée Greuze at Tournus (No. 38; Martin-
Masson, No. 29). It is a crowded composition the meaning
of which is unclear.

109   Portrait of Napoleon Buonaparte

Oil, on canvas, 22$\frac{1}{16}$ x 18$\frac{1}{8}$ in. (56.0 x 46.0 cm)
Paris, M. Fabius

Collections: Caroline Greuze, Paris; her sale, Paris, January
25–26, 1843, lot 3, sold for 2,000 francs (bought in?);
Susse, Paris; his sale, Paris, March 26–29, 1844, lot 62,
bought in at 1,500 francs; marquis de Las Cases, Paris, 1883
   Exhibitions: Paris, Portraits d'un siècle, 1883, No. 111
   Bibliography: Martin-Masson, No. 1060

It is frustrating to be unable to recount the circumstances
that brought together in 1792 the budding military and
political genius Napoleon Buonaparte (1769–1821) and the
aging Greuze, an encounter that resulted in this brooding
but curiously tender portrait.

The painting can be dated on the evidence of the uniform
Buonaparte wears, that of captain in an artillery regiment, a
rank to which he was elevated on August 30, 1792. As
Buonaparte was in Paris that year only from May until
shortly after the September Massacres, and as he did not
return to the capital until after he had been made general
the following year, the portrait must have been executed
very soon after he was appointed captain.

Buonaparte's moodiness, which must have appealed to
Greuze's own emotional sensitivity, was already apparent
in his *Réflexions sur la vie* written in 1786: "*Toujours seul au
milieu des hommes, je rentre pour rêver avec moi-même et me livrer
à toute la vivacité de ma mélancolie. De quel côté est-elle tournée
aujourd'hui? Du côté de la mort. Dans l'aurore de mes jours, je
puis encore espérer de vivre longtemps.*"[1]

Greuze's later, full-length portrait of Napoleon as First
Consul (Versailles) repeats the head as shown in the present
picture. A drawing for the Versailles portrait appeared in
the marquis de Valori sale, Paris, November 25–26, 1907,
lot 116, sold for 500 francs, and a painted study for it is in
the Bibliothèque Thiers, Paris, formerly in the Frédéric
Masson collection, Paris.[2]

It is worth noting that Thoré, who prepared the catalogue
for the Caroline Greuze sale, and Bonnefons de Lavialle
and Schroth, experts for the Susse sale, both specified that
the head in the present portrait was "*terminée*" and "*du
plus grand caractère*" but that the garments remained "*à
l'état d'esquisse.*"[3] This difference in finish probably resulted
from Napoleon's lifelong dislike for sustained posing.

1   "Always alone in the midst of
men, I retire to dream with myself
and surrender myself to all the
intensity of my melancholy. In
what direction is it turned today?
In the direction of death. In the
dawn of my days, I can still hope
to live a long while." Napoleon,
Mémoires et oeuvres, ed. T. Martel,
Paris, 1910, p. 412. See also E.
Munhall, "Portraits of Napoleon,"
Yale French Studies, Fall-Winter,
1960–61, pp. 3–20
2   Information kindly supplied by
M. Jacques Foucart
3   "finished." "of the highest
quality." "in the sketch stage."

110 Saint Mary of Egypt with a Skull

Brush, black ink wash, black chalk, heightened in white gouache, over pencil, on tan paper, 12 x 16⅛ in. (30.5 x 40.8 cm)

Inscribed on an old label attached to the mount: "*Voyez sur cette Sainte Marie Egyptienne par Greuze correspondant de l'Académie de Dijon, Galerie de Portraits du XVIIIè siècle par Arsène Houssaye, 1848, 2è série, p. 263*"[1]

Dijon, Musée des Beaux-Arts

Collections: Anatole Devosge, Dijon (d. 1850) (?); acquired by the museum in the nineteenth century

The inscription on the mount of this drawing identifies the subject as Saint Mary of Egypt, whom Greuze also represented in a painting of 1801 included in this exhibition (No. 113). As in the painting, the Saint is depicted kneeling on a rolled mat, but instead of a crucifix she holds a skull, and her attitude of rapt introspection in the painting is replaced here by one of passionate concentration on the source of the light that illuminates her cave. While both of these works are related in mood and subject matter to Greuze's earlier study of an old woman reflecting on the life of Mary Magdalen (No. 61), another repentant sinner who achieved sainthood, they transcend the genre limitations of that drawing through the immediacy of their religious emotion.

Greuze also painted a version of *Saint Mary of Egypt* showing the subject with blond hair (see No. 113). As that work appeared in the Duclos-Dufresnoy sale of 1795, a tentative date of around 1790 might be considered for the present drawing.

The so-called *Penitent Magdalen*, clothed and holding a skull, in the Fogg Museum of Art, Cambridge (No. 1955.100), should be compared with the present sheet for its similarly bold execution and fervor. A drawing of a skull appeared in the Caroline Greuze sale, Paris, January 25–26, 1843, lot 92.

1 "On this Saint Mary of Egypt by Greuze, corresponding member of the Académie of Dijon, see Galerie de Portraits du XVIIIè siècle by Arsène Houssaye, 1848, 2è série, p. 263"

111 Portrait of Bernard Dubard

Oil, on oval panel, 26⅜ x 21⅜ in. (67.0 x 54.3 cm)
Signed and dated on back of panel: *J. B. Greuze 1799*
San Francisco, The Fine Arts Museums of San Francisco,
Archer M. Huntington Purchase Fund

Collections: Wildenstein and Co., New York, 1913; purchased
by the museum in 1935
   Exhibitions: Paris, Galerie Philipon, Tableaux anciens de
la Galerie Wildenstein, 1913, No. 17; Saint Louis, City Art
Museum, French Art of the XVIII Century, 1923, No. 11;
San Francisco, California Palace of the Legion of Honor,
French Paintings from the Fifteenth Century to the Present
Day, 1934, No. 32; New York, Wildenstein and Co., The
French Revolution, 1943, No. 11; Cleveland Museum of
Art, Style, Truth and the Portrait, 1963, No. 61
   Bibliography: Brookner, p. 132, Pl. 92; G. D. Davisson,
"Portrait of Citizen Dubard, Painting by Jean Baptiste
Greuze," *California Palace of the Legion of Honor Bulletin*,
March, 1944, pp. 98–100

Bernard Dubard (1767–1829) served as private treasurer to
Napoleon while the latter was First Consul. After 1800
Dubard was general treasurer for the French army in Italy.
   Cooly elegant in its simple design, this portrait resembles
in some respects the important contemporary one by Greuze
in the Musée des Beaux-Arts at Saint-Omer (Martin-
Masson, No. 1251), described variously as representing
Talleyrand, Napoleon or Barbaroux, all three identifications
having been contested. The clothing in that portrait and
the position of the torso are nearly identical to those in the
present one, an indication that in his late years Greuze
sometimes tended to repeat successful motifs rather than
invent new ones.

112 The Departure for The Hunt
(*Le Départ pour la chasse, portrait du C.****
et de sa femme, dans un paysage)
Brush, gray ink wash, over pencil, on tan paper, 15⅛ x
13¾ in. (38.3 x 35.0 cm)
Paris, Musée du Louvre, Cabinet des Dessins

Collections: Edmond and Jules de Goncourt, Paris (Lugt
1089), purchased for 75 francs in 1877;[1] their sale, Paris,
February 15–17, 1897, lot 118, acquired for 900 francs by
the museum (Lugt 1886)
   Exhibitions: Salon of 1800, No. 173; Paris, Ecole des
Beaux-Arts, Dessins de maîtres anciens, 1897, No. 564;
Paris, Gazette des Beaux-Arts, Les Goncourt, 1933,
No. 203; Paris, Musée Carnavalet, La Révolution française,
1939; Paris, Musée des Arts Décoratifs, Les Goncourt, 1946
   Bibliography: Brookner, pp. 86, 132, Pl. 94; E. de
Goncourt, *La Maison d'un artiste*, Paris, 1881, I, p. 89;
Martin-Masson, Nos. 130, 308, 1287

At the age of seventy-five Greuze chose to demonstrate his
powers as a draughtsman by including this sheet as the
only drawing among his eleven entries in the Salon of 1800,
his first since 1769. The artist's reappearance in the Salon
provoked numerous articles but no specific reference to this
drawing.
   The garden setting with classical architecture in the
distance recalls that of the 1767 *Votive Offering to Cupid*
(London, Wallace Collection). Similar to *The Departure for
the Hunt* but less brilliantly executed is the contemporary
A Family in a Park (Rotterdam, Museum Boymans-van
Beuningen).

1 Ms. catalogue of Edmond de
Goncourt's collection of French
drawings, Paris, Fondation Custodia,
Institut Néerlandais, p. 30

113 Saint Mary of Egypt (*Le Repentir de sainte Marie l'Egyptienne dans le désert*)
Oil, on canvas, 71½ x 57¼ in. (181.6 x 145.4 cm)
Norfolk, Chrysler Museum at Norfolk

Collections: Lucien Bonaparte, prince de Canino, Paris, 1800; his sale, London, May 14–16, 1816, lot 26 (bought in?); T*** and L*** sale, Paris, March 20–21, 1840, lot 30 (?); Durand-Duclos, Paris; his sale, Paris, February 18, 1847, lot 29, sold for 3,500 francs to Simonet; Prousteau de Montlouis, Paris; his sale, Paris, May 5–6, 1851, lot 74 (?); marquis de Maison, Paris; his sales, Paris, June 10–12, 1869, lot 4, bought in, and Paris, February 24, 1896, lot 2, sold for 6,300 francs to Durand-Ruel; Durand-Ruel et Cie., Paris; acquired by Walter P. Chrysler, Jr., February 17, 1954

Exhibitions: Salon of 1801, No. 158; Salon of 1804, No. 219 (?); Dayton Art Institute, French Paintings 1789–1929 from the Collection of Walter P. Chrysler, Jr., No. 2

Bibliography: Brookner, p. 133; A. Houssaye, *Galerie de Portraits du XVIIIè siècle*, Paris, 1848, p. 263; Martin-Masson, No. 2; Smith, No. 64; Valori, pp. 371–72

Engraving: Angelo Testa

Saint Mary of Egypt is Greuze's last known figure painting. In it the artist demonstrated that at the age of seventy-five he could still paint a nude of heroic proportions, treat a grand if obscure theme in a manner consistent with the tenets of history painting and convey a fully convincing tragic expression. The picture also shows Greuze's continuing preoccupation with the vicissitudes of the spirit, in this case possibly reflecting the contemporary turmoil in his own life.

The title under which Greuze exhibited this painting at the Salon, as well as the inscription on the engraving Testa made from it while it was still in the Lucien Bonaparte collection, make it clear that the artist intended to represent the fifth-century Saint Mary of Egypt rather than Saint Mary Magdalen, the other penitent sinner with whom the subject of the picture has at times been confused. Saint Mary of Egypt, after a debauched career in Alexandria, was converted on the threshold of the Holy Sepulchre at Jerusalem and withdrew to the desert east of Palestine, where she spent the rest of her life in isolation. After many years she received communion from a priest named Zosimus, who returned a year later to find her dead. According to tradition his efforts to bury her were failing when a lion appeared and helped dig her grave with his paws. Saint Mary of Egypt is often depicted with a lion beside her, as here.[1]

The history of this picture has been confused by the existence of another painting, now lost, depicting the same Saint with blond hair rather than brown and with a reclining lion. That canvas is first recorded in the Duclos-Dufresnoy sale, Paris, August 28, 1795, and reappeared, with the present one, in the marquis de Maison sales of 1869 and 1896. At the 1896 sale both were acquired by Durand-Ruel, who sold the blond version to a Huntington on April 17, 1897.[2] A half-length study for the blond version, which also appeared in the marquis de Maison sale of 1869 (lot 5, sold for 9,990 francs), is now in the Claude Dreyfus collection.

Apparently Greuze decided to execute a copy with variants of the earlier, blond *Saint Mary of Egypt* when he received in 1800 a commission from Lucien Bonaparte, then minister of the interior, who owned at least three other paintings by him. By this time, however, Greuze's situation was so desperate that he had to write requesting a partial payment in advance. His second such letter, once published as autograph but now believed to be in his daughter's hand, reads as follows: "*Le tableau que je fais pour le gouvernement est à moitié fini. La situation dans laquelle je me trouve, me force de vous prier de donner des ordres pour que je touche encore un à-compte pour que je puisse le terminer. J'ai eu l'honneur de vous faire part de tous mes malheurs; j'ai tout perdu, or le talent et le courage. J'ai soixante-quinze ans, pas un seul ouvrage de commande; de ma vie je n'ai eu un moment aussi pénible à passer. Vous avés le coeur bon, je me flatte que vous aurés égard à mes peines le plus tôt possible, car il y a urgence. Salut et respect. Ce 28 pluviôse, an IX.*"[3]

Baron Boutard, writing for the *Journal des débats* in 1805, stated that though it was listed in the Salon catalogue this *Saint Mary of Egypt* did not actually appear in 1804, even after the exhibition had been rehung so that the public could see at close range the larger paintings, which were originally skied. Nevertheless, the critic described Greuze's painting sympathetically, presumably remembering it from the Salon of 1801: "*Les tableaux de Greuze, de tout temps recherchés et acquis à grands frais par les étrangers, sont rares en France, et celui dont il s'agit est peut-être unique dans son genre. Je ne crois pas du moins qu'on connoisse de ce maître beaucoup de figures nues et de grandeur naturelle comme est celle de cette Sainte-Marie-Egyptienne. . . . Le sujet du tableau de la Sainte-Marie-Egyptienne, est le même au fond que celui de la Magdelaine; cependant, comme cette sainte pénitente est bien moins connue que la Magdelaine, et qu'elle n'a pas comme elle une physionomie de tradition, le peintre pouvoit se livrer sans contrainte à son imagination. Greuze a usé de cette liberté pour donner à sa sainte Marie un caractère de dévotion douce et affectueuse qui est bien plus touchant en lui-même, et bien mieux du ressort de la peinture que l'expression des angoisses et des remords de la pécheresse; et il s'est ainsi ménagé de moyen de développer en un sujet grave tout le charme d'une nature jeune et gracieuse, sans manquer à la première des règles de la composition historique, qui veut que la physionomie et le choix de nature de chaque*

personnage soient en rapport avec son caractère connu. Nous n'entrerons pas dans de plus grands détails sur un tableau que trop peu de personnes ont vu, nous attendrons pour en rendre compte, que le public ait été mis à même d'en apprécier tout le mérite."[4]

A number of drawings by Greuze related to *Saint Mary of Egypt* are known. In addition to the two in this exhibition (Nos. 58, 110), these include: a red and black chalk drawing, stumped, in the van Sitter sale, Paris, May 3–5, 1838, and the Burat sale, Paris, April 28–29, 1885, lot 80; a red and black chalk drawing with ink wash in the Revil sale, Paris, March 29, 1842, lot 112, sold for 92 francs, and the Prousteau de Montlouis sale, Paris, May 5–6, 1851, lot 75; an ink wash drawing in the Daigremont sale, Paris, April 3–7, 1866, lot 244, and the Walferdin sale, Paris, April 12–16, 1880, lot 31, and a red chalk and ink wash study in the Calendo sale, Paris, December 11–12, 1899, lot 86.

1 G. Ferguson, *Signs and Symbols in Christian Art*, New York, 1954, pp. 21, 240–41
2 Letter from Durand-Ruel et Cie. dated October 19, 1963
3 "The picture I am working on for the government is half finished. The situation in which I find myself compels me to beg you to authorize another advance so that I may complete it. I have had the honor of informing you of all my misfortunes; I have lost everything, except talent and courage. I am seventy-five years old, not a single commissioned work; all my life I have never had so painful a moment to live through. You have a good heart, I flatter myself that you will have consideration for my sufferings as soon as possible, for it is urgent. Greetings and respect. This 28 pluviôse, year IX." Quoted in Goncourt, I, p. 329
4 "The pictures of Greuze, perenially sought after and acquired at great expense by foreigners, are rare in France, and the one in question is perhaps unique in its genre. At least I do not believe that one knows from this master many life-sized nude figures like that in this *Saint Mary of Egypt.* . . . The subject of the picture of *Saint Mary of Egypt* is basically the same as that of *the Magdalen*; however, as this penitent saint is considerably less familiar than *the Magdalen*, and as she does not have like her a traditional appearance, the painter was able to deliver himself without constraint to his imagination. Greuze has used this liberty to give to his Saint Mary a character of gentle and affectionate devotion which is much more touching in itself, and much more within the province of painting than the expression of the pangs and remorse of the sinner; and he has thus found the means to develop in a serious subject all the charm of a youthful and gracious nature, without breaking the first rule of historical composition, which requires that the appearance and the choice of temperament for each subject be in agreement with his known character. We shall not enter into greater detail about this picture, which too few people have seen; we shall wait to report on that until the public has been able to appreciate all its merit." M. B. [baron Boutard], "Beaux-Arts, Salon de l'an XIII," *Journal des débats*, January 5, 1805, pp. 5–6

114 Portrait of the Artist (*Le Portrait de l'auteur*)

Oil, on panel, 20½ x 17¹¹⁄₁₆ in. (52.0 x 45.0 cm)
Marseille, Musée des Beaux-Arts

Collections: marquis de Valori-Rustichelli, Paris; his sale, Paris, April 16–18, 1866, lot 87, sold for 3,000 francs; Félix Abram, 1885; bequeathed by him to the museum in 1925
Exhibitions: Salon of 1804, No. 211; Pau, Musée des Beaux-Arts, L'Autoportrait du XVIIè siècle à nos jours, 1973, p. 31
Bibliography: Brookner, pp. 87, 133, Pl. 96; Martin-Masson, Nos. 1139, 1143; P. Rosenberg, in *French Painting 1774–1830: The Age of Revolution*, exhib. cat., Detroit, 1975, No. 86, p. 465; J. Vergnet-Ruiz and M. Laclotte, *Les Petits et Grands, Musées de France*, Paris, 1962, p. 238; G. Wildenstein, "Table alphabétique des portraits peints, sculptés, dessinés et gravés exposés à Paris au Salon entre 1800 et 1826," *Gazette des Beaux-Arts*, January, 1963, p. 36

As a farewell portrait this ranks among the finest. Greuze, who had written in 1800, "*j'ai tout perdu, or le talent et le courage,*"[1] proved his words by painting himself the year before his death in the very same pose, pointing to himself with his portcrayon, that he had employed in an optimistic self-portrait of his youth (Tournus, Musée Greuze).[2] In contrast to the earlier work, he appears here as shrunken, fragile, even pained, but with an air of lasting self-confidence equal to the challenge laid down by the writer to whom he has so often been compared, Jean-Jacques Rousseau: "*Je veux montrer à mes semblables un homme dans toute la vérité de la nature; et cet homme, ce sera moi.*"[3] With reason Arsène Houssaye would compare this self-portrait to Rembrandt: "*On s'étonna de la vigueur d'un peintre de quatre-vingts ans; cela est franc et vrai comme une tête de Rembrandt; c'est moins fier et moins beau, mais il s'y trouve ce sentiment attendri qui anime toutes les têtes de Greuze.*"[4]

C.-L. F. Lecarpentier stated that the portrait had been completed shorty before the Salon of 1804: "*on applaudit sur-tout à son portrait qu'il venoit de peindre lui-même.*"[5] That this was the *Portrait de l'auteur* exhibited in the Salon that year is attested to by Monsaldy's sketch of it, made in reverse in anticipation of an engraving.[6] Less intense versions of the portrait are in the Hermitage and the Phoenix Art Museum,[7] and a miniature reproducing it is in the collection of baron Walckenaer, Paris.

Two other self-portraits, painted approximately forty and twenty years earlier, also are included in this exhibition (Nos. 36, 95).

225

1 "I have lost everything, except talent and courage." See No. 113

2 Brookner, Pl. 1

3 "I want to show my fellow creatures a man in all the truth of nature; and that man will be me." J.-J. Rousseau, *Oeuvres complètes: Les Confessions*, Paris, 1959, I, p. 5

4 "One was astonished by the vigor of an eighty-year-old painter; it is frank and true like a head by Rembrandt; it is less proud and less beautiful, but there is in it that compassionate sentiment that animates all of the heads by Greuze." A. Houssaye, *Galerie de portraits du XVIIIè siècle*, Paris, 1848, p. 267

5 "One applauded especially the portrait he had just painted of himself." C.-L. F. Lecarpentier, *Notice sur Greuze lu dans la séance de la Société libre d'Emulation de Rouen*, [Rouen], 1805, p. 7

6 Paris, Bibliothèque Nationale, Cabinet des Estampes. On Monsaldy's project, see G. Wildenstein, "Un Tableau attribué à David et rendu à Mme Davin-Mirvault: 'Le Portrait du violiniste Bruni,'" *Gazette des Beaux-Arts*, February, 1962, pp. 94–95

7 *French Paintings and Sculpture from the Phoenix Art Museum Collection*, Phoenix, 1965, No. 24

Bibliography of Works
Referred to in Abbreviated Form

L. P. de Bachaumont, *Mémoires secrets pour servir à l'histoire de la république des lettres en France. . .* , London, 1777–89

J. Bouchot-Saupique, *J.-B. Greuze: Quatorze dessins*, Paris, 1939

A. Brookner, *Greuze: The Rise and Fall of an Eighteenth-Century Phenomenon*, London—Greenwich, Connecticut, 1972

E. Dacier, *Catalogues de ventes et livrets de Salons illustrés par Gabriel de Saint-Aubin. . .* , Paris, 1909

D. Diderot, *Correspondance*, ed. G. Roth, Paris, 1955–

———*Oeuvres complètes*, ed. M. Tourneux and J. Assézat, Paris, 1875–77

———*Salons*, ed. J. Seznec and J. Adhémar, Oxford, 1957–67

D. Diderot and J. d'Alembert, *Encyclopédie, ou dictionnaire raisonné des sciences, des arts et des métiers. . .* , Paris, 1751–65

M. Fried, "Absorption, a Master Theme in Eighteenth-Century French Painting and Criticism," *Eighteenth-Century Studies*, IX, No. 2, Winter, 1975–76, pp. 139–77

E. and J. de Goncourt, *L'Art du dix-huitième siècle*, I, Paris, 1880

J. Guiffrey and P. Marcel, *Inventaire général des dessins du Musée du Louvre et du Musée de Versailles*, Paris, VI, 1911

L. Hautecoeur, *Greuze*, Paris, 1913

F. Lugt, *Les Marques de collections de dessins et d'estampes*, Amsterdam, 1921; *Supplément*, The Hague, 1956

J. Martin and C. Masson, *Catalogue raisonné de l'oeuvre peint et dessiné de J.-B. Greuze*, Paris, 1908

C. Mauclair, *Jean-Baptiste Greuze*, Paris, [1905?]

F. Monod and L. Hautecoeur, *Les Dessins de Greuze conservés à l'Académie des Beaux-Arts de Saint-Pétersbourg*, Paris, 1922

E. Munhall, "Greuze's Frontispiece for *Sophronie*," *Gazette des Beaux-Arts*, October, 1961, pp. 237–42

———"Greuze and the Protestant Spirit," *Art Quarterly*, Spring, 1964, pp. 1–21

———"Les Dessins de Greuze pour 'Septime Sévère,' " *L'Oeil*, April, 1965, pp. 22–29, 59

———"Quelques découvertes sur Greuze," *La Revue du Louvre*, No. 2, 1966, pp. 85–92

———"Savoyards in French Eighteenth-Century Art," *Apollo*, February, 1968, pp. 86–94

R. Portalis and H. Béraldi, *Les Graveurs du dix-huitième siècle*, Paris, 1880–82

F. Reiset, *Notice des dessins, cartons, pastels, miniatures et émaux exposés . . . au Musée Impérial du Louvre*, Paris, 1866–69

P. Rosenberg, N. Reynaud and I. Compin, *Musée du Louvre: Catalogue illustré des peintures: Ecole française XVIIè et XVIIIè siècles*, Paris, 1974, I

W. Sauerländer, "Pathosfiguren im Oeuvre des Jean Baptiste Greuze," in *Walter Friedlaender zum 90. Geburstag*, Berlin, 1965

J. Smith, *Catalogue raisonné of the Works of the Most Eminent Dutch, Flemish and French Painters*, VIII, London, 1837; *Supplement*, London, 1842

C. de Valori, "Notice sur Greuze et sur ses ouvrages," in *Greuze, ou l'Accordée de village*, Paris, 1813; reprinted by A. de Montaiglon, ed., in *Revue universelle des arts*, XI, 1860, pp. 248–61, 362–77

J. G. Wille, *Mémoires et journal. . .* , ed. G. Duplessis, Paris, 1857

C. Wright, *Old Master Paintings in Britain. . .* , London, 1976

Exhibitions at the Royal Academy, London
Referred to in Abbreviated Form

1871, Exhibition of the Works of the Old Masters

1932, Exhibition of French Art 1200–1900

1946–47, Exhibition of The King's Pictures

1954–55, European Masters of the Eighteenth Century

1968, France in the Eighteenth Century

Annan, Glasgow: Nos. 15, 44; Atelier Municipal de Reprographie, Marseille: No. 114; René Basset, Lyon: Nos. 2, 3, 67; Bibliothèque Nationale, Paris: fig. 16, Nos. 4, 11; E. Irving Blomstrann, Hartford: Nos. 10, 80; L. Borel, Marseille: No. 29; Brenwasser, New York: No. 104; Bulloz, Paris: Nos. 24, 30, 72; Studio P. Cadé, Paris: fig. 6, Nos. 1, 99, 102; Galerie Cailleux, Paris: figs. 9, 22, Nos. 18, 66, 83; Cooper, London: Nos. 6, 23, 41, 42; Documentation Photographique de la Réunion des Musées Nationaux, Paris: figs., 5, 15, 19, 20, 21, 23, 24, Nos. 34, 37, 38, 46, 53, 60, 69, 70, 77, 84, 87, 88, 95; Jean Dubout, Paris: No. 71; Fasch Studio, Milton, Massachusetts: No. 40; John R. Freeman and Co., London: No. 13; Studio Gérondal, Lille: Nos. 48, 49; Giraudon, Paris: fig. 1, Nos. 52, 100; Guy et Aillet, Tournus: Nos. 61, 90; Peter Heman, Basel: No. 51; Richard di Liberto, New York: figs. 7, 8, Nos. 28, 32, 101; Sydney W. Newbery, London: No. 55; Photoscope Corp., Dallas: No. 107; Eric Pollitzer, Garden City Park, New York: No. 25; Herbert P. Vose, Wellesley Hills, Massachusetts: fig. 18